THE RECONSTRUCTION OF
PALESTINIAN NATIONALISM

MANCHESTER
UNIVERSITY PRESS

New Approaches to Conflict Analysis

Series editor: Peter Lawler, Senior Lecturer
in International Relations, Department of Government,
University of Manchester

Until recently, the study of conflict and conflict resolution remained comparatively immune to broad developments in social and political theory. When the changing nature and locus of large-scale conflict in the post-Cold War era is also taken into account, the case for a reconsideration of the fundamentals of conflict analysis and conflict resolution becomes all the more stark.

New Approaches to Conflict Analysis promotes the development of new theoretical insights and their application to concrete cases of large-scale conflict, broadly defined. The series intends not to ignore established approaches to conflict analysis and conflict resolution, but to contribute to the reconstruction of the field through a dialogue between orthodoxy and its contemporary critics. Equally, the series reflects the contemporary porosity of intellectual borderlines rather than simply perpetuating rigid boundaries around the study of conflict and peace. *New Approaches to Conflict Analysis* seeks to uphold the normative commitment of the field's founders yet also recognises that the moral impulse to research is properly part of its subject matter. To these ends, the series comprises the highest quality work of scholars drawn from throughout the international academic community, and from a wide range of disciplines within the social sciences.

PUBLISHED

Karin Fierke
Changing games, changing strategies:
critical investigations in security

Deiniol Loyd Jones
Cosmopolitan mediation?
Conflict resolution and the Oslo Accords

The reconstruction
of Palestinian nationalism

Between revolution and statehood

HELENA LINDHOLM SCHULZ

Manchester University Press

MANCHESTER AND NEW YORK

distributed exclusively in the USA
by St. Martin's Press

Published by Manchester University Press
Oxford Road, Manchester M13 9NR, UK
and Room 400, 175 Fifth Avenue, New York, NY 10010, USA
http://www.man.ac.uk/mup

Distributed exclusively in the USA by
St. Martin's Press, Inc., 175 Fifth Avenue, New York,
NY 10010, USA

Distributed exclusively in Canada by
UBC Press, University of British Columbia, 6344 Memorial Road,
Vancouver, BC, Canada V6T 1Z2

British Library Cataloguing-in-Publication Data
A catalogue record for this book is available from the British Library

Library of Congress Cataloging-in-Publication Data applied for

ISBN 0 7190 5596 2 *hardback*

First published 1999

06   05   04   03   02   01   00   99   10   9   8   7   6   5   4   3   2   1

Typeset in Photina
by Graphicraft Limited, Hong Kong
Printed in Great Britain
by Bookcraft (Bath) Ltd, Midsomer Norton

CONTENTS

v

PREFACE

In a protracted, bitter and on-going conflict such as that between the Palestinians and Israel, affecting approximately 7 million Palestinians (including the diaspora) and 5 million Israeli Jews – not to mention the people in the remainder of the Middle East and diaspora Jewry – there will always be aspects and events that are not adequately discussed and understood. Not only does the Palestinian–Israeli conflict, the 'archetype' of national(ist) conflict, affect those immediately concerned, that is, the Palestinians and the Israeli Jews, the Arabs and world Jewry, but this conflict has always been intimately intertwined with world events, both as cause and consequence. International actors, states, organisations and individuals have had, and continue to have, an immediate impact upon the course of events in the Palestinian–Israeli conflict, although it is also true that international powers and actors have never been completely able to control their Middle Eastern allies. Matters in the Middle East have a particular and peculiar way of taking unexpected turns not foreseen by international politicians and analysts.

During the 1990s, the Palestinian–Israeli conflict has surely entered a new historical era with the mutual recognition, the Declaration of Principles, secretly negotiated in the fjelds of Norway and jubilantly signed on the South Lawn of the White House on 13 September 1993, and the process that has since unfolded. However, there is still a long and arduous road to travel for peace to be achieved, as underlined by the slowdown in the process from 1996 to 1999. Although peace has not yet been achieved, we are in a period of declining Palestinian–Israeli conflict.

Palestinian nationalism and national identity are issues rarely problematised in theories on the creation of national identities and nationalisms. Two extreme modes of analysis have monopolised the debate. In Israeli and pro-Israeli Western eyes, the Palestinian population is segmented, fragmented and divided. The deep divisions within the Palestinian movement (which undoubtedly exist) are taken as a pretext for why the Palestinians should not have a state of their own. They are not a 'real nation'; hence they do not need a state. On the other hand, Palestinian and Western writers sympathetic to Palestinian suffering argue that there is a Palestinian 'nation', cohesive or not, and that, on the basis of this nationhood, the Palestinians have a right to self-determination and statehood. Both arguments have their basis in the ideology of nationalism, in the sense that each 'people' or 'nation' should have their own state. The two sides differ only in their conclusion about Palestinian nationhood.

Since the mutual recognition by Israel and the Palestine Liberation Organisation (PLO), the nationhood of the Palestinians has finally been accepted by Israel. Nevertheless, the fact that researchers through their writings tend either to enhance Palestinian nationhood, and hence their political rights to statehood, or deny their national identity and strip them of political rights, is, I think, a sign of the prevalence of nationalism as an ideology. Sympathy for the Palestinians and their predicament, being the victims of another nationalist movement – Zionism – of wars and refugee flows, of Arab governments' fear of the impact of the Palestinian refugees, of international power plays, of regional power ambitions, and of occupation and gross violation of their human rights, has contributed to a lack of theorising about Palestinian nationalism. Instead, Palestinian nationalism has frequently been seen as a unique case from which it is impossible to draw general conclusions. In reality, national movements constantly and painfully reshape and re-identify themselves.

Despite people's claims, there is nothing inherent in nationhood, and nothing inherent in rights to statehood, control over territory, a flag, a national anthem, and so on. Hence the Palestinian claim for self-determination is not based on natural or objective grounds. Neither is there anything inherently right, natural or objective in Israeli Jewish statehood. Neither of the claims can, however, be denied or ignored. Nationalist ideology and its predominance as an organising structure of the international system have made an imprint upon both Palestinians and Israeli Jews to such an extent that the only solution to the conflict must lie in either an abolition of nationalist ideology (which is, needless to say, hard to foresee) or the fulfilment of the nationalist aspirations of both Palestinians and Jews. That is to say, Palestinian self-determination in the form of statehood, without compromising Israel's security needs, is the only solution possible today.

This book therefore does not attempt to discuss who is right and who is wrong. In dealing with protracted and violent conflicts, however, it is inevitable that the researcher is affected or intrigued by the conflicts themselves. No writer/researcher on the Palestinian movement is unaffected by, or is able to stand completely aside of, the overall conflict. The traumas on both sides, the real and perceived images of threat and insecurity, the wars, those killed, those injured, the hatred, the military occupation, repression and violence are all part of the make-up of all research concerning Palestinians and Israelis. This has been an inherent part of the fieldwork for this book that was carried out between July 1994 and July 1995. Living the conflict for one year, not like Palestinians or Israelis, but as an outside observer, caused emotional stress and despair many times, such as when experiencing the huge collective suffering in Israel in the immediate aftermath of terror attacks in Tel Aviv or Beit Lid, causing distrust of the peace process. Or when riding the Palestinian collective taxis from the village outside Jerusalem where I stayed, and facing the military repression and humiliating identity checks to which Palestinians are exposed at any one of the numerous military checkpoints, symbolising the borders between 'us' and 'them', between the West Bank and Israel. Or when entering the Gaza Strip through the Eretz Checkpoint on a sunny day in March with the orange blossom and mimosa competing in filling the light air with sweet smells. But the Eretz Checkpoint exhibits itself as a deep cut in the earth with its ever extending security arrangements, turning Eretz into one of the Checkpoint Charlies of the 1990s. Or when turning back from Gaza, and seeing endless lines of trucks filled with tomatoes and strawberries rotting in the sun awaiting their turn for security check-ups and frustrated drivers giving up, throwing their cargo in the ditch and returning home. Or the sounds of sirens and sights of ambulances rushing injured Palestinian demonstrators to the hospital after *intifada*-like confrontations with the Israeli soldiers outside the Jneid prison in Nablus, clearly showing the coexistence of continued conflict and peace negotiations.

The other side of the coin also had an impact on me as a researcher, however. That is, the leisurely life on Gaza's beach on Fridays with thousands of people swarming the beach, a sight unthinkable six years ago, the coffee drunk together with a family from Sha'ati camp who had moved to a new apartment complex outside Jabaliya, the hopes and wishes of people that if peace had not arrived, it was at least on its way. My year in the village of Abu Dis, outside Jerusalem, taught me a great many things about living a national(ist) conflict.

Most of the time, however, life is not nearly as dramatic as described above or as displayed on the news. In the midst of conflict and traumas, people go on, leading their own lives, struggling for employment to make ends meet, to get the olive harvest done in time, to achieve education for their children without constant reflection on the conflict which determines their lives.

ACKNOWLEDGEMENTS

A number of people have been indispensable in assisting me in my work. First of all, I would like to express my deep gratitude to my supervisor, Professor Björn Hettne, for highly valuable and substantial comments and criticism. His never-ending encouragement and trust, as well as critical comments and reflections on inconsistencies in my arguments and concepts, have been invaluable. His patient and careful reading of different versions of the manuscript is tremendously appreciated. Sune Persson (Associate Professor of Political Science, Göteborg University) read parts of the manuscript, previously presented in a licentitate thesis, and his exacting knowledge of the Palestinian–Israeli conflict and Palestinian nationalism surely helped me to overcome important inconsistencies.

I would also like to thank my colleagues at the Department for Peace and Development Research at Göteborg University for an inspiring research environment and fruitful seminar discussions over the last few years. The Seminar for Ethnic Studies has been an invaluable forum for discussions and debates on themes of ethnicity and nationalism as well as methodology. I am especially indebted to Bent Jørgensen and Maria Stern Pettersson, who read and gave valuable criticism on the text at various points in its production. My colleague and husband, Michael Schulz, was my harshest critic, with his never-ending questioning of theoretical reasoning and concepts, which forced me constantly to reflect on my own assumptions and premises. His long-time knowledge about the Palestinian–Israeli conflict also provided assistance in the interpretation of empirical events and data. He has also been my staunchest supporter, and without his moral backing during times of confusion in fieldwork, it is possible that this book would never have been written – for better or for worse.

Many thanks also go to the anonymous reviewers of the proposal for this book, for whose careful reading and constructive points I am exceedingly grateful. To the series editor, Peter Lawler, thanks for encouragement.

While carrying out fieldwork, I was associated as a research fellow with the Department of Sociology at BirZeit University. My deepest gratitude goes to Vice-President Ibrahim Abu-Lughod and his former assistant, Dr Riyad Amin, as well as Professor Aziz Heidar for organising the arrangement. Professor Aziz Heidar also took time to discuss issues of Palestinian nationalism and identity, and I appreciate his sharing of his thoughts with me. Professor Salim Tamari also engaged in discussions on my research topic, and I have certainly gained from taking part of his ideas and analyses. Dr Ziad Abu-Amr helped me better to understand the role of the Islamic movements in Palestinian political life. I would also like to thank Dr Ali Jarbawi at BirZeit University, Dr Iyad Barghouti of an-Najah University, Nablus, Dr Liza Taraki, Dr Islah Jawwad, and Dr Eileen Kuttab of BirZeit University, and Dr Mahdi Abdel Hadi of the Palestinian Academic Society for the Study of International Affairs (PASSIA) for discussions and reflections. Part of the material used in this book was published by PASSIA in 1995, and I would like to express my thanks for that opportunity. A special mention goes to Dr Saleh Abdel-Jawwad-Saleh of the BirZeit Research and Documentation Centre. Also, I particularly want to thank Yousef and Ahmed for never letting me down when I needed information or help of any sort. And thanks to Atieyeh, who provided countless information and knowledge and friendship with him and his family.

I would also like to express my gratitude to the Harry S. Truman Research Institute for the Advancement of Peace at the Hebrew University of Jerusalem for providing similar arrangements as a research fellow as did BirZeit University. I especially wish to thank Professor Moshe Ma'oz for interesting discussions and for fruitful cooperation. Thanks go to Idit Avidan and Dal'ia for friendly technical assistance. Warm thanks also to Professor Baruch Kimmerling of the Department of Sociology at the Hebrew University for support, interesting discussions and a warm reception. Likewise, Professor Sammy Smooha at Haifa University has engaged in discussion on the topic.

Many thanks also to the staff of the library of the Arab Studies Society, to the Jerusalem Media Communication Centre and *al-Tal'ia* for assisting me in finding *intifada* leaflets. I am also grateful to copy-editor Diane Jones for her highly capable handling of the manuscript.

Above all, I want of course to express the deepest gratitude to those people interviewed, most of whom appear and speak in this text, for sharing their time and thoughts with me. Without them, this book would not have come about. Should anyone feel offended or misinterpreted by what I have written, I am to blame and I apologise sincerely should that be the case. Needless to say, I alone am responsible for the interpretations and analyses.

To Ulrika Persson, thank you for being the best of neighbours, for never-ending moral support and for being a friend who was always there.

Besides my husband, one person stands out, on whom I have been especially dependent for the fulfilment of this task, and that is my mother, Annika Lindholm, never ceasing in encouragement as well as practical support.

Although the bulk of the research was carried out using private funds, I wish to thank Göteborg University for important grants and donations. During the finalisation of the book, I was able to draw on a generous grant from the Knut and Alice Wallenberg Foundation, intended to support young women researchers in Sweden. I thank the Wallenberg Foundation for this opportunity.

Acknowledgements

An actualisation of the interviews was done in 1997, as part of another project, dealing with potentials for democratisation of Palestinian politics. This project was financed by the research board of the Swedish International Development Authority, which I kindly thank for its support.

Helena Lindholm Schulz

ABBREVIATIONS

AHC	Arab Higher Committee
ALF	Arab Liberation Front
ANM	Arab Nationalist Movement
CPRS	Centre for Palestine Research and Studies
DFLP	Democratic Front for the Liberation of Palestine
DOP	Declaration of Principles
al-Fateh	Palestinian National Liberation Movement
Fida	Palestinian Democratic Federation Party
GUPS	General Union of Palestine Students
IDF	Israeli Defence Forces
JMCC	Jerusalem Media and Communication Centre
MCA	Muslim-Christian Association
OET	Occupied Enemy Territories
PASSIA	Palestinian Academic Society for the Study of International Affairs
PCBS	Palestinian Central Bureau of Statistics
PCP	Palestine Communist Party
PDFLP	Popular Democratic Front for the Liberation of Palestine
PDU	Palestinian Democratic Union
PECDAR	Palestinian Economic Council for Development and Reconstruction
PFLP	Popular Front for the Liberation of Palestine
PFLP–GC	Popular Front for the Liberation of Palestine – General Command
PLC	Palestinian Legislative Council
PLF	Palestinian Liberation Front
PLO	Palestine Liberation Organisation
PNA	Palestinian National Authority
PNC	Palestine National Council
PNF	Palestinian National Front
PPP	Palestine People's Party
PPSF	Palestinian Popular Struggle Front
UN	United Nations
UNLU	Unified National Leadership of the Uprising

1

Introduction: nationalism and the Palestinians

We are thrown from one airport to another and nobody wants to accept us.

I am nobody. I want to be somebody.

When I struggle against the occupation I am a Palestinian.

The above quotations from prominent Palestinian political leaders and activists illuminate some of the main representations of Palestinian national identity. Embedded in all of these brief, but painfully clear, notions are concepts of acute significance in defining Palestinianism from within. Palestinian identity constitutes a denied and excluded entity, but also a collectivity which struggles to achieve what it does not yet have: statehood, independence and international legitimacy as a people. In 1998, five years after the jubilant handshake between the two arch-enemies, Israel's Prime Minister Yithzak Rabin and PLO Chairman Yasir Arafat, the Palestinians mourned *al-nakba*, the catastrophe which has been paramount in shaping their political identity.

This book deals with the urgent task of shedding light on the creation of Palestinian nationalism(s) and national identity. The study elucidates how Palestinian nationalism is constantly being re-created and illustrates the very meaning of Palestinian national identity. It covers the ups and downs of the making of Palestinianism from the early part of the century onwards. The bulk of the material, however, relates to contemporary times and the immediate history, ranging from the simultaneous change and strengthening of Palestinianism during the *intifada* to the present era of identity crisis in the midst of state-building. Although the peace process between Israel and the Palestinians has, at the time of writing, reached a stalemate, there is still a case to be made on its allowance of Palestinian *de facto* state-making. The peace process and the (restricted) circumstances of state-building imply a completely new environment for identity and nationalism. A revolutionary liberation nationalism is to take on the responsibility of administration and governance, a step which

1

implies a profound change in both the form and the content of nationalism. This book depicts the Palestinian movement precisely in this moment of dramatic and uncertain change.

Although there is a vast literature on the Palestinian national movement – 'doing Palestine' has become a fashion – studies on Palestinian society are generally under-theorised. A constructivist perspective has in fact only recently reached research on Palestinian identity and nationalism (see Kimmerling and Migdal, 1993; Khalidi, 1997; Sayigh, 1997a). The Palestinian sociologist Salim Tamari aptly described the situation:

> One can say without much hesitation that no Arab society has been researched, analysed and written about as much as Palestinian society, and yet remained so poor in the theoretical treatment of its subject. There is a dominant implicit theme directing its conceptualisation in local literature which claims that Palestinian society is completely unique, that it has had a historical experience that is unparalleled and, therefore, that the theoretical literature on stratification, development, gender studies, ethnicity, etc., is not directly relevant to Palestine. (Tamari, 1997: 18)

Palestinian history is usually seen as a unique, exceptional case of nationalism and national identity, narrated in an historical, chronological mode. The Palestinian case is, of course, unique in its dramatic turns of history and in the violent changes it has experienced. There is actually a great lacuna to fill in research on Palestinian nationalism and national identity, despite the existence of many excellent historical works.[1] Research has, rather, served two contradictory political purposes. On the one hand, it has contributed to present a picture of a split and divided population, not really in possession of a 'genuine' national identity – whatever national consciousness may exist is in this primarily Israeli literature seen as a reaction only – (e.g. Porath, 1974, 1977). On the other hand, it has provided a discourse emphasising Palestinian essentialism in trying to prove an authentic nation with innate rights and immanent connections to the land since time immemorial (Khalidi, 1971; Frangi, 1982; Muslih, 1988). Palestinian identity and nationalism have rarely been problematised or analysed in line with theories on what constructs such politics. It will here be argued that Palestinian identity and nationalism are neither completely the result of their significant 'other', that is, a reaction, nor are they natural givens. Instead, Palestinian identity and nationalism are constancy constructed and re-created in the very meeting point between external and internal factors, in the intersection where structures, processes and actors convene. Through illuminating what actually takes place in terms of identity creation at this junction, the Palestinian condition(s) could add to a general understanding of nationalism and how national identities are crafted. On a more general level, the Palestinian case can teach us that, in order to understand nationalism, one must understand the complexities of the combination of external and internal events in changing the direction of nationalist political discourse.

There are naturally exceptions to this general trend of lack of theorising. Important contributions include Sayigh (1979, 1994), who focuses on the Lebanese refugee experience combined with class and gender perspectives. Although trained as a sociologist, Sayigh's perspective is largely ethnographical/ hermeneutic, and she demonstrates brilliantly what it means and has meant to be a Palestinian and to live Palestinianism in the agony of exile in Lebanon. Johnson (1982) studies Islam as an ideological system of meaning in Palestinian nationalism. Also his perspective is hermeneutic/anthropological, but lacks a relating of ideological systems to political and economic structures and institutions. Kimmerling and Migdal (1993) use similar points of departure as this work, reading the history of Palestinianism through an analysis influenced by constructivist theories of nationalism, although their work sometimes suffers from a lack of hermeneutic understanding of the driving forces in Palestinian society. Based on archival sources, the work remains, despite its pioneer status, somewhat detached. Recently, two outstanding works have come on to the market, drawing on constructivist theories on nationalism and national identity, and it appears that there is now a new opportunity to approach issues related to Palestinian experience in a more theoretical manner. One of these works is the exacting contribution of Khalidi (1997), who covers in detail the formative years of Palestinian nationalism using modern theories on nationalism. The second is the magnificient opus by Yezid Sayigh (1997a), who in immense detail describes how armed struggle was the foundation stone of nation-building. It is of substantial importance that these contributions are from Palestinians. Other works have assumed an approach more directed towards institution-building (Brand, 1988a) and the PLO as a structure and organisation (Cobban, 1984; Nassar, 1991), or have dealt with political and social processes in the occupied territories and the *intifada*, without explicitly addressing how the *intifada* relates to the constant process of identity construction (e.g. Lockman and Beinin, 1989; McDowall, 1989; Nassar and Heacock, 1990; Robinson, 1997).

This book deals with the process of constant re-creation of Palestinian nationalism from three perspectives. The first is to examine the dynamics of external and internal factors in formulating nationalism. The second is inspired by Barth (1969) and others, and attempts to come to terms with the relationship between content/meaning and form/boundary in identity discourses. Barth's revolutionary contribution to ethnicity studies was to implicate ethnicity/ cultural identity as a form of social organisation rather than as 'culture' or 'essence'. How has Palestinianism occurred in the interplay between external factors, the meeting with the 'other(s)' and internal factors, and the role of the national(ist) elite and its followers? What meaning do actors bestow on identity in terms of 'self' and 'other'? Out of which structuring of concepts and ideas has Palestinian nationalism emerged and how does it reshape itself in new contexts? How does a change in context such as the peace process and the decline of the Palestinian–Israeli conflict from 1993 onwards influence nationalism as an ideology? How do people define their identity? What do Palestinians themselves consider to be at the core of Palestinianism? What is the relationship between form/organisation and culture/meaning?

The third issue relates to internal negotiations, compromises and conflicts over national identity. In all (or most) national/nationalist movements there is an internal contestation of the *meaning* of nation and the organisation of the state or, in this case, the state-to-be; that is, there are competing nationalist discourses, informed by relations of dominance and power. National identity and nationalist ideologies/discourses take on different meanings, related, for example, to social stratification, gender issues and regional location. There are dominating and challenging discourses of nationalism and identity. As stated by Eric Hobsbawm: '"national consciousness" develops *unevenly* among the social groupings and *regions* of a country; this regional diversity and its reasons have in the past been notably neglected' (Hobsbawm, 1990: 12). Hence nationalism and national identity are not monolithic but multi-faceted and often contradictory; neither are they static, but dynamic, and they change with historical processes. One cannot therefore speak of *one* Palestinian nationalism, just as one cannot speak of *one* Zionism. What competing ideas and representations exist within the Palestinian movement? What internal challenges and cleavages influence the nationalist discourse?

One of the urgent reasons for contributing to the study of Palestinianism is the over-mystification of Palestinian-ness that exists among its apologists as well as its adversaries. Palestinian identity suffers from stereotypes and stigmatisation, and a deconstruction of its ideology and meaning may add to a much-needed demystification.

> As much as any people in the world, the Palestinians have suffered from media stereotypes: 'terrorists' and 'freedom fighters', 'murderers' and 'victims'. At times, the Palestinian leadership has reinforced such images by insisting on a national consensus denying the rifts in their society. (Kimmerling and Migdal, 1993: xix)

The ideology of nationalism is throughout this book to be seen as the main explanatory factor for the Palestinian–Israeli conflict, and here I am in agreement with Portugali, who has formulated this point most explicitly: 'Zionism and Palestinianism were the very origins, the very generative forces which have brought into existence both Israeli and Palestinian societies as well as the conflicts between them' (Portugali, 1993: 36). It is nationalism that creates the nation rather than being the outcome of a 'natural' nation (cf. Gellner, 1983; Hobsbawm, 1990; Anderson, 1991). In fact, Israeli society and Palestinian society 'enfold each other to the extent that neither is definable today independently of the other' (Portugali, 1993: 39). Israeli and Palestinian society and identity are mirror images of each other and part of each other, although it needs to be pointed out that Zionism was initially formed as a European phenomenon; that is, as a reaction against nationalism in Europe, antisemitism and pogroms, persecution and extermination. There is today no Israeli society which 'exists' completely independently of the Palestinian, and *vice versa*. It is as though both societies carry with them the other, as a perceived burden but also a potential asset. However, a national identity is not formed exclusively or in absolute terms in the relationship. Internal processes of negotiation and elite politics are equally important, as is popular sentiment.

Both Palestinianism and Zionism are in a way *ideologies of conflict*, in their direct relation to the 'other'. It is therefore of great importance to find out the content of ideology in conflict; that is, to what extent ideologies advocate negative perceptions of 'others', and what the 'other' represents, what function it fulfils, and so on.

Although this study drafts the long historical lines of the Palestinian formation of a national identity, its main focus is recent history and the bulk of the material relates to contemporary history; that is, from the late 1980s, from the *intifada* to self-government. The main emphasis is further upon the West Bank and Gaza.

Nationalism as an ideology of boundedness

Nationalism[2] is an ideology of such force that peoples from all over the globe and in different historical configurations have unhesitatingly willed themselves to kill and to die for the nation. After World War II, and particularly following the collapse of the bipolar world order and the end of the Cold War, most conflicts in the world have been intra-state wars rather than inter-state and have centred around issues of government and territory; that is, they have been concerned with state- and nation-building, making nationalism and identity fundamental ingredients of such conflicts.

Nationalism is Janus-faced – as emphasised by most studies. On the one hand, it provides peoples with means for collective security, belonging and identity. Nationalism may be emancipatory, as in the national liberation movements throwing off the yoke of colonialism. It may be inclusive and embrace different ethnic/cultural groups in one movement under the umbrella of citizenship. It may also, and on the contrary, be expressed as exclusivist, chauvinistic, aggressive and expansionist. All nationalisms embrace both these sides at the same time like two sides of a coin, although in different degrees. Furthermore, nationalism is universalist in its function as a general ideology. According to the international structure, everyone should have a nationality and belong to a certain nation-state formation, in order to, for example, be able to cross international borders. Nationalism must be related to the external arena, or the sphere of the international system, also owing to the prevalence of nationalism as a value system in the international system: 'Nationalism is not merely an ideology . . . It is rather an articulation related to the real setting of the modern international system. Nationalism refers to the nation-state as an organisational unit of this international system' (Tibi, 1971: 11).

In the sense that the international system takes as its starting point nationalism as an ordering principle, nationalism is an ideology of a different order than Marxism, liberalism, socialism, and so on. Nationalism is an ideology of paradigmatic or super-paradigmatic nature. It is, to use Portugali's terminology, 'generative social order' (Portugali, 1993: 44). It is also, however, particularist in the sense that each nationalism is limited and restricted – not everyone can be included (Anderson, 1991: 5) – and it is thus an ideology of *boundedness*.

Nationalism is the main instrument for the state in creating needed homogeneity. As both Gellner (1983) and Hobsbawm (1990) have asserted, it is *nationalism* that creates the *nation* and not the other way around. Nationalism is a political *ideology*, both in the sense of legitimising existing states and power-holding elites – '*official* nationalism' (cf. Anderson, 1991: 83 ff.) – and in the sense in which it opposes current state structures – *oppositional*[3] or *popular* nationalism, as evident in the rise of ethno-nationalist movements. Most recent works on nationalism emphasise the connection between nationalism and the modern state. There are also, however, aspects of nationalism which are connected to the level of 'society' and informal ways of imagining the 'nation', and do not have their origin in state structures (Eriksen, 1992a: 142; 1993).

Space and time

The main elements of nationalism are 'territory, place and environment (i.e. spatial entities), in relation to people and their collective memories (i.e. temporal entities)'. Nationalism focuses on the 'distribution of land among nations' (Portugali, 1993: 37).

'Space' and 'time' are thus *the* fundamental components of the ideology of nationalism which draws heavily on history or historicism. Through imagining a wholeness throughout history, nationalism provides people with a sense of security. Continuity and a sense of long-time presence on the land, in a certain space, are the main justification used for nationalist claims. In that sense, nationalism is a mechanism of defence against the disruptive changes of modernity (Eriksen, 1993: 105). History is utilised to justify claims to territorial land and claims to statehood. The narrating of history is subject to myths and legends, and hence part of ideology. Hobsbawm states: 'Nationalism requires too much belief in what is patently not so' (Hobsbawm, 1990: 12). Ernest Renan expressed the same thing: 'Getting its history wrong is part of being a nation.'[4] Nationalism regards the nation (at least one's 'own') as antique, as everlasting, as thriving on a glorious history. Naturally, different 'nations' have different access to a readily available history. If there is no history that can easily be utilised, then a history is invented. However, the reinterpretation or remaking of history in present-day circumstances is not wholly voluntaristic, but occurs in relation to contexts, historical processes and significant 'others'; that is, agents and peoples construct history, but not solely at their own will or through their own making, as Marx once phrased it (see Eriksen, 1993: 37). Relations of power are embedded in this process.

Nationalism also relies on a shared vision of a common future for success in the mobilisation of movements. '[N]ationalism . . . places its golden age firmly in the future' (Smith, 1979: 126), and the dreamed of or planned future is thus as important in the formulation of the nationalist movements as the past. The goals are connected to statehood or, at least, to the control of a land, of a specific territory – of the 'homeland', the *patrie* (Smith, 1979: 2 f.).

Space, that is, the territory embraced by state borders, is important both in the sense of providing modes of production and in the sense of emotional attachments. One concrete function of nationalist ideology is its relation to providing feelings of security and belonging. A territory, a 'homeland', is crucial in determining a nation's location. Territory is therefore imbued with meaning and the homeland is subject to history-creating and myths. Landscape is romanticised in arts and poetry as nature is 'nationalised'. The importance of geography is highlighted by the central place given to the map in nationalist ideologies (cf. Anderson, 1991; Krishna, 1996). Through projecting a map with one's own nation at the centre of the world or region, geography and world territory are hierarchised. If divided, the homeland must be reunited. If its members are dispersed, they must return to the homeland, which is perceived as 'Paradise Lost'.

Nationalism is thus an ideology of *boundedness* and a belief in or claimed congruity between people, territory and state, or population, geography and politics. Nationalism addresses questions such as 'what people?', 'how should "the people" be defined?', 'what territory?', 'what is the relation between people and territory?', and so on. The general belief of nationalism is that the world is organised and divided into 'nations' which *possess* territories (cf. Smith, 1991: 40). It is in this sense that nationalism is the main ideology of the modern state.

Homogenisation and state-building

Barry Buzan distinguishes between three main elements of the state: the legitimating *idea* of the state, which is usually expressed as the will and intention to create a nation out of the population inhabiting a certain territory; the *institutions* of the state, embracing the executive, legislative, administrative, judicial and repressive apparatus of the state; and the *physical base* of the state, equalling the population, the territory and the resource base of the state. The idea is of profound importance for cohesion and integration. If the idea on which a coherent ideology is based is weak, that is, not legitimate enough, this is frequently compensated for by an over-development of institutions and the repressive apparatus (Buzan, 1991: 83). The idea most commonly used is nationalism, implying that *nation* is the glue which holds the modern state together. Hence it could be argued that, from the perspective of the state, nation *is the idea*. This could be related to Benedict Anderson's concept of 'imagined community', implying that the nation is an abstract idea or construction in our minds (Anderson, 1991), although it may be real enough for the members of the group constituting the 'nation'. A 'nation' is thus both an idea *and* a group of people holding that idea as real for themselves.

A large part of the literature divides the practices of nationhood into two main categories. On the one hand, a nation can be defined according to a perceived or claimed *cultural identity* and a common belonging (or *ethnicity*); on the other hand, it can be defined as related to *citizenship*, that is, the population within a certain territory belongs to the same nation, regardless of cultural 'belongingness'. Anthony Smith (1991) labels this the 'civic' or 'territorial' model. Historical territory, which corresponds to the 'homeland', a community of laws in which all members (citizens) are equal, and a common, civic culture (Smith, 1991: 9 ff.) are important aspects of this way of perceiving the 'nation'. Territory and geography, however, frequently become culturalised or essentialised and connected to a certain group through the ideology of nationalism. In the *culturalist* way of defining the nation, what is stressed is common descent rather than civic legality (Smith, 1991: 11 f.). The national idea therefore contains principles of both *inclusion* and *exclusion*. Civic nationalism builds ideally and in theory on the principle of invitation; that is, one can become a member of a nation through acquiring citizenship. However, culturalist and essentialist ideas also flavour more civically oriented nationalisms and nation-building projects. There are no definite distinctions between the two. As Smith points out, there is a 'profound dualism at the heart of every nationalism. In fact every nationalism contains [both] civic and ethnic elements in varying degrees and different forms' (Smith, 1991: 13) and, it could be added, at different times.

In order to achieve cultural homogenisation, the dominant political elite needs to be legitimised by its population. Thus the idea or ideology which is to be used in order to integrate a population must be convincing to a majority of the population. The ideology of nationalism as expressed in the nation-state project (or 'official nationalism', to use Anderson's (1991) term) and its mission to homogenise its population often fails in legitimacy and gives rise to contending ethno-nationalisms, or conflicts over the content of nationhood, which in turn may threaten the nation-state project. Nationalisms frequently contain mechanisms of exclusion, that is, *vis-à-vis* their own citizens, depending on which ideology of homogenisation is used. Frequently, elites define the 'nation' in hierarchical ways, placing themselves at the centre as those who are 'better' nationals, that is, those who have the privilege of defining the nation.

Nationalism is thus about homogenisation, about attempts to make people similar, to create a common identity out of whatever building blocks lie within a certain space. Official nationalism is based not only on assumptions of who are 'we' and who are 'they', on mechanisms of exclusion and inclusion, but on conscious attempts at homogenisation; it thrives on myths of homogeneity so as to legitimate administrative functions of statehood. Institutional and adminis-trative aspects of statehood are used in the process of homogenisation. Gellner emphasises the importance of a modern education system in the spreading of nationalism. 'At the base of the modern social order stands not the executioner but the professor. Not the guillotine, but the (aptly named) *doctorat d'état* is the main tool and symbol of state power' (Gellner, 1983: 34). Nationalism is also about socialisation, about 'making good citizens' out of a population. Homo-genisation projects therefore set out to apply norms of conformity to a society. In that sense, nationalism is about conforming with norms; it is to be 'like others and do what others do' (Bauman, 1995: 112).

The military institution is another example of the role of institutions. The role of the military apparatus in nation-building can be divided in the following way: (1) as the ultimate symbol of statehood, in its legitimate use of violence in Weber's (1947: 156) definition of the state; the role of its personnel is to defend the nation; (2) in bringing together different parts of a population in the com-mon goal of 'defending the nation'; and (3) in the use of coercive methods in order to suppress unrest or politics of difference.

Language is another instrument used in defining or shaping a nation, not least by nationalists themselves (cf. the early German tradition of Fichte (1808 [1995]) and von Herder (1784–97 [1995])). Although in reality there is no straightforward relationship between language and national identity, or language and ethnicity (Anderson, 1991), language is important in its role of providing a system for meaningful communication and in this sense serves as a vehicle for cultural integration. It is through a vernacular, administrative lan-guage that a nation is imagined. Tradition, language, religion and so on are, however, like the nation, 'inventions' and constructions. Their importance lies in the role they play in nationalist discourses; that is, what importance is bestowed by the group or nationalist ideology in relation to 'language', 'religion', 'history' and 'territory'.

Through the process of homogenisation, difference becomes visible and stands out as problematic. Those who fail to have this 'something', however defined, in common tend to become marginalised (Verdery, 1994), in what Hettne (1992) has called the 'nation-state' project and Connor (1972) has called 'nation-destroying' rather than 'nation-building'. Stavenhagen (1990) elaborates the notion of 'ethnocide' to describe the process of homogenisation whereby cultural systems are marginalised. Hettne, Connor and Stavenhagen all view this process with a bias towards sympathy for 'ethnic groups' and 'nations', without problematising on the idea of ethnicities as fundamental principles of group identity. Nevertheless, they all emphasise the role of the state in creating ethnic tensions or reactions in abortive attempts at homogenisation. The state is 'the frame for producing visibility through differences whose significance it creates' (Verdery, 1994: 45), and politics of difference are frequently the result of state ambitions to make similar or to eradicate or subjugate difference. The failure lies in the paradox that it is precisely the *process or project of creating homogeneity which renders difference more important*. It is this process, and the role of the state in this process, rather than difference in itself which lie at the root of ethnic conflict and the new wave of nationalism and 'fundamentalism'.[5]

The nation is worshipped and glorified. Kapferer (1988) emphasises the emotional, religious aspects of nationalism. Seton-Watson (1977: 465) states that nationalism in some cases has become an 'ersatz religion' in its worshipping of the nation and the self. In a sense, it is a narcissistic ideology, in its political self-love (cf. Anderson, 1991).

In its emphasis on legitimating claims on territory and in its constant endeavour of defining 'in' and 'out' groups, nationalism lacks a coherent theory on how state and polity should be organised. Among, for example, the liberation movements of the 1950s, as well as the separatist and ethno-nationalist movements of the 1980s and 1990s, there was a conviction that if only self-determination were to be established then a glorious future was ensured. The question for nationalism is not so much *how* a society should be ruled as *who* should rule it. In mobilising processes, issues of liberation, self-determination and independence have prevailed over issues of what choices should be made post-liberation or post-independence. Focus has been placed on external relations. The neglect of the 'transition *after* decolonisation to a period when a new political order achieves moral hegemony is symptomatic of the difficulty that millions of people live with today' (Said, 1993: 284). Fanon also addressed this issue: an unguided nationalism will simply repeat itself, it will 'crumple into regionalisms inside the hollow shell of nationalism itself' (Fanon, 1968: 159), implying that the ideology and struggle of nationalism are a repetition of the imperialist argument turned around and, when enforced, nationalism will provoke reactions in the form of regional identities and politics of difference within states. Liberation nationalisms or ethnic nationalisms do not therefore provide a coherent alternative. Rather, they are based on the same parameters as the structures they fought or fight against.

National identities

Contemporary research and academic debate on ethnicity and national identity by and large concur that ethnicity as well as national identity – both 'ethnic groups' and 'nations' – are socially and culturally constructed and that they build on *imaginings*.[6] However, when discussing imaginings and constructions, one inevitably reaches a point where the question has to be posed, why are these constructions so important to people? Why are people prepared to sacrifice their lives for the idea of the nation? Furthermore, although the primordialist perspective on ethnicity and national identity is largely 'outfashioned' in social science, the principle of ethnicity and nation becomes absolute and essential to the agents and actors of ethnicity and nationalism: there is, in day-to-day representations of identity, an objectification and reification of culture by groups and peoples themselves.

Leaving both essentialism and instrumentalism aside as oversimplified analytical frames, identity will be seen throughout this book as constantly open to change. People are flexible and adjust their actions according to contexts and circumstances, although not always as functionally as suggested by Cohen (1974). The changing of identity is not completely open; neither is it primarily strategic. Rather, there are a number of potential options for each individual. In certain circumstances, ethnic and national identities may shift and slide easily and there is a relatively free choice, whereas in other cases structural barriers and fixed social boundaries and categories make any shift near inconceivable. Emphasis varies over time; it is the *context* and *situation* which determine how a group as well as individuals may identify and define itself/herself/himself.

Since Barth's path-breaking work on ethnic boundaries in 1969, the main point of departure for ethnicity studies has been to see ethnicity as a form of social organisation. Barth underlined the continuity of boundaries despite potential shifts of cultural content:

> the nature and continuity of ethnic units ... depends on the *maintenance of a boundary*. The cultural features that signal the boundary may change and the cultural characteristics of the members may likewise be transformed, indeed, even the organisational form of the group may change – yet the fact of continuing dichotomisation between members and outsiders allows us to specify the nature of continuity, and investigate the changing cultural form and content. (Barth, 1969: 14)

National identity is thus not static or fixed but is partly fluid and boundary-exceeding, in a constant process of fulfilling itself. National identity and nationalism are *processes*, that are contextually and situationally defined. They depend on certain historical social and politico-economic situations, as well as the overall context (see Eriksen, 1992a), but cannot be reduced simply to interests or motives. In fact, as post-modernist literature has it, it is more appropriate to talk about constant processes of identification than about identity as a fixed category (Hall, 1992). Hobsbawm (1990: 11) states that 'national identification and what it is believed to imply can change and shift in time, even in the course of quite short periods. In my judgement this is the area of national studies in which thinking and research are most urgently needed today.' Shifting national identities and what these changes imply in particular cases are thus an area which has not been thoroughly investigated, according to Hobsbawm. An important research focus ought to be how identities are described and defined by actors and how these internal notions change and are contested. The interpretation of national identity is not equally distributed within a population. Many of today's conflicts ultimately boil down to the questions 'which borders?', 'what population?' and 'what national idea?'. Fragmentation is the result of increasingly shallow ideas of homogeneity. A relevant starting point is to investigate how the concept of 'nation' is internally contested and negotiated; that is to say, how is it defined among potential members and what competing ideas and definitions exist.

'Self' and 'other'

Barth's work moved ethnicity studies away from culture and content as defining ethnicity, and focused on *boundary* and *form/organisation*. In that sense, ethnicity came to be recognised as more similar to 'nation' than previously, when nation was portrayed as modern and ethnicity as pre-modern. Ethnicity was a social organisation of *difference*, and hence interaction with the 'other' became crucial. However, Barth also saw ethnic identity as 'superordinate' to other identities, as 'imperative' (Barth, 1969: 17); a standpoint which has been criticised since, despite Barth's emphasis on boundaries, it leads the thoughts to primordialism. The focus on the 'other' as an inseparable part of identification processes implied, however, a significant change in ethnicity studies.

It is only in relation to an 'other' that it becomes meaningful to identify a 'self' (Said, 1978; Derrida, 1981; Laclau, 1990; Hall, 1996). 'The constitution of the "I" is acknowledged to come about only through the discourse of the "other", that is through signification' (Giddens, 1979: 38). Identity is constructed in polarisation, exclusion and power hierarchisations. Identities are formed in interactive dyadic relationships. Often, a negative stereotyping is emphasised, but 'others' does not necessarily mean 'strangers' or 'aliens', but could involve co-residents in encompassing social systems and lead more often to questions of how 'we' are distinct from 'them', rather than to a hegemonic and unilateral view of the 'other' (Barth, 1994: 13). In addition, a 'them' must not refer to a specific group of people; it must not be well defined or delimited but must rather refer to a general 'them', a non-us, 'out there' (Roosens, 1994: 85). Roosens' clarification is important in the sense that through emphasising boundaries between 'us' and 'them', there is a risk of overemphasising differ- ence and negative interaction or conflict. There are, however, 'others' of differ- ent kinds; 'others' could also be defined through positive interaction. Stereotypes, however, carry information which helps individuals to structure and order a chaotic 'reality' (cf. Eriksen, 1993). 'Other' represents those who are not 'we', and relations with 'others' can be friendly/characterised by amity, or hostile/ characterised by enmity, or just indifferent. Furthermore, ethnic or national identities are, like other identities, not only formed in relation to an 'outside', to something which is different, but involve attempts of being *similar* to the 'in'- group; to recognise oneself in the behaviour of others is also to sense security. To conform with a norm is a way to enhance security. 'Self' and 'other' thus represent similarity and difference.

Despite the landmarks doubtless gained by the focus on boundaries, Eriksen warns against overemphasising what he calls 'formalism' through overestim- ating the boundary. By the agents of ethnicity and nationalism, ethnicity and culture are perceived as properties and not constructs, and for agents and social formations, a perceived cultural substance *is* important. A formalist/ constructivist approach may thus partly miss the point in leaving out aspects of ethnicity and national identity that are important to agents (Eriksen, 1992a: 31; cf. also Smith, 1991, 1994). It should be emphasised that ethnicity and national identities *are* constructed and created, which is not to be mistaken for make-believe and creations out of thin air. To construct should rather be seen as an active, creative process, carried out in the interplay between intending agents and larger structures. Also, something which is produced in a relatively short time period may carry profound social meaning. Continuity and meaning should not be (mis)taken to mean the same thing.

The nation/ethnicity as family

If ethnicity/national identity is related only to boundary, people's self- definitions would be (anew) disregarded. If the problem previously was that anthropologists, colonial powers and outside actors invented ethnicities through an overemphasis on demarcation through language, race, tradition, culture, religion, and so on, the issue could now be that scholars throw the baby out with the bath water, in claiming that all there is to ethnicity is a construction of social boundaries. If so, what would distinguish ethnicity from other modes of identity, be they gender, class, age group or subculture? It is here that the con- cept of a perceived common genealogy is fruitful. Ethnicity and nationalism are *kinship ideologies*, ideologies which prescribe that the members of a community or group constitute an extended family, with a common ancestry similar to those of families. It is the family 'writ large' (cf. Horowitz, 1985; Smith, 1991: 19 ff.; Roosens, 1994). It is within the family that one is secure.[7] The most forceful explanation of Anderson's question of why it is that so many people are prepared to kill and to die for the nation is this analogy with the 'family', rather than the 'deep, horizontal comradeship' which Anderson himself suggests (Anderson, 1991: 7). It is the ideology of family relations (also emphasised by Anderson, however) between members of a nation which comes closest to explaining the attraction of nationalism. It is also this analogy which makes national identity a useful tool for providing security. The nation is thus seen as a large, imagined family or kinship group. Perceptions of biological reproduction thus become crucial. The ethnic or national group has been 'born' at a particular time in history, and thus the very terminology of ethnicity and nationalism leads one to think of the structuring of gender roles.[8] Women are the very reproducers of people, and it is thus women who produce Swedes, Palestinians, Jews, French men and women, Poles, and so on. Symbols of the nation are often feminised, and when nationalist discourse talks about the 'nation' as an object, as that which is to be protected and fought for, women provide the connotations and images. However, when talking about the 'nation' as an acting unit, a subject, then it is men that are referred to.

It should also be emphasised that nationalism and national identity are to a large extent dependent on the *internal* distribution of power and resources. Nationalism is also shaped by the dynamics and social power structures and class relations within each community. Marxist authors interpret nationalism by analogy with class analysis, implying that nationalist movements are seen as a result of deprived interests and socioeconomic circumstances. It is doubtless the case that socioeconomic and material discontent is part of the reason for the rise of contemporary nationalist movements. Seton-Watson (1977: 10) states:

> Nevertheless the discontent was directed by the nationalist elites into nationalist movements rather than towards economic change. Where this happened, one may say that the masses accepted nationalist rather than social revolutionary leadership . . . Without the discontents there would have been no movements; but without the nationalist elites the movements would not have been nationalist.

It is therefore of major importance to bring class analysis into the study of nationalism. National politicisation is often defined by 'cultural brokers', or a political leadership, capable of providing mobilising resources. Anderson shows eloquently how popular nationalism in Europe in the 1820s–1920s was formed by the social strata who had language as their profession (i.e. writers, journalists, lexicographers, etc.), and how the nationalism that was produced was consumed by the 'reading classes' (i.e. the bourgeoisie) (Anderson, 1991: 74 ff.).

Key issues and analytical scheme

To analyse nationalism, I have divided the concept into three main components. Nationalism is an ideology of boundedness, implying desired coherence between the borders/boundaries of a certain geography or territory, of a population consisting of a 'people', a 'nation', and of the polity, that is, the administrative/functional apparatus of statehood. In its constant aspiration for establishing and securing borders and boundaries, nationalism is also an ideology of identity and about constructing identity. The three themes refer to political goals, images of the 'self' and ideas of the 'other'.

1 *Political goals* as related to territory and statehood: what does a particular nationalism claim that it wants to achieve in terms of establishing state structure; defending the state against external threats; gaining independence, autonomy, self-rule, liberation of territory from foreign rule; separation from the state; merging with other movements and/or states, and what are the strategies to achieve this goal – through military struggle; diplomatic negotiations; mobilisation of the 'masses'; through gaining international support; through legal measures; or through parliamentary struggle? What should be the political and geographical borders of a particular nationalism? Related to the Palestinian case, questions could be elaborated as follows. What are the definitions and descriptions of the kinds of arrangement that are desired for the territory that is called 'Palestine'? What are the most ideal goals in terms of a solution to the Palestinian–Israeli conflict? Since Palestinian nationalism is an integral part of the conflict itself and cannot be separated from it, we need to address issues of long- and short-term goals.

2 *Perceptions of the 'self'*: who are the 'wes', the 'in'-group, those who remain within the boundary; what is the meaning of 'self'; what kinds of mechanism of exclusion–inclusion exist so as to distinguish 'us' from 'them'; what are the internal contestations of definitions of 'self'; how are internal boundaries between different kinds of 'us' established and maintained and how do such boundaries change; how does 'self' relate itself to 'others'? In relation to the Palestinian case, how are the Palestinian nation and identity described and defined? What is the meaning that actors place on their identity and how does that meaning differ and vary between different internal actors? How do they describe 'Palestine' and 'Palestinians'? What is Palestinian nationalism? Integral to this issue are perceptions of internal relations. How are sources of power and structures of dominance, such as the newly established Authority as well as the PLO, perceived? How are internal relations and potential for conflict perceived and described? How do members of different factions perceive competing factions? How do

15

'insiders' perceive 'outsiders' returning in the wake of the agreements, and how do the 'returnees' perceive the 'inside' structure?[9]

3   *Perceptions of the 'other'*: who are the significant 'others' and how are they defined and described; what is the meaning of 'other'; what kinds of mechanisms of exclusion–inclusion exist in order to distinguish and maintain 'others'; how are perceptions of 'others' changed in the contextual flux; how are boundaries established and maintained so as to keep 'others' at a distance, or vice versa; how do 'others' represent a 'friendly' 'non-we', that is, how are boundaries created so as to encompass mutual empathy? Applied to the Palestinian case, this may look as follows. How are the state of Israel, Israelis and Jews described and perceived? What does Israel represent? How is the international system described? How are Arabs and Arabism described? Has there been a change since the implementation of the agreements? What are the differences between the different factions?

A discussion of method

The focus of the book is thus on ideas, self-perceptions and descriptions, meaning, identity and ideology. In order to capture this, two main methods are used: (1) qualitative interviews with representatives of the political leadership; and (2) text analysis of primary sources such as leaflets, documents, charters and political programmes. Qualitative interviews were conducted during a year of field study between the summer of 1994 and the summer of 1995, a period which saw unprecedented change and which breathed enthusiasm and optimism, despite undoubted backlashes. During that time Yasir Arafat arrived in the Gaza Strip and the Palestinian National Authority (PNA) gradually assumed partial control over Gaza and Jericho. The interviews were updated in the autumn of 1997, in a different setting altogether, characterised by apathy and despair in relation to the faltering peace process since mid-1996. The highly volatile and rapidly changing Middle Eastern political arena also changed the context of research during such a time span. Since the interviews deal with the political situation and opinions/descriptions of political events, it is inevitable that they are influenced by the ups and downs of the peace process, the closure of the West Bank and Gaza, deadly military attacks by Hamas or Islamic Jihad, and so forth.

I conducted fifty interviews with the political leadership in the West Bank and Gaza. 'Political leadership' is defined as individuals in high positions in the various factions and members of the PNA. Factions included in the study are al-Fatah, the targest faction of the PLO, the Popular Front for the Liberation of Palestine (PFLP), the Democratic Front for the Liberation of Palestine (DFLP), the Palestine People's Party (PPP), the Palestinian Democratic Federation Party (Fida) or the Palestinian Democratic Union (PDU) (all PLO factions, although the PFLP and DFLP have refused to participate in PLO meetings since the Oslo Accord), and Hamas and Islamic Jihad. I interviewed at least two representatives of each faction. In some cases being a representative of a faction and being a member of the PNA coincided. Representatives of Fateh constituted, however, the bulk of those interviewed, simply because of its dominance in Palestinian political life. Some factionally independent people were also included, some of them within the PNA and others independent critics of the current process. 'Independent' in this context means independent of factional 'belongingness', but could imply strong family (*hamuleh*, that is, extended family) affiliations. The motivation for choosing to interview leaders and the political elite was that they are active in producing formal nationalism and my main concern is official nationalism and how it is contested. Naturally, this creates a bias in the sense that informal or popular nationalism is not given equal attention. This material was supplemented by interviews with local Fateh activists.

Although none of those interviewed has declined to be named, I have decided to let the respondents remain anonymous throughout the text. The prime reason for this is that quotations and interpretations may appear to be out of context to the respondents. Of course, to me the interviews, after transcription, come out as texts, and are interpreted. Thus in interpreting text and oral narrative and responses I have used basically the same mode of procedure.

The top echelon of political representatives of the various factions were all astonishingly generous with their time and in sharing their views and opinions with me, although they all had hectic schedules. Most made genuine efforts to find a way to meet in the midst of pressing circumstances. What must be kept in mind is that the interviewees are politically active, and hence their responses are also political and official. Such replies are also, however, individually independent. The way interviewees interpret, analyse and describe is dependent on their own life situations. In addition, the purpose of my study is to present the official political discourse as it is presented by actors in the form of factions, movements and individuals. However, one has to bear in mind that the replies may at times be given for a reason, and the researcher must try to put the answers into a context. Why is it that this person tells me these things and why is it that he/she uses those terms? A failure to do this may mean the researcher being captured by political processes and used as a vehicle for carrying political messages. The same goes for how methodologically to approach ethnicity and nationalism, essentialised by actors but seen as socially constructed by analysts.[10]

> If nationalisms and ethnicities are seen as 'natural' entities which are not dealt with critically by investigators, then they will not be able to understand how social realities can be social products and in what ways they are ideological. If they fail to regard folk concepts of national and ethnic identity critically, analysts can easily become the hostages of nationalists wishing to justify violent and discriminatory

practices. The analytical deconstruction of ethnicity and nationalism can therefore be politically important. (Eriksen, 1992a: 12)

On the other hand, it is equally necessary to take the agents of ethnicity and nationalism seriously, to consider internal self-perceptions as tantamount importance to the critical approach (cf. Eriksen, 1992a: 32). The dilemma of combining as close and accurate as possible an interpretation of what actors voice with a critical approach has in this study been very concrete from a methodological point of view. That is, how to take actors seriously and let their narrative stand in focus, without falling prey to their potential stereotypisation and a politically charged discourse? Through being perceived as a representative of structures of Western dominance, however unintended, the researcher from the 'West' puts her-/himself in a position of narrating/analysing/interpreting which implies a great deal of power. In the process of communication, it is not only what people say that is of interest, but in what context they say it. That is to say, that respondents conveyed what they did to *me* is naturally of tremendous importance. Who am I and how am I perceived by respondents? Power thus works in (at least) two ways in any interview situation.

My attempt to describe the Palestinian movement as far as possible from 'within' – that is, how Palestinian political leaders themselves describe the meaning of nationalism – is also guided by the will and intention to overcome simplified and reductionist approaches, as well as explanations coloured by shortcomings related to the fact that I am an 'outsider'. However, it may be argued that an outside observer has the benefit of distance, being apart from the movement and its political discourse.

The dilemma is double. On the one hand, I seek to describe Palestinianism from the actors' point of view, that is, to understand and interpret, rather than to explain or seek to master the Palestinian discourse. On the other hand, my intention is to analyse critically, and my interpretations may not correspond with respondents' interpretations. The question of what 'right' the distant observer has to describe a complicated political process and interpret and critically examine the actors' points of view is thus legitimate. Why become one more of a number of 'others' who unilaterally place themselves in the position of describing, telling and writing about the Palestinians? The only answer is to contextualise statements and polarised attitudes so as to make them comprehendable and not add to their mystification. In addition, this is the dilemma of all research, only in this case made worse by the fact that an asymmetrical international system acts upon the process. Analysts do have a right to try to systematise and analyse perceptions and interpretations of the 'relatively deprived'. Nevertheless, it has to be done with care. To claim that only Arabs can write about Arabs, Palestinians about Palestinians, Swedes about Swedes and Westerners about the West would be to give in to nationalist/essentialist politics of difference and feed exclusivist presumptions of cultures as bounded entities with little capacity for empathy.

The text

Qualitative interviews are complemented by an interpretation of text that was utilised in analysing documents, statutes and charters from Palestinian political organisations.

Furthermore, the production of nationalist discourse during the *intifada* was analysed mainly through a selection of leaflets and communiqués (the *bayanat*) from the Unified National Leadership of the Uprising (UNLU), as well as separate leaflets and communiqués from Hamas and Islamic Jihad.[11] During the *intifada*, the *bayanat* were, together with political graffiti (cf. Steinberg and Oliver, 1994), the most common way of political communication and directing the population in various actions. The *bayanat* contained both ideologised analyses of the current situation and concrete directions of, for example, strike days and specific activities. Leaflets have been an ingredient of Palestinian nationalist/political life at earlier times in history (Mishal and Aharoni, 1994), but with the UNLU *bayanat* they gained a new intensity. The production of leaflets under one 'heading', the UNLU, rather than previous factional ones, was an achievement in itself.[12]

Texts (including the interviews) are reproduced in the process of reading and interpretation, and not only the context in which a text is written, but the context in which it is read, contributes to the production of meaning of the text. Not only the social activities which are studied, but the social activity of studying subjects and agents and the material they produce, are situated temporally, paradigmatically and spatially (cf. Giddens, 1979: 54). This is not to say that subjectivism and relativism are all there is to it, however. Conceptual tools and the theoretical approach guide my readings of texts and interviews and, hopefully, provide a more generalised framework and set of understanding. Also, in order to interpret discourse in the form of oral and textual statements meaningfully, an historical and situational contextualisation is needed. Only in so far as we can gain a deeper level of understanding of the context in which a text was produced can we understand its meaning. In this study, there is therefore an explicit intention to connect context and internal meaning. As in interviews, interpreting texts requires an active communicative process guided by intersubjectivity, where the text is not an object to be studied but a subject with a multitude of things to say.

Of course, and as already underlined, texts are only part of reality. In order to understand and explain my problem area, actions as well as institutions must be included. And, as Habermas (1988) argues, meaning and action are interwoven. In order to explain action, we have to understand meaning, and in order to understand meaning, we have to observe actions. As Tibi (1991: 123) states:

> A sociologist who knows Islam only as a *fait social* is no more likely to provide an appropriate understanding of the subject than a traditional Orientalist. The researcher must be familiar with both the texts *and* the sociostructural reality that corresponds to them in order to achieve an adequate understanding of how that sociocultural system functions.

Although the focus in this book is on identity and ideology through text in different forms, this is done in a constant relation to institutions, structures and actors. Institution-building, concrete politics and strategies and internal disputes are interwoven in the analyses, as is Israel's and other actors' behaviour.

Although the study of change always implies an historical perspective, it should be emphasised that the perspective is not evolutionary, that is, Palestinian nationalism is not going through predetermined stages. Rather, histories of nationalism should be seen as dynamic, non-linear processes. Frequently, when historical material is presented, history looks more organised and 'neat' than it really is. In addition, actors reinterpret history and use it in determining actions for themselves; history is never neutral, but used, invented and reinvented. Writing at a time in history when rapid change is taking place in the political scene of the Middle East and about a time, the history of which is not yet written but which will inevitably be deemed historical, those lines should be kept in mind.

Structure of the book

The following chapter turns the focus on the Palestinian case and outlines how a specific Palestinian identity was formulated at the beginning of the twentieth century, in relation to the collision with the Zionist project. It should be noted, however, that Palestinian identity was also influenced by larger-scale processes such as the dissemination of nationalism as an idea in the region and structural reforms in the Ottoman empire. The chapter describes the fragmentation of identity, nationalist politics in the aftermath of the 1948 disaster, and how a territorialised Palestinianism gained a mass following after the 1967 war. It was then that Palestinian identity in effect came to mean to 'struggle' and to 'suffer', two concepts of acute significance in the structuring of Palestinian identity.

Chapter 3 moves from the exile experience of longing to the inside situation of occupation, and discusses how the *intifada* changed the character of Palestinian identity as well as the ideology of nationalism. The main representation of Palestinianism as manifested in struggle and suffering now reached the West Bank and Gaza in a direct and concrete way.

The remaining parts of the book – the lion's share – focus on the post-Oslo period, when self-government again changed the form of Palestinian identity. Chapter 4 deals with the agreements with Israel, self-government and state-building, and how these processes are seen by the different political trends in Palestinian life. Chapter 5 analyses in depth the meaning and content of Palestinian identity as narrated by the interviewees. It also brings into focus the ways in which identity is not only in acute interaction with an 'other', but always internally contested and negotiated. Political trends in Palestinian politics are divided into four categories: official or mainstream nationalism (largely represented by Fateh), oppositional leftist nationalism, Islamism and reformism.

Chapter 6 deals with perceptions of the 'other', since no one identity can be seen in isolation from its significant 'others'. How do Palestinians perceive Israelis and Jews? Here, what may be called Palestinian inferiority complex is brought into focus, as well as the dichotomy between perceptions of Israel as an enemy and a neighbour.

The final chapter discusses two main themes. First is how Palestinian nationalism and identity must be seen as both a result of the violent and catastrophic meeting with Zionism and Israel, and as the consequence of active production by political elites capable of providing images and visions. Both conventional wisdoms of Palestinian identity – that is, the Palestinian claim of a primordial, essential identity and the Israeli instrumentalist, reactive interpretation – are insufficient to provide us with an understanding of the Palestinian predicament. Second, it reflects on the debate on boundary versus 'cultural stuff' (Barth, 1969: 204), form versus content, social relations versus cultural meaning in identity discussions, strongly emphasising that the two are interrelated.

NOTES

1 Contributions to the study of Palestinian nationalism have until recently been mainly historical. Among the most noteworthy are Quandt, Jabber and Lesch (1973); Porah (1974); Lesch (1979); Johnson (1982); Muslih (1988); Kimmerling and Migdal (1993); and Khalidi (1997). We need also to mention Rosemary Sayigh's (1979, 1994) contribution to the understanding of the creation of Palestinianism from a bottom-up camp experience, using narratives from Sabra and Shateela. There are, of course, many other works which contribute to our understanding of the Palestinian story, but they will not be mentioned here since they do not deal explicitly with nationalism.

2 For the history of nationalism as an ideology or doctrine, see Smith (1972, 1979, 1983, 1986); Armstrong (1982); Gellner (1983); Hobsbawm (1990) and Anderson (1991). Seton-Watson's (1977) classical work focuses more on nationalist movements and nations than on nationalism. One of the main debates in the nationalism discourse is whether nations are to be seen as modern only (Nairn, 1977; Gellner, 1983; Hobsbawm, 1990; Anderson, 1991) or whether (at least some) nations are pre-modern (Seton-Watson, 1977; Armstrong, 1982; Smith, 1986, 1994; Hastings, 1997).

3 Oppositional nationalism does not necessarily have to be popular, but rather a challenging elite project.

21

4 In his lecture *Qu'est-ce que c'est une nation?* at the Sorbonne in March 1882.

5 The casting of ethnicity, nationalism and the politics of identity in the 1990s is also entangled with the process of globalisation and its creation both of an eclectic, timeless, spaceless world culture and of intense production of particular identities (e.g. Featherstone, 1990).

6 Rather than 'inventions' and fabrications. The standard work on the 'invention of tradition' is Hobsbawm and Ranger (1983).

7 Although, of course, domestic violence is one of the main threats to the security of women and children.

8 Anderson (and others) does not discuss how the nation is gendered. For such an analysis cf. Yuval-Davies (1997). In the study of the relationship between nationalism and gender, it is also important to ask whether national identity is experienced differently by men and women. One obvious difference is that, for the most part, it is men who are prepared to die for the nation (Anderson, 1991: 141); it is men who are socialised and trained through military apparatuses, military service and guerrilla warfare to love and defend the nation. In a military sense, women are important as the bearers of potential national soldiers. This obviously ought to make a difference in the experience of ethnicity and nationality.

9 The conceptual pair 'inside' and 'outside' is structuring internal Palestinian relations in a very real sense. 'Inside' refers to those living under occupation and 'outside' refers to exiles. 'Outside' often refers mainly to the exiled PLO leadership, but also to the Palestinian diaspora at large. 'Inside', 'inner' or 'interior' is *dakhli* in Arabic and 'outside', 'outer' or 'exterior' is *kharji*.

10 In the primordialist era of studies of ethnicity and nationalism, the problem was that researchers ran the risk of themselves creating 'ethnicities' in their search for them. The problem inherent in constructivism is rather the other side of the coin, that is, to think ethnicity away or neglect it, since it doesn't 'really' exist anyway.

11 The UNLU consisted of al-Fateh, the PFLP, the DFLP and the Palestine Communist Party (PCP). *Bayanat* means statements or declarations. The term is used for both UNLU and Hamas leaflets, but in the headings of the leaflets the UNLU used the word *nida*, which means 'call', whereas Hamas used *bayan*. The first leaflet by the UNLU was produced on 8 January 1988. Islamic Jihad produced the first leaflet related to the outbreak of the *intifada* on 10 December 1987, that is, only one day after its outbreak. A leaflet signed 'Hamas' appeared on 14 December 1987.

12 The Palestine National Front (PNF) also produced unified leaflets during the 1970s.

2

From elite proto-nationalism to mass-based revolution

The modern ideology of nationalism crystallised in Palestine in the early part of the twentieth century. It is often claimed that Palestinian identity and nationalism emerged as a reaction against Zionism, the encounter with Jewish immigration and the political processes at hand during the British mandate. As has already been underlined, it is true that Palestinianism is unusually clearly formulated in entanglement with its main significant 'other': 'Zionism', 'Israel' and expressions of Israeli Jewish collective identity. However, the emergence of Palestinianism must also be understood in the context of the spread of nationalism in the region at large (cf. Khalidi, 1997). The structural changes of Ottoman rule – the Tanzimat reforms, when centralisation occurred and new institutions were created in order to facilitate tax-collecting – served as a background variable in the sense of an increasingly Westernised education system, and the emergence of a new press, political organisations and clubs with a profound impact upon intellectual and political life in Palestine (Khalidi, 1997). One of the most important changes was the introduction of the Ottoman Land Law in 1858, which required a title of ownership for all land, which in turn placed large parts of the land under the control of the city notables and clan leaders. A new landowning class was slowly created, based on property – a process similar to that in the rest of the Middle East (cf. Zubaida, 1989: 87 f.). Power shifted from rural tribal chiefs, the *sheyoukh*, to city notables (the *a'yan*), holding political, economic and cultural influence. New taxes were imposed upon the peasantry, who found themselves deeply indebted. The *a'yan* was also the credit-giving institution. The elite was linked to the Ottoman rulers as an intermediary political structure which facilitated the rule of the empire.

Although Jewish immigration and land purchase remained at a low level during the pre-World War I period, it increased, and two separate economies were slowly formed. At the same time, contacts with Europe increased through missionaries and Christians settling in the Holy Land, as well as rapid integration in the world economy. An economic boom in the coastal areas drew rural migrants from the hinterland to the new economic centres.

World War I meant disruptive change, in particular for the peasantry, as land alienation and urbanisation had begun to transform Palestinian society. During the war, most notable Palestinian families supported the Ottoman empire and identified with 'Ottomanism' (Muslih, 1988: 89). The word 'Palestine' (*Filastin*) was in use, however, in the latter part of the Ottoman empire, being used to denote either the whole of Palestine or the *sanyaq* of Jerusalem, mainly by an educated stratum (cf. Porath, 1974) and in print media (Khalidi, 1997).

During the war, Great Britain and France manipulated growing anti-Turkish sentiment in the Arab world, and early variants of Arab nationalism were inspired by French and British models. After the war, the final fall and decay of the Ottoman empire and the division of the Middle East into British and French mandates and protectorates, the British and French could no longer serve as the national model and ideal for the germinating national movement, as during the mobilisation against the Turks. Disappointment over the non-fulfilment of the McMahon–Husayn correspondence in 1915[1] and the division of the Middle East into mandates and protectorates (the Sykes–Picot Agreement of 1916, the Treaties of Sèvres and San Remo (1920) and Lausanne (1923)) and Western colonialism provided an impetus for anti-imperial nationalism. The task was no longer to fight the Ottomans but to free the Arab world from Western rule. When King Feysal's rule of Syria ended in disaster, defeated by the French in 1920, this marked the 'awakening of the Arabs', according to George Antonius, a Christian Palestine Arab. The Arab awakening was the result of a catastrophe, an unprecedented disaster when Syria was crushed and the Arab world divided (Antonius, 1938). An emotional, anti-French Arab nationalism based on the German notion of an eternal 'nation' emerged, largely under the influence of Sati' al-Husri (Hourani, 1962: 312 ff.; Tibi, 1971: 117 ff.). The new Arab nationalism held that *language* was the defining component of a 'people', a 'nation', and hence the Arab nation extended over the whole of the geographical area, the population of which had Arabic as their mother tongue (Tibi, 1991, 1997).

In its early life, Arabism had only marginal appeal in Palestine (cf. Porath, 1974: 20 ff.). During the Arab revolt, most leaders in Palestine continued to identify with Ottomanism and quiescently supported the Young Turks, although hajj Amin al-Husayni (the importance of whom will be discussed below) was to join the Arab Revolt (Mattar, 1988: 12). Muslih argues that Palestinian nationalism or patriotism began to take shape in the 1910s, and that it was easier for the Palestine Arab elite at the time to subscribe to local patriotism than to the Arab nationalist framework, due to the interconnectedness between Ottomanism and the Palestinian elite (Muslih, 1988: 104).

Factionalism and early elite mobilisation

The Balfour Declaration of 1917 sparked widespread opposition, anti-Zionism and fear, although anti-Zionist resistance had actually occurred prior to the Declaration (Khalidi, 1997). Mobilising forces were the increasingly dispossessed peasantry, the print media and urban intellectuals (Khalidi, 1997). Muslih argues that the role of peasants in the formation of the anti-Zionist Arab movement was already evident in the 1910s, when land alienation as a process began (Muslih, 1988: 72). In addition, since land was sold by local landowners to Jewish immigrants, internal tension was aggravated.[2] The Balfour Declaration was perceived as contradicting the McMahon–Husayn correspondence and resulted in a wave of disappointment and consequently anti-imperialist Arab nationalism (cf. Antonius, 1938). The British conquest implied that the new separate administration over all Palestine enforced the concept of 'Palestine' as a single unit (Porath, 1974), with the exception of Trans-Jordan.

In the 1920s, and with the establishment of British mandatory rule,[3] the domestic socio-political system in Palestine – and large parts of the Arab world – was heavily influenced by the *a'yan*. The rural population, a large proportion of whom were share-croppers, was attached to the *a'yan* through patron–client relations, and the villages became increasingly dependent on the city notables. Horizontal cleavages in the form of family and clan identities were also of primary importance, and personal loyalties were a major factor in deciding politics. Factionalism and family rivalries characterised the politics of the Arab community in Palestine (Johnson, 1982: 18). The two most prominent Jerusalem families that fought for influence were the Husaynis[4] and the Nashashibis.[5]

The British mandate pursued a policy of creating political alliances with the local elite, based on the religious institutions which were under British control.[6] The granting of rights to the Supreme Muslim Council and the appointment of hajj Amin al-Husayni as its president were a lead in this policy. The British adopted a 'divide and rule' strategy and separated the Muslim, Christian and Jewish communities in order to keep intact the *millet* system of Ottoman rule.[7] Not only did Jewish land purchase increase, but the British administration introduced new legal and administrative practices at odds with the traditional system, causing further fragmentation and disorientation, among both the peasantry and the urban notables.

Social boundaries were thus in the early part of the twentieth century in a period of change, from tribal, clan, notables–peasantry, and so on, to marking Palestine Arabs from Jews, the British and other Arabs. Crucial in this formative period was structural change in the form of rapid socioeconomic integration into the world economy, the gradual emergence of an 'other' and the increasing role of print media, such as the press, textbooks and novels (cf. Lesch, 1979; Kimmerling and Migdal, 1993; Khalidi, 1997). Poetry played a leading role in transferring images of the soil, an 'idealised image of the village', and hence the gradual imagining of a people (Kimmerling and Migdal, 1993: 55). Still, the nourishment of nationalist ideals – whether Palestinian or pan-Arab – was largely confined to the elite. A 'proto-national' elite with a nationalist programme was thus formed during this period, although this nationalism was indecisive and oscillated between Ottomanism, Arabism and Palestinianism; it was also severely hampered by fragmentation. The focus of national(ist) considerations was decided more by political and economic interest (Sayigh, 1997a) than by deep sentiments of belonging.

The formulation of Palestinian nationalism

A nationalist agenda was formulated partly through the Muslim–Christian Associations (MCAs), formed in Jaffa in 1918. The central principles of the MCAs were, according to Kimmerling and Migdal, anti-Zionism and 'Palestinism':

> Palestinism meant the assertion of Palestine as a common homeland at a time when political boundaries were new and still quite uncertain. After a brief flirtation with the notion of their incorporation into Syria, the new organizations began to proclaim emphatically the existence of a distinct Arab people in Palestine. Even when some adopted pan-Arab programs, they took care to distinguish Palestine's Arabs from those outside the country. (Kimmerling and Migdal, 1993: 53)

In a similar fashion, Muslih argues that the MCAs represented 'the first generation of Palestinian politicians whose ideals formed the basis of Palestinian nationalism' (Muslih, 1988: 162). An important feature of those new forms of organisation was to distinguish Palestine's Arabs from other Arabs. What took place in this period was the first attempt to create a national political body based on the territory of Palestine as the organising principle and to mobilise an identity connected to this territory.

Nevertheless, at the First Arab Congress in 1919, the delegates, including the MCAs, adopted a resolution stating that Palestine was part of Syria, thus reflecting the influence of Arab nationalism and the close links with the southern Syria notion:

> Resolution of the First Palestinian Arab Congress
> (1) We consider Palestine nothing but part of Arab Syria and it has never been separated from it in any stage. We are tied to it by national [*qawmiyya*[8]], religious, linguistic, moral, economic and geographic bonds. (Quoted in Muslih, 1988: 181 f.)

Since the population of Syria was promised a national government of its own in the Anglo-French Declaration of 1918 but the Palestine Arabs were not, the population of Palestine thus opted for unity with Syria. Political clubs were formed, drawing support from the young, educated Muslim section of the population. The political goals of the organisations were the same (anti-Zionism and the unification of Palestine with Syria), but their messages were somewhat different. In 1920, conflicts occurred between the two main clubs, marking the commencement of the 'great conflict between the Husayni and Nashashibi families' (Porath, 1974: 101). Both clubs lost influence after the Third Arab Congress in 1920, after which the MCAs were considerably strengthened.

At the Third Arab Congress (which took place in Haifa), no reference was made to Greater Syria. Thus by 1920, when King Feysal's rule of Syria was shattered, Palestinian nationalism and the idea of an independent Palestine had gained the upper hand over Arab nationalism among the local elite (Lesch, 1979; Muslih, 1988: 201), and a romantic nationalist rhetoric emphasising the 'love' of Palestine was being nurtured (Khalidi, 1997: 168 ff.). This was the first time that the Palestine Arabs had declared the goal of establishing a national government (Porath, 1974: 46). The appeal of the Syria idea was substantial only as long as it could visualise some strength.

When the British mandate came into force in 1922, a 'paralysis of the national movement' occurred (Porath, 1974: 183). Gradually, however, new social and political forces in the form of younger intellectuals began to mobilise and become articulate. By the Seventh Arab Congress in 1924, a radical new generation had emerged as a social and political force to be reckoned with. This radical group allied itself with hajj Amin al-Husayni and the Arab Executive. In the latter half of the 1920s, religious matters were brought to the fore with dissension over al-Haram al-Sharif in Jerusalem and the massacres of Jews in Jerusalem, Hebron and Safed.

The political elite did not, however, respond to the grievances of the uprooted and dispossessed Palestinian peasantry, who, owing to the loss of land, were drawn increasingly to urban localities. Hence during the early 1930s a vertical class cleavage between the *a'yan* and the Palestinian masses became increasingly obvious (Khalaf, 1991: 33).

The Great Revolt and popular proto-nationalism

In the mid 1930s, then, Palestinian politics were characterised by, on the one hand, institutionalised family factionalism and, on the other, peasant grievances. Six political parties existed in the early 1930s, one of which, Istiqlal (Independence), challenged the family structure. Istiqlal had a radical, pan-Arab, anti-British and non-cooperative approach and had its leadership in the north of the country, in the cities of Nablus and Jaffa.[9] It managed to mobilise both young professionals and the *shabab* – a new social force in the form of young men who, in the social context of land dispossession, Jewish immigration, British rule and incorporation into the world market, took on the meaning of men no longer bound by family or clan ties.[10] Istiqlal provided the first organised opposition against the *a'yan*. The main support was drawn from professionals, intellectuals and government officials (Lesch, 1979). The political weakness of the middle class, however, impeded a more broad-based recruitment by the six parties. Increased Jewish immigration and the connected land alienation did, however, provide fertile ground for popular political action. Neither the institutionalised elite nor the new intellectual stratum managed to channel peasant and worker grievances into cohesive collective action. Instead, the vacuum was to be filled with actions by Sheikh 'Izz al-Din al-Qassem (see Milton-Edwards, 1996), a Syrian-born student at the al-Azhar University in Cairo and a student of Muhammad 'Abduh.[11] al-Qassem's political message was that of a reform of Islam; only the faithful could be successful in the struggle for Palestine.

The peasant rebellion, or Great Revolt, which broke out in 1936 was preceded by a call for revolt by al-Qassem and Ikhwan al-Qassem (the Qassem Brotherhood), which gathered a large number of uprooted peasants and part of the poorer urban strata – the *shabab* – as followers in an Islamic-nationalistic militancy. The sheikh was, however, killed in a confrontation with the British police force before his request was carried out. The Great Revolt was a response to al-Qassem and the unrest of the 1930s. His own organisation and the unrest which took place in the aftermath of his death were also directed against the traditional elite; this is why popular Islam also became an instrument in internal class relations (cf. Johnson, 1982: 45 ff.). al-Qassem's impact lay in his direct linkage to the poor, the uneducated, the landless and the peasantry (Milton-Edwards, 1996: 12 f.).

The Great Revolt was a popular uprising which started spontaneously and without direction from the political elite. It consisted of a general strike which lasted for six months, as well as violent attacks on the Jewish population and Jewish institutions. The leaders of the uprising were to a large extent drawn from the ranks of al-Qassem (Johnson, 1982: 53). Its main social forces were the peasants, the *shabab* and the emerging working class, although the Western-educated intelligentsia and city merchants also played a role. The local elite was eventually driven to support the uprising. By then hajj Amin al-Husayni had become increasingly radical.[12]

After six months, the uprising was brought to an end, but it was revived in September 1937. The village and the rural hinterland became the base for the struggle, posing a threat to the *a'yan* and the cities. A popular culture romanticising the peasants and the lower classes emerged (Kimmerling and Migdal, 1993: 113). During the latter part of the uprising, fragmentation and internecine violence were aggravated, as were religious tensions. Such tensions were manipulated by the British mandatory power, in turn intensifying already existing divisions (Kimmerling and Migdal, 1993: 114 f.). Like the *intifada* fifty years later, the revolt and the general strike also implied increased economic hardship for large sections of Palestinian society.

The uprising lasted until 1939, when it was crushed by harsh British repression. The end of the revolt left the Palestinian movement void of effective leadership. The Great Revolt demonstrated, however, that the British felt obliged to take into consideration Arab grievances, and in 1939 a White Paper was produced, limiting Jewish immigration and proposing a unitary state and full independence after ten years. After pressure from the *mufti*, the Arab Higher Committee (AHC)[13] rejected the White Paper because it did not put an immediate halt to immigration, since the land policy was seen as flawed and because independence for Palestine would be conditioned by Jewish cooperation (Khalaf, 1991: 73 ff.).

The real impact of the revolt was that it marked a nationalist politicisation of the Palestinians, and the spread of nationalist ideas to unprivileged social strata, such as the peasantry (Sayigh, 1979: 45). Socioeconomic deprivation merged with national(ist) grievances. Islamic symbolism was used in formulating a nationalist discourse. Religious discourse did not stand in opposition to nationalism; rather, religiousness augmented nationalist sentiments in an effective combination of the use of symbols connected to the land, the peasantry and religious idioms. 'Paradoxically, the revolt was a distinct watershed, crystallising the Palestinian national identity as nothing before. It offered new heroes and martyrs – most prominently Sheikh Qassam – and a popular culture to eulogise them [. . .] the revolt helped to create a nation' (Kimmerling and Migdal, 1993: 123). The revolt implied the formulation of a 'folk nationalism', similar to that of European nationalisms in the late 1800s, as a reaction against the nationalism of the intelligentsia and the elite (cf. Hobsbawm, 1990). It represented a folk Islam in opposition to the Islam of the learned, as well as a folk nationalism versus elite definitions. Both Hamas and the PLO today draw on the self-sacrifice, the martyrdom and the struggle which were provided by Sheikh Izz al-Din al-Qassem.

The catastrophe and the dispersal

Between 1939 and 1948, there was a stalemate in the political activism of Palestine Arabs, largely due to harsh British repression of the Revolt. During the 1940s, far-reaching socioeconomic changes were taking place; a working class was formed, as was an emerging bourgeoisie consisting of entrepreneurs and merchants as well as professionals and intellectuals, challenging the notability's economic power. Despite these changes, the traditional elite kept tight political control, and there was a discrepancy between economic and political power. No longer was it the landholding strata that dominated the economic life of Arab Palestine (see Khalaf, 1991: 45–60). This situation thus differed from most other anti-colonialist nationalisms of the 1940s, where it was primarily the newly emerging Westernised elite which took the leading role in nationalist movements. In Arab Palestine, the traditional elite maintained legitimacy through its anti-Westernism (Khalaf, 1991: 63 f.). Hajj Amin al-Husayni increased his support even though he spent the years between 1941 and 1946 in Europe, having fled to Lebanon in October 1937.[14] In the second half of the 1940s, the *mufti* became a widely respected leader throughout the Arab world as Palestine became increasingly important in Arab nationalist discourse.

During World War II, the Arab economy in Palestine grew considerably. Great Britain's mobilisation in the war gave rise to a growing construction sector, drawing workers to the cities. A new Arab working class and organisation of labourers emerged. Although the Arab economy experienced a boom during this period, British policies clearly favoured the Jewish economic sector (Khalaf, 1991: 47 ff.).

From 1945 onwards, the involvement of the Arab states in the Palestine question increased. The Palestine question contributed to the spread of Arab nationalism among a younger, educated generation in the Arab world, forcing Arab regimes to take action (Khalaf, 1991: 163). King 'Abdallah of Trans-Jordan manoeuvred to expand territorially and to include Palestine, or parts of Palestine, in Trans-Jordan, as part of his plans to resurrect the Greater Syria idea. The United Nations (UN) vote in favour of partition of Palestine in 1947 aggravated communal violence and terror, and British rule soon disintegrated. According to Sayigh, it was in fact only now that the political elite began in earnest to territorialise their claims and ideas (Sayigh, 1997a: 10). For large parts of the Arab population, fleeing the scene became the sole option, as violence and turbulence permeated the country.

With the establishment of the state of Israel in 1948, and the first Arab–Israeli war in 1948–49 leading to the mass exodus (see Morris, 1987, 1990),[15] the dispersement – *shatat* in Arabic – of the Arab Palestinian population became a reality. One of the most important symbols of the *nakba*,[16] 'the catastrophe', was the massacre of village residents in Dair Yasin by Jewish Irgun[17] forces in April 1948, when some 200 villagers were killed. Dair Yasin was crucial in heightening Palestinian fears and the refugee flow, and has had a profound impact on the narration of Palestinian history.

It was in the 1950s that the politics of Arab nationalism became a common ideological denominator for the Arab states, although this commitment was more on the ideological than the practical level. Politics have instead been firmly based in the inter-state system.

Arab nationalism as dominant discourse, 1948–67

Because of the *shatat*, it became increasingly difficult to organise a coherent Palestinian leadership. Instead, the Palestinians were susceptible to the political ideologies of the states in which they resided. The liberation of Palestine was in the late 1940s an element of a broader Arab nationalism and anti-Western tendency. This movement can be seen as analogous with the national liberation movements in Africa and Asia during the decolonisation process in its anti-imperialism, the search for recapturing lost land and claimed authentic traditional symbols and values.

Universities were one of the main bases for the spread of new ideologies, and the large number of well educated Palestinians contributed to the diffusion of Arab nationalism in Palestinian ranks. Arab nationalism served as an ideology of rescue for the Palestinian movement, which was fractured by disasters. Competition between Jordanian Arab nationalism based on the conception of confederal unity, and the more radical Arabism of Egypt's President Gamel Abdel-Nasser and Syria, advocating the establishment of a single political Arab unity, crippled any potential for consistent action. A number of small Arab organisations and guerilla groups – *fedayeen*[18] – were formed, many of them drawing on experiences from pre-1948. More modern ideological movements were, however, unable to attract a mass following.

One of the most influential movements was the strongly anti-Hashemite Arab Nationalist Movement (ANM) and the unitary philosophy of Nasser. The goals of the ANM were to unify the Arab nation, liberate it from the 'imperialists' and take revenge for the humiliation of the 1948 war (cf. Cohen, 1982). In its early phase, the rhetoric of the ANM could be placed within a fascist framework in its 'absolutist nationalism and iron discipline' (Sayigh, 1997a: 72). 'It was also evident in its choice of main political slogan – "unity, liberation, and revenge" – and in its dramatic battle cry: "blood, iron, and fire"' (Sayigh, 1997a: 73). Its goal was to liberate Palestine, but only after complete Arab freedom from the yoke of colonialism. After the cessation of the confederation between Syria and Egypt, the ANM began to separate the issues of Arab unity and Palestinian liberation. During the 1950s and 1960s, the ANM to an increasing extent advocated a socialist agenda, and after Nasser's nationalisation of the Suez Canal in 1956, it became a staunch supporter of Nasser's Arabism. In 1964, it was bitterly opposed to the first Palestine National Council (PNC).

> Perhaps no Arabs had more to gain than the Palestinians from denigration of specific loyalties . . . in favor of devotion to broader Arab unity, and they became among pan-Arabism's most fervent exponents. . . . Pan-Arabism's emphasis on national liberation, both social and political, transformed the Palestinian dilemma from the particular to the general – it placed this dilemma in the broader historical context of the regeneration of the entire Arab people, their shedding of imperialism's shackles. (Kimmerling and Migdal, 1993: 196)

There was, however, also Palestinian institution-building, which was to serve as the base for the Palestinian national movement which re-emerged in the late

1950s. In 1948, the All-Palestine Government,[19] led by the *mufti*, al-Husayni (who was now, however, seated in Damascus), was formed in Gaza. A Palestine National Council was also formed during that year, consisting of Arab mayors hostile to the Hashemite kingdom. Also in 1948, the PNC issued the first Palestine Declaration of Independence, stating: 'Based on the natural and historical right of the Palestine Arab people to freedom and independence [...] [we declare] total independence of all Palestine [...] and the establishment of an independent, democratic state whose inhabitants will exercise their liberties and rights' (al-Husayni quoted in Mattar, 1988: 132).

Gradually the *mufti* lost influence and, with Jordanian rule over the West Bank, Jordan became the main actor (Migdal, 1980a: 36; see also Mattar, 1988). In Jordan, political Islam was the main current in the refugee camps throughout the 1950s (Sayigh, 1997a: 49). Camp politics were more prone to Islamism, while the intellectuals and the middle class were influenced by Arabism.

The nationalism of al-Fateh

Palestinian territorial nationalism in its modern form originates in al-Fateh, which was formed in Kuwait in 1959[20] by radical students from Cairo and the Gaza Strip, one of whom was Yasir Arafat. al-Fateh is the reverse acronym for al-Harakat al Tahrir al-Watani al-Falastin, which means the 'Palestinian national liberation movement'. The use of *watan* rather than *qawm* indicates a shift to Palestinian territorialism and patriotism rather than Arab nationalism.

The basic idea of Fateh was that Palestine was an issue first and foremost for the Palestinians, rather than the Arab states. Specific Palestinian nationalism ran contrary to the larger principle of pan-Arabism. Arab unity would come about only as a result of the Palestinian liberation of Palestine, and hence Palestine was to come first – the reverse strategy to that of the pan-Arabists (Cobban, 1984: 24; Sayigh, 1997a). Concerning relations with the Arab states, Fateh's strategy was non-interference in the internal affairs of the states and Arab non-interference in the life of Fateh, although al-Fateh was also to become deeply entrenched in Arab politics.

It was also al-Fateh that was first to mention the idea of a Palestinian state. Article 5 of Fateh's 'Seven Points', passed by the Central Committee of al-Fateh in January 1969, reads: 'Al Fateh, the Palestine National Liberation Movement, solemnly proclaims that the final objective of its struggle is the restoration of the independent, democratic State of Palestine, all of whose citizens will enjoy equal rights irrespective of their religion' (Laqueur and Rubin, 1984: 372).[21] al-Fateh thus called for a non-sectarian state for Jews, Christians and Muslims in all of Palestine, indicating a certain pragmatism and accommodationist strategy *vis-à-vis* Israel. One of the strengths of al-Fateh has been its purely nationalist message. This has enabled the organisation to gain

widespread support from large and diverse sections of the Palestinian population, including traditional elites, conservative Islamists and radical left-wingers.
Its outlook has been mainly non-ideological in terms of right–left argumenta-
tion and there has been no reference to, or elaboration of, what will happen
after liberation. The future state was defined in abstract grand terms as 'independent' and 'democratic', but no real political standpoint was formulated of
how this state should be organised. al-Fateh's *raison d'être* was its revolutionary
national liberation ideology, inspired by Vietnam, Algeria, Cuba and China,
although Fateh had not learned the importance of organisation and mobilisation. Neither was there a coherent theory on the social, economic and political
requirements of the armed struggle (Sayigh, 1997a: 199). The foremost task
was to keep the people united during the revolution. Ideological influences and
party politics were seen as potentially divisive (cf. Chaliand, 1972: 67 f.; Nassar,
1991: 81 ff.; Sayigh, 1997a: 90).

The PLO: between nationalism and patriotism, between unity and liberation

When the PLO was formed in Jerusalem by the Arab League in 1964 – led by
Ahmed al-Shuqayri – it was primarily organised under the influence of Egyptian President Gamel Abdel-Nasser.[22] The ANM was critical of the enactment of
the PLO, as was the GUPS (Brand, 1988a: 75; Sayigh, 1997a). The reason for
its establishment was partly an Egyptian intention to control the *fedayeen* movement, in accordance with Nasser's regional power ambitions, but it was also a
response to calls for a 'Palestinian entity' by the All Palestine Government and
to the 'statist' ambitions of its first leader, al-Shuqayri. The first PLO was heavily
biased towards the traditional elites, landowners and the professional sections
of the middle class (Sayigh, 1997a: 99).

In the 1968 Palestinian National Charter[23] – which has served as the frame
of reference for Palestinian politics and identity – the pan-Arab influence is
reflected, with no reference to a Palestinian state. Instead it reads: '1. Palestine
is the homeland of the Arab Palestinian people; it is an indivisible part of the
Arab homeland, and the Palestinian people are an integral part of the Arab
nation' (Laqueur and Rubin, 1984: 366). The Arab people – *qawm* – are seen
as an organic whole, a unity which contains parts in the form of territorial
homelands. The connection between land and people is organic and nationalism is almost a biological necessity. On the relationship between the Arab unity
and Palestine, the Charter states:

> 13. Arab unity and the liberation of Palestine are two complementary objectives,
> the attainment of either of which facilitates the attainment of the other. Thus, Arab
> unity leads to the liberation of Palestine, the liberation of Palestine leads to Arab
> unity . . .

14. The destiny of the Arab nation, and indeed Arab existence itself, depend upon the destiny of the Palestinian cause. From this interdependence spring the Arab nation's pursuit of, and striving for, the liberation of Palestine. The people of Palestine play the role of the vanguard in the realisation of this sacred national goal. (Laqueur and Rubin, 1984: 366)

The relationship with the Arab world at large was part of the Palestinian movement. 'Arab' and 'Palestinian' were entangled with each other. The liberation of Palestine was for the sake of Arabs. Still, the Charter refers to the 'people of Palestine', indicating also Palestinian nationalism or patriotism. In addition, the ANM was critically attuned to the idea of establishing a 'Palestinian entity' (Sayigh, 1997a: 100). Fateh expressed criticism of the early PLO, but for different reasons altogether; that is, for being too much controlled by the Arab states and for not exhibiting enough revolutionary zeal (Sayigh, 1997a: 101 f.).

Although the Palestinian National Charter did not refer to the goal of establishing a state, it was to a large extent preoccupied with Palestinian national identity. The Palestinian nation was defined:

4. The Palestinian identity is a genuine, essential, and inherent characteristic; it is transmitted from parents to children. The Zionist occupation and the dispersal of the Palestinian Arab people, through the disasters which befell them, do not make them lose their Palestinian identity and their membership in the Palestinian community, nor do they negate them.

5. The Palestinians are those Arab nationals who, until 1947, normally resided in Palestine regardless of whether they were evicted from it or have stayed there. Anyone born, after that date, of a Palestinian father – whether inside Palestine or outside it – is also a Palestinian.

6. The Jews who had normally resided in Palestine until the beginning of the Zionist invasion will be considered Palestinians. (Laqueur and Rubin, 1984: 366)

The PLO defined the Palestinian nation in a romantic, cultural sense as being 'genuine'; as everlasting, transmitted from parents to children in the cyclical life of the family. The metaphor of biological genealogy and the portrayal of a common ancestry, and therefore a common destiny, structure nationalist history-making and narratives of selfhood. Palestinian self-description as the descendants of the Kanaanites is part of such Palestinian myth-making and legitimisation through the production of history (e.g. Khalidi, 1971; Frangi, 1982).

Embarking from this territorial baseline, Palestinians are distinguished from other Arabic-speaking peoples and from Arab nationalism. According to Article 6, Jews could also be Palestinians; that is, if they settled in Palestine prior to the 'Zionist invasion'.[24] Jews were perceived as belonging to the religious category of 'Judaism' and did not, according to the PLO, constitute a nation of their own (Article 20 of the Palestinian National Charter; Laqueur and Rubin,

1984: 369).[25] The Charter is thus part of a conscious nation-building strategy, forming the official discourse and politics of inclusion versus exclusion.

Arabism and the Marxist fronts

Arabism continued to be a troubled part of Palestinian nationalism. An important feature of both the PFLP[26] and the DFLP[27] is that Palestine is part of Arab unity. This is particularly so for the PFLP, while the DFLP has been more inclined towards Palestinian territorialism. The PFLP sprang from the pro-Nasser ANM, in which PFLP leader George Habash was one of the main personalities.[28] The PFLP has been tormented by internal strife and divisions.

For the Marxist–Leninist fronts, the struggle for Palestine is first and foremost a *class* struggle. In the late 1960s, this was formulated in terms of a joint strategy of 'Arab and Palestinian masses'; a 'people's war' was to be fought, for which the PFLP was to provide the revolutionary ideology:

> The national struggle reflects the class struggle. The national struggle is a struggle for land and those who struggle for it are the peasants who were driven away from their land. The bourgeoisie is always ready to lead such a movement, hoping to gain control of the internal market . . .
>
> Therefore, the fact that the liberation struggle is mainly a class struggle emphasises the necessity for the workers and peasants to play a leading role in the national liberation movement. If the small bourgeoisie take the leading role, the national revolution will fall as a victim of the class interests of this leadership. It is a great mistake to start by saying that the Zionist challenge demands national unity for this shows that one does not understand the real class structure of Zionism.
>
> The struggle against Israel is first of all a class struggle. Therefore the oppressed class is the only class which is able to face a confrontation with Zionism. ('Platform of the Popular Front for the Liberation of Palestine', 1969, in Laqueur and Rubin, 1984: 381)

Although the main battleground was to be Palestine, the liberation of Palestine was not all. Rather, the Arab masses were to be liberated from the yoke of the Arab reactionary regimes and the bourgeoisie. The PFLP further emphasised the special relationship between Jordan and Palestine; in order for Palestine to be liberated, Jordan must be liberated from the Hashemite King Husayn and 'This is the only way in which Amman can become an Arab Hanoi: – a base for the revolutionaries fighting inside Palestine' (Laqueur and Rubin, 1984: 382). The Arabism of the Marxist front is also related to the argument that the Palestinians would need the Arab states in order to challenge Israel (Sayigh, 1997a: 198). To the PFLP, more resources were needed than could be provided by the Palestinians themselves, and therefore a thorough mobilisation of the Arab masses was needed. The PFLP bases its ideology on a 'scientific revolutionary' model, inspired by Mao Sedong. The DFLP, in its early phase, portrayed itself as the vanguard of radicalism and criticised Fateh for leaning on 'reactionary Arab states'. DFLP radicalism contributed to push the PFLP further to the left.

Although the PFLP never posed a real threat to al-Fateh dominance, the organisation contributed to the nationalist discourse in the PLO and the debate between Palestinianism and Arabism. There were thus two main ways of imagining and portraying Palestinianism. One was the depiction of the Palestinians as part of a broader cause and identity, and the other emphasised the particularities of the Palestinian plight based on what had happened to the territory of Palestine. Both ways, however, thrived on the loss, the exile, the catastrophe as catalysing forces, in fact implying that the Palestinian Arabs who had remained in Israel were detached from Palestinianism (cf. Smooha, 1989; Kimmerling and Migdal, 1993: 179; Schulz, 1996).

Struggle, revolution and exile

The 1960s became a revolutionary turning point for Palestinian nationalism, through the gradual change of PLO ideology and increase in its institution-building. It was yet another catastrophe which led to the embodiment of struggle as the main political principle and a main ingredient in Palestinian nation-building (cf. Sayigh, 1997a). As Sayigh has put it, 'The experience of *al-nakba* made for a distinct Palestinian*ness*, but not necessarily for Palestinian*ism*' (Sayigh, 1997a: 666). The 1967 war and the disastrous defeat for the Arab states caused a wave of embitterment among Palestine's Arabs. To Palestinians, the Arab states had proved themselves incapable of assisting the Palestinians in their plight. As a counterbalance against the disasters befalling the Palestinians, the meaning of Palestinian identity was now increasingly crafted through the influence of the *feday* ideology. Guerrilla activities had increased in the preamble of the 1967 war and there was already a rebellious foundation to build upon. PLO Chairman Ahmed Shuqayri was discredited, partly by his association with Nasser, who had suffered a devastating defeat, and partly because of his inability to elaborate a political and military programme to counter the occupation that was the lasting consequence of the 1967 war. In December 1967, Shuqairy resigned (Sayigh, 1997a: 147). Popular support for al-Fateh and for the *fedayeen* grew, and in 1969 al-Fateh gained the upper hand in the PLO. (It is still the largest single organisation in the PLO, which it effectively controls.) With this step, the Palestine Resistance Movement, which had been established in the refugee camps in the Arab world through the *fedayeen* and their activism, and the PLO merged into one, blending the kind of nationalist legitimacy which had been bestowed upon the guerrillas with the institutional legacy of the PLO.

36

In February 1969, Yasir Arafat was elected Chairman after a short (six months) period of leadership by Yahya Hammuda. 'Fateh's capture of the parastatal structure of the PLO was a major step towards the consolidation of a common political arena and consequently of Palestinian proto-nationalism' (Sayigh, 1997a: 220 f.).

In the aftermath of the war, al-Fateh, headed by Yasir Arafat, promoted a 'popular war of liberation' in the occupied territories, and unsuccessfully sought to promote military activity from within the West Bank (Cobban, 1984: 37; Sayigh, 1997a: 161 ff.). Until the spring of 1968, the PLO saw the 'inside' as the baseline for guerrilla movement (Sayigh, 1997a: 207).

Successful mobilisation was, however, rather to occur in the 'outside'. In the two decades following the *nakba* in 1948, what it meant to be a Palestinian had been subject to re-creation; the definition of Palestinian identity now emerged from the refugees and the camp population, finding themselves deprived of land and property. Palestinian identity was re-created from an exile experience. Loss was a defining component of Palestinian national identity. In the 1960s, 'camp' and exiled Palestinians 'gained a new understanding of themselves as *jil-al-thawra*, the revolutionary generation' (Kimmerling and Migdal, 1993: 220). The *jil-al-thawra* was to turn the humiliating experiences of the *jil-al-nakba* to assertiveness and action. 'The mere fact that Palestinians acted and organized was a positive assertion and an aim in itself' (Sayigh, 1997a: 91). The task was to create a new Palestinian.

In 1968, with the battle of the Jordanian village of Karameh (*karameh* is also Arabic for 'honour'), when Palestinian *fedayeen* challenged the Israeli army, Palestinian guerrillas became the daring and fighting heroes of the Arab world; they had proved themselves capable of providing a threat to the Israelis in a sense that the Arab armies had not. Although it was in fact the Jordanian army which had been the main actor in challenging Israel in Karameh, Karameh still represents the 'pride' and 'honour' of Palestinian identity. It had now been proved that, despite the fact that Palestinians were deserted, left alone and fought against by one of the strongest armies in the Middle East, despite their loss and suffering, they would not surrender. 'So powerful was the new myth of the heroic guerrilla that even King Husayn joined in, avowing in a televised speech that "we are all *fida'iyyun*"' (Sayigh, 1997a: 179).

A military, revolutionary culture was formed and enhanced during the exile through education and youth organisations, as well as graffiti, folk songs, poetry, and so on. There was a 'quasi-mystical icon of the feday' (Kimmerling and Migdal, 1993: 233). Hence a new image of the Palestinian came into being as the revolution was launched, catalysed by the 1967 war (Sayigh, 1979: 147). A basic dichotomy of 'struggle/resistance' and 'suffering/sacrifice' gradually came to embody a Palestinian narrative of selfhood and history. Palestinian identity was formed out of the trauma of loss as well as the active identity creation of al-Fateh. Struggle now became a fundamental core ingredient of Palestinian national identity.

> [I]t is against this background that the relationship between Palestinian nation building and the armed struggle needs to be understood. No political force grasped this better than Fatah [. . .]. It regarded the link between national identity and the practice of armed struggle as fundamental, and it was upon this core understanding that it proceeded to construct a broad constituency and assert its dominance in Palestinian national politics in the following years and decades. (Sayigh, 1997b: 25)

'Revolution' and armed 'struggle' were not only political strategies but became crucial identifying principles of nationhood and served as main discursive strategies. Fateh drew inspiration from revolutionary experiences in Vietnam, Algeria and Cuba, and was directly inspired by the writings of Franz Fanon (1968) and the 'cleansing' effect of violence (Sayigh, 1997a: 91).

Sayigh (1997b: 26) notes that Fateh's way of emphasising the 'event' or 'act' of armed struggle was important in itself; irrespective of the results of the 'act', it was critical in this crafting of identity.

> The dramatic arrival on the scene of the guerrillas after the June 1967 War therefore confirmed the self-perception of Palestinians as strugglers. Military action confirmed that the Palestinians, to themselves above all, were active participants in shaping their own destiny, rather than passive victims. True, Palestinian armed struggle had a negligible physical impact on Israel and was afflicted by wild exaggeration and jealous rivalries on the part of the guerrilla groups. Yet the excessive hyperbole and symbolism only went to show that military action served a different function entirely: to consolidate a national myth and imagined community. (Sayigh, 1997b: 27)

The real impact of the struggle was therefore not any effect it might have on the external arena, but its internal consequences and the fact that the Palestinians now *did* something, they acted on their own behalf. Thus its main task was not to inflict pain on Israel but to create and maintain a specific Palestinian identity. It was through military action that Palestinian identity was manifested. The new Palestinian was to turn the humiliating trauma into pride and dignity. 'The ethos, or defining quality, of the Palestinian culture of resistance was militancy or struggle (*nidal*), whose concrete expression was the PLO in all its myriad forms and armed struggle. The words *nidal* and *al-qadiyyah* (the cause) pervaded Palestinian discourse' (Peteet, 1991: 31).

'This was the heyday of the guerrillas, their "honeymoon" as they called it' (Sayigh, 1997a: 147). Fateh started to launch attacks against Israel on 1 January 1965,[29] which is often used as the 'birth-day' of the revolution. In its 'Communiqué No. 1', Fateh stated that 'the armed revolution is the way to Return and to Liberty . . . the Palestinian people remains in the field . . . has not died and will not die' (Cobban, 1984: 33). Despite proud declarations of the scale and scope of military operations, the attacks were initially disastrous in military terms (Sayigh, 1997a: 119).

> The driving force in the philosophy and ideological outlook of Fateh, to the extent that they existed, was profoundly existential. It derived overwhelmingly from the physical circumstances and deep alienation of the majority of uprooted and exiled refugees, rather than the minority of Palestinians who still resided in their original homes after the end of the 1948 war. The same existential drive imbued Fateh's notion of 'revolution'. 'With revolution we announce our will [hence existence], and with revolution we put an end to this bitter surrender, this terrifying reality that the children of the Catastrophe [of 1948] experience everywhere.' (Sayigh, 1997a: 88)

In 1969, several hundred attacks were carried out against Israel (Sayigh, 1997a: 147). It is often argued that Fateh's nationalism was reactive nationalism, its basic enticement lying in the concept of liberation and active resistance. However, Fateh nationalism was also actively created. The very core of Palestinianism was formed in this period of hectic revolutionary zeal.

The struggle, resistance and revolution also degenerated into sheer terrorism. The PFLP became in the late 1960s[30] the forerunner in advocating terrorism (or 'external operations') as a legitimate instrument in the resistance (Sayigh, 1997a: 213 ff.). The PDFLP at the time considered 'external operations' dysfunctional (Sayigh, 1997a: 234). PFLP terror in the late 1960s, such as hijacking, was one of the main factors contributing to the devastating civil war in Jordan. After the war, PLO international terrorism peaked in the early 1970s as the Palestinian revolution was seriously crippled. Other external factors also contributed to a frustration of the nationalist revolutionary discourse and strategy.[31] It was now Fateh which adopted the course of international terror, primarily through the 'Black September' organisation, formed as a response to the Jordanian debacle. Terrorist acts by Black September and other guerrilla organisations included airline hijackings, the 1972 Munich Olympics attacks when the Israeli team was hijacked and killed, an attack against Ben-Gurion airport and a 1974 attack against a school in Ma'alot. In the PLO discourse of the time, there was no real distinction between civilian and military targets, since Israeli society was militarised and since the Israeli army was based on conscription (Kimmerling, 1997: 246). Terrorism fed into an Israeli discourse demonising the PLO, now represented as the arch-terrorists of the world (Kimmerling, 1997: 231).

Institution-building

PLO institution-building has reached a substantial level and serves as the foundation of state formation. The PLO's structure includes a 'parliament' (the

PNC), a 'government' (the Executive Committee) and a military apparatus (the Palestine Liberation Army), and the various departments could be equalled to a 'quasi-governmental' apparatus (Cobban, 1984: 12). The PLO has also been engaged in building an elaborate civilian infrastructure for Palestinian refugees in the Arab states, such as health clinics, schools, factories and research institutes (cf. Brand, 1988a, b). The statist ambitions of the PLO are evident in the Charter, resembling a constitution, various government departments, the army and military training system, the education system, the flag, the anthem, the existence of an economy with a certain taxation system, economic enterprises, foreign representation, and so on. Institution-building was also enhanced by the GUPS, the General Union of Palestine Workers and the General Union of Palestinian Women (see Brand, 1988a). In exile, the education system provided fertile ground for the production of nationalism. Apart from the state-resembling deterritorialised institutions and the challenging institution-building, primarily in Jordan and Lebanon, it was relatively easy for the Palestinians to organise in the conservative Gulf states, whose policy towards the Palestinians was more liberal than that of the 'front-line' states with shared borders with Israel. Thus certain Palestinian institutions have been able to form more extensively. One of the most important Palestinian institutions in Kuwait was the PLO schools, established in 1967 (Brand, 1988a: 120).

Statist aspirations were further underlined in the late 1970s, partly enabled by the increasing influx of money from Arab states after 1978. This 'steadfastness' money allowed the amplification of bureaucratisation as well as a particular mode of neo-patrimonial politics and the personalisation of politics around Yasir Arafat (Sayigh, 1997a: 455). Increased Saudi aid after 1983 further imbued PLO politics and institution-building with patronage loyalties (Sayigh, 1997a: 603).

In the first years of the resistance, factional rivalry was not an issue, since it was the resistance movement itself with which people identified, rather than with this or that faction. This period was marked by a hectic, 'feverish mass activism . . . during which everyone rushed to affiliate himself/herself in a group' (Sayigh, 1979: 170). 'There was a mood of total identification with the Resistance' (Sayigh, 1994: 91). Despite the political differences that were to increase, there was agreement between the factions on the nationalist symbols, used by all in equal ways: the flag, the gun, the fighter and the martyr. Songs were invented and mixed with traditional, rural songs. Funerals of martyrs became important nationalist symbols (Sayigh, 1994: 103). Nationalism in the form of the revolution served to overcome dispersal and to integrate a shattered population under one ideological heading.

Palestinian society today is an entity for which one is hard put to find parallels in recent history. It is a *society* by any accepted definition of the term: with a common language, a range of shared norms, a great deal of shared experience, but most important of all a *concept of selfhood, of being a community*. But it is a scattered society, its members either in exile or under occupation, and this makes its selfhood an object of constant attention and its boundaries the focus of much probing and shoring-up. It is, in the final analysis, an anti-structure – a liminal body defining its presence in terms of its past and its future in terms of inversions of normality and with reference to what it has lost. (Johnson, 1982: 65; emphasis added)

In the tradition of Victor Turner (1969), Nels Johnson describes Palestinian society as a 'liminal body', as an 'anti-structure'. What was lost – the homeland – was connected to self-definition. The Palestinians *'were'* what they had lost. Further, finding themselves in new surroundings, a process of alienation materialised; both from the past, from what used to be, and from the present, from the host society. Thus the future must be described as a reversal of the present. It was what the Palestinians *used* to be and what they *would* become that was important. The present was merely a transitional period, a *'rite de passage'*. The current was temporary, it was too filled with suffering to be defined as normality.

The dramatic rise of the guerrilla movement after the battle of Karama created a new myth. 'To declare Palestinian identity no longer means that one is a "refugee" or second-class citizen. Rather, it is a declaration that arouses pride, because the Palestinian has become the *fida'i* or revolutionary who bears arms.' Armed struggle was the source of political legitimacy and national identity, the new substance of the 'imagined community' of the Palestinians. (Sayigh, 1997a: 195)

Class, gender, refugees

Nationalism and national identity as struggle/revolution versus suffering/ sacrifice also interacted with other modes of identification such as class, gender, refugees, family and faction. Concerning gender roles, women's issues were subordinated to the overall nationalist discourse, and although the image of woman as guerrilla fighter was a widely held ideal, women were mostly projected as 'sisters of men' or 'mothers of martyrs' (Jawwad, 1990: 72). Being a 'mother of martyr' became a specific assignment in the Palestinian national struggle, representing both pride at the sacrifice for the cause and a symbol of Palestinian suffering. Women became an important symbol in paintings and in posters: a Palestinian woman in traditional dress carrying a gun was a frequent symbol of nationalism (Sayigh, 1994: 103). The nation that was to be protected, that is, the nation as the land, as the 'object', was gendered; the nation was a woman to be liberated and defended by the active fraternity of *fedayeen*. In a highly generalised way, men 'struggle' and women 'suffer' in their capacity as 'mothers of martyrs', and national identity is clearly gendered. Women's contribution to the nation and the cause is represented by their sacrifice of sons being martyred. The very symbols of Palestinian-ness are the active (male) struggler, the guerrilla, the *intifada* fighter and the suffering woman, representing the defeats, the traumas and the pain in a genderisation of the two poles of Palestinian national identity. Although women underwent military training (Sayigh, 1994: 106), their share in the defence of the camps in Lebanon was rarely as fighters but more often as suppliers of food, cooking for guerrillas, taking care of the wounded, but also doing, for example, agricultural work usually conducted by men. Said one woman in Tel al Zatar: 'Now a girl knows what she should do. She is doing the right thing. She is being of benefit to the revolution, to her people' (Peteet, 1991: 74). 'The struggle is a man's battle, and women's role is to help by encouraging him and taking care of him' (Palestinian woman in Lebanon; in Peteet, 1991: 92). Militancy is also, however, a way in which Palestinian women define themselves (Peteet, 1991: 76). The national cause also suppressed any form of gender agenda.

Although some argue that the revolutionary form of nationalism exhibited a more explicitly 'bottom-up' character (Kimmerling and Migdal, 1993: 187) than the earlier form of elite mobilisation, the class dimension of the exile and the struggle is striking. Forty-seven per cent of the refugees of 1948 were peasants or agricultural workers. Workers and petty employees amounted to 25 per cent (Hilal, 1992: 56). Loss of land led to both economic and social deprivation, since identity in a peasant community is deeply connected to images of earth (e.g. Sayigh, 1997a: 47).

However, the upper echelons in formulating struggle as identity were middle class, while the poorer strata and former peasants in exile were to provide the fighters. The PLO was largely an urban, bourgeois phenomenon. Urban–rural dichotomies were not overcome by the resistance movement; such polarities were rather re-created in the 'Land of Longing and Exile'. Refugees of urban origin shunned their Palestinian compatriots of peasant or rural origin (Shamir, 1980; Sayigh, 1997a: 47). The revolution was an urbanised movement, juxtaposed with rural popular culture. As in many nationalist movements, it was the intellectual, urban strata which nurtured rural culture as a specific guardian of the land (cf. Anderson, 1991; Eriksen, 1993).

> On the one hand, in much Resistance oriented writing and art, the people of the camps were presented as symbols of the misery of exile . . . and of resistance and rootedness in the land . . . Yet at the same time, the camps were perceived as areas of total deprivation, in need of social assistance and political organisation. There was also a widespread Resistance view of camps as 'reservoirs of men for the Revolution'. Such perspectives suggest the class/culture gap between [Palestine Resistance Movement] cadres and the people of the camps. Even though the Resistance leadership adopted elements of peasant culture – the *keffieyeh* and *agal*, the rural naming system – as mobilising symbols and signs of 'authenticity', in its hierarchies, ethos and mentality the Resistance was nevertheless deeply urban, as much in its leftist wing as in Fateh. (Sayigh, 1994: 102)

One uniting factor was (arguably) the *ghourba*,[32] which served to strengthen Palestinian national identity. To the Palestinian refugees, a return to 'Palestine', to 'Paradise Lost', was the paramount goal (e.g. Sayigh, 1979). Memories of the homeland and the telling of history serve as a bond keeping the Palestinians together. This is a way of 're-creating Palestine' and a way of transferring the content of being Palestinian from one generation to the next (Sayigh, 1979: 10 f.).

Although, in the first years of exile, traditional ways of making politics and organising were reconstructed, strengthening the power base of the *mufti* and the AHC, gradually, political parties and factions came to replace village and clan structures as bases of loyalty (Sayigh, 1994: 62). Although the family remained an important base for identity and loyalty, and although family relations and structures served as a base of security, there was also change in family relations. Identification with the resistance or with specific political factions sometimes outmoded family identification. Usually, however, the members of one family or household joined the same organisation (Sayigh, 1994: 106 f.).

To have the status of 'refugee' implies a specific dilemma of identity. Socially, refugees are often downgraded in host societies. Being a refugee becomes a social stigma, not least because social status and position have traditionally been derived from possession of land. The loss of land has meant a loss of identity, of a sense of direction and of perceived social status (Shamir, 1980: 149 f.).

The experience of being refugees and living in camps provided the Palestinians with an identity distinct from that of the various host populations; this is one of the reasons why Palestinian refugees often have not wanted to live outside the camps and give up their refugee status (cf. Johnson, 1982). Their refugee status gives Palestinians in exile political rights, a fact which has also been used by the PLO. The 'exile identity' served both instrumental, political purposes and provided meaning to the idea of being Palestinian. This is how the phenomenon was explained to Johnson by his Palestinian respondents: 'if the Palestinians move from the camps, or accept citizenship in another country, they will cease to have a distinct identity after a few decades, and if they permit this to happen, they will lose their struggle for rights in their own land' (Johnson, 1982: 65). The loss of land was a prime factor in giving rise to and promoting a national identity of 'struggling' and 'suffering'. 'Suffering' arose because of catastrophes befalling the Palestinians and because of the action of 'struggle'. The martyr, the *shahid*, became another image, another 'cultural hero' (Kimmerling and Migdal, 1993). Suffering was the result not only of passive submission but of the active role of resistance.

Thus al-Fateh's achievement was a major one, virtually forming a new content of the ruptured and disconnected Palestinian identity out of disasters and resistance. Palestinian nationalism in the late 1960s found a base in a mass movement for the first time. Disasters played a significant role in the production of meaning. The consciousness of this strategy is revealed in the following quotation from Arafat: 'The Palestine Liberation Organisation was a major factor in creating a new Palestinian individual, qualified to shape the future of our Palestine' (Address to the UN General Assembly, 13 November 1974, quoted in Laqueur and Rubin, 1984: 514). Thus Palestinian nationalism as formulated in the exile years created an identity *between* disasters and struggle, between what happened to the Palestinians by the way of other actors and their own ways of countering disasters. Between and betwixt, Palestinian identity and nationalism were moulded in the very midst of processes which were out of their control and their own creativity, activity and reaction. Identities are created in such spaces, neither totally reactive, operational or strategic nor the result of givens. 'Self' is created both in the actual meeting with the 'other' and in the strategies invented to deal with the 'other'.

Arab states and the PLO

The Fateh and the Fateh-dominated PLO have also been bedevilled by the contradiction between Palestinian and Arab nationalism – a dialectic between specific territorial nationalism (*wataniyya*) and a larger, unifying nationalism based on Arabism (*qawmiyya*). This contradiction proved a dilemma for the Palestinian movement, stuck as it was between the need to respond to the Palestinian masses, the need for international recognition and sympathy, and the need for Arab verbal, political and financial support. The PLO was dependent on the Arab states for the building of a social and economic infrastructure, for financial and political support and for access to territory for guerrilla activities against Israel. Palestinian refugees in the Arab world also increased Palestinian dependence on the Arab states. Arab support for the Palestinians has, however, been more ideological than real. PLO alliances with Arab states have been shifting, as the latter's interests have altered and in accordance with their politics *vis-à-vis* the Palestinians. Arab state politics have been a considerable factor contributing to the fragmentation of PLO politics, in its incessant manipulation with various guerrillas. The base for guerrilla action was initially Jordan.

With the resistance of the late 1960s, the PLO became more of a problem to the Jordanian regime, with military attacks carried out against Israel from Jordanian territory, as well as open contestation and defiance of the Jordanian hegemony within its state borders (Sayigh, 1997a: 243–81). Following the September 1970 civil war, when PLO bases and infrastructure were virtually eliminated, ensuing increased *fedayeen* activities from Jordanian territory, including the PFLP hijacking of international aircraft, meant that relations between Jordan and the PLO became increasingly strained. The expulsion of the resistance movement increased the vulnerability of Palestinians in Jordan. In fact, the 1970–71 war left the revolution in an atmosphere of siege (Sayigh, 1997a: 148, 282–92). In 1972, King Husayn outlined his United Kingdom Plan, whereby the West Bank would be granted autonomy within a scheme of overall Jordanian control (cf. Ma'oz, 1984: 101), which caused strong reactions from al-Fateh and the PLO, which became increasingly anti-Husayn. After the civil war, PLO factions resolved to perform more terror attacks and the group Black September was formed (e.g. Gresh, 1983; Sayigh, 1997a).

The Jordanian debacle of the early 1970s led to an intensification of the PLO presence in Lebanon, coinciding with the disintegration of the Lebanese state and the subsequent civil war between 1975 and 1989. Until the beginning of the 1980s, this further strengthened Palestinian institution-building, rendering the PLO some kind of *de facto* sovereignty and control over territory (Brand, 1988a: 233 ff.). During the resistance period, the camps were 'liberated zones' ruled by Palestinian militia, legitimated by the Cairo Accords of 1969.

The war in Lebanon and Palestinian involvement in the war added another layer to Palestinian history and identity creation. Events such as the 1976 Christian Falangist attack against the Palestinian refugee camp in East Beirut (Tal el Zataar), with the knowledge of the Syrians, underlined the vulnerability of the Palestinian diaspora and, as in Jordan in 1970–71, 'the assailants were fellow Arabs' (Cobban, 1984: 73). Syria, previously the main ally of Fateh, now proved its staunchest enemy, as it manipulated with Fateh dissidents in its own regional ambitions and concerns. Syria also feared the implications of Fateh's and the PLO's Lebanese presence as well as the rapprochement between Egypt and the PLO. Syria has arguably been the most influential Arab actor in determining PLO politics.

After the October War in 1973, the PLO attempted to involve itself in the negotiation process between Israel and the Arab states which resulted in military disengagement agreements between Israel and Egypt. The 'peace process' gained a forward push by the coming to power of the American Democratic President Jimmy Carter in 1976, who also made statements indicating a certain openness towards the PLO. In relation to this, some PLO leaders entered into an unofficial dialogue with leftist Israelis, as the PLO sought to jump on the bandwagon of US diplomacy without deserting its strategy or its identity based on struggle. The PLO was, however, seriously divided on this issue, and rejectionist attitudes as well as PFLP rapprochement with Syria hampered moves in this direction. A role for the PLO was also stalled by the Camp David Accords between Israel and Egypt, catching the entire Arab world by surprise. For the PLO, Israeli–Egyptian peace implied a serious dilemma.[33] The Egyptian–Israeli peace treaty in 1979 implied a rapprochement between Jordan and the PLO, also sparked by a new alliance between Syria and Iraq. Other peace initiatives which were welcomed by a mixture of opinions in the Palestinian ranks were the Fahd Peace Plan of 1981 and the Reagan Proposal of 1982. The Fahd Plan, or Fez Plan, envisaged an independent Palestinian state along with recognition of all states in the region, and was eventually approved by Arafat and the mainstreamers, while the rejectionists opposed it. Although the Reagan plan ruled out the prospect of a Palestinian state, it did assert the Palestinian right of autonomy and was received with ambivalence in the Palestinian ranks.

Following the second Israeli invasion of Lebanon in 1982 (the first occurred in 1978), the next Palestinian tragedy occurred in the direct fighting with the Israelis and the forced evacuation from Lebanon which brought the Beirut era to a close. When the PLO left Beirut, the Palestinian refugees were left largely without protection, as grimly underlined by the Falangist massacre, facilitated by the presence of the Israeli Defence Forces (IDF), of Palestinian refugees in the camps of Sabra and Shateela in September 1982 (see Sayigh, 1994).

The two Israeli invasions, the Falangist massacres and the Syrian attacks against PLO forces added up to a Palestinian disaster in Lebanon. Not only was the military foothold lost, but the political and civilian infrastructure which had reached unprecedented levels, the 'a state within state', was also destroyed. As in Jordan, the PLO organisation with its statist ambitions and a large population adhering to its ideological call had challenged the authority of the host state.

With the Syrian–PLO rapprochement in the early 1980s, Jordan again severed its relations with the PLO. In 1983–85 relations were improved, and in 1985 the Amman Accord between Jordan and the PLO suggested a confederation between Palestine and Jordan. The Accord was strongly criticised by the rejectionist groups in the PLO. After 1985, Jordan sided with Syria, however, and together they attempted to manipulate and divide the PLO.

The Lebanon years also witnessed a Palestinian disintegration when al-Saiqa[34] and the PFLP–GC withdrew from the PLO and a mutiny occurred within al-Fateh – a 'civil war within a civil war' (Kimmerling and Migdal, 1993: 236) through Abu Musa's al-Fateh Uprising, supported by Syria. Fateh's increasing divergences and internal fights were being acted out in Lebanon, the vulnerability of an injured and fragmented society providing a fertile ground for internal rivalry. 'This episode of intra-Palestinian fighting was taken by the community as an ominous sign of future battles, many judging the Fateh split as a more serious blow to the national struggle than the Israeli invasion or the evacuation of Beirut' (Sayigh, 1994: 210). The Lebanon experience and the Syrian assault left the PLO seriously fractured and divided. As if this were not enough, Shi'ite anti-Palestinianism expressed by the Amal movement linked with Syrian interests of power in an attempt to oust the PLO. This led to another disaster, the Battle of the Camps, consisting of three assaults, or sieges, by the Amal on the Shateela camp during the period 1985–86.[35] The sieges served, however, to reunify the Palestinian ranks, and Fateh and Arafat came out stronger than before. Again, disaster fed into identity construction. Defeat was turned into triumph in asserting itself as a national collectivity, and again there was a conscious use of the catastrophe. By the late 1980s, '[t]he PLO was completely adrift' (Sayigh, 1997a: 547). Not until the PNC meeting in Algiers in 1987 did the PLO regroup its ranks.

The rifts between Jordan and the PLO reached a low with the breakdown of the joint Jordanian–PLO agenda in the peace process in the mid 1980s. In July 1986, the Jordanian government closed the PLO offices in Jordan. In April 1987, the PLO Executive Committee formally cancelled the Amman Accord. A renewed improvement of the relationship occurred in 1988 and the withdrawal of Jordanian claims on the West Bank as a response to the *intifada*. With the Jordanian disengagement from the West Bank, changes were also made regarding Jordanian citizenship for West Bankers. Jordanian passports were to be issued for a period of two years for Palestinians in the West Bank at Palestinian request. As a sign of acknowledging the strength of Palestinian identity, West Bank Palestinians were from now on to be considered Palestinians and not Jordanian nationals.[36] In the political communiqué adopted by the 19th PNC meeting in Algiers in November 1988 (at the same occasion as the Declaration of Independence was issued), the link between Jordan and the Palestinians was again underlined in the call for a confederation. In the 1990s a confederation was again discussed in relation to the peace process and the establishment of Palestinian self-rule.

Steps towards shifting goals and strategies, 1974

In 1974 – the same year that the PLO gained increased international recognition[37] – it partly and officially changed its direction concerning goals and strategies. Until then, the PLO had declared that the goal of the organisation was to 'liberate all of Palestine'.

At the 12th PNC meeting in Cairo in 1974 (see Gresh, 1983), the PLO adopted, after intense debate, a resolution stating that it would struggle to 'establish the people's national, independent and fighting authority on every part of Palestinian land that is liberated. This requires a major change in the balance of power in favour of our people and its struggle' (Article 2 in 'Palestine National Council, Political Programme, 8 June 1974', in Lukacs, 1992), implying that intermediate steps could be aspired to as parts of the national goal. This decision was preceded by activity by, for example, the PDFLP, which advocated the establishment of a 'national authority' in the West Bank and Gaza Strip. The PDFLP was also the main organisation working for Palestinian participation in the negotiation process following the October War of 1973. Also Fateh voices, foremost of whom was Salah Khalaf, or Abu Iyyad, argued that the best way to force Israel to relinquish territory was to participate in the negotiation process and to end the era of rejectionism (Sayigh, 1997a: 336).[38] Both the idea of complete revolution that of joining cause with Jordan were rejected by the PDFLP, which focused more directly on the 'homeland' (statements by General Secretary of the PDFLP, Nayef Hawatmeh, Defending the Establishment of a Palestinian National Authority in Territories Liberated from Israeli Occupation, 24 February 1974, in Lukacs 1992: 307 f.). The PDFLP differed from the PFLP and was openly advocating a Palestinian state alongside the state of Israel as early as 1969. Although Judaism was considered a religion, the PDFLP also recognised the 'legitimacy of Jewishness' and the rights of the Jewish community (cf. Cobban, 1984: 154). One of the instrumental factors in determining the PDFLP's outlook was its close association with the Soviet Union, which pushed its ally further towards pragmatism (Sayigh, 1997a: 342).

This discussion also involved statist aspirations, hence the conflict between those who believed a statist structure to be necessary to institutionalise the struggle and those who saw a state or 'authority'[39] as anathema to the revolutionary ideal (Sayigh, 1997a: 335).

The PNC declaration was the outcome of a compromise between the 'moderates' and the 'radicals'.[40] The compromise was not, however, long-lived and the PFLP resigned in that same year from the Executive Committee of the PLO. It was in the early 1970s that factionalism began to be a problem, with loyalties being increasingly directed towards individual factions at the expense of the overall resistance.

Following the 1974 decision, the PLO in practice accepted the liberation of parts of Palestine, as an intermediate step. This was an important step towards recognising Israel and accepting a two-state solution. The development of a two-state solution was further cemented in the PLO's 'Six Point Programme' of 1977, when it was determined that the Palestinian right to self-determination should be established in 'an independent national state on any part of the Palestinian revolution' (quoted in Lukacs, 1992: 336).[41] No longer were military means to have sole priority; the struggle also had to be political. Still, however, *al-thawra*, the revolution and the struggle, served to inform identity. That is to say, the alteration of goals and strategies did not in any significant way shift the focus of the meaning of Palestinian identity. The continuity of the symbolism of armed struggle is also to be related to its use as a bargaining position (Sayigh, 1997a: 337).

NOTES

1 The letter from McMahon, the British High Commissioner in Cairo, states that an independent Arab state was to be created with the exception of those parts of Syria west of the districts of Damascus, Homs, Hama and Aleppo. Palestine was not mentioned, and opinions diverged between the British and the Arabs over whether Palestine was to be part of the independent Arab state or not.

2 During this time, most Jewish purchases of land stemmed from large absentee land-owners (amounting to 52.6 per cent of the total of land purchased up to 1936). Only 9.6 per cent was bought from the peasantry, while the remaining land was sold by large resident owners (24.6 per cent), government, churches and foreign companies (Granott, 1952, quoted in Sayigh, 1979: 27).

3 British rule over Palestine commenced in 1918 as a military administration of the area east and west of the River Jordan. Palestine became a British mandate in 1922, following the division of the Middle East between France and Great Britain at the San Remo Conference in 1920. In 1918, Syria, Lebanon and Palestine had been divided into three areas called the Occupied Enemy Territories (OET), based on the Sykes–Picot Agreement of 1916. Palestine became the OET-South. When the British mandate was approved in 1922, the area east of the River Jordan was separated from the mandate and established as Trans-Jordan under Amir 'Abdallah.

4 The Husayni family is of Sharifian lineage, claiming links to the Prophet Muhammad. The family held the office of *mufti* of Jerusalem for the first time at the beginning of the seventeenth century and also held the office of mayor of Jerusalem for long periods. In 1921 hajj Amin al-Husayni (1895–1974) was appointed *mufti* of Jerusalem by the British rulers. (*Mufti* refers to a Muslim expert who gives non-binding legal opinions on *shari'a*, the Islamic system of law and way of life.) In 1929, he was appointed President of the Supreme Muslim Council. There were also, at times, splits within the family between 'moderates' and 'radicals'. See Mattar (1988) for a detailed biography of the *mufti*.

5 See Porath (1974), Lesch (1979), Muslih (1988), Khalaf (1991) and Khalidi (1997) for detailed accounts of the influential families of this time. Cf. also Kimmerling and Migdal (1993). Amin al-Husayni changed his political outlook over the years, from being quiescent pro-British to radical anti-imperialist and anti-Zionist. The Nashashibis, on the other hand, were during the initial period more radical, but turned to a pro-British position and were involved in discussions with the Zionist movement.

6 Although British rule of course drew Palestine closer and closer to the world economy, it should be noted that British interests in Palestine were not primarily economic, as in colonies elsewhere, but mainly strategic. In terms of the economy, one of the most tangible results of the British presence was the transport system and road networks, which served to foster British defence interests. This favoured primarily merchants and Christians (Divine, 1980: 225).

7 The Ottoman *millet* system was based on local autonomy for religious groups, and was in a way an Ottoman variant of the Arabic/Islamic *dhimmi* system, the protected 'People of the Book'.

8 The concept used is *qawmiyya* and not *wataniyya*. *Qawmiyya* is usually connected to the wider sphere of Arab nationalism, whereas *wataniyya* applies to patriotism, which came to mean state nationalism.

9 One of the leading personalities of *Istiqlal* was Ahmad al-Shuqayri, later to become the first Chairman of the PLO.

10 Literally, *shabab* means young, unmarried men, but also refers to gang members.

11 Muhammad 'Abduh was a modernist Islamist active in Cairo.

12 He was at this time increasingly seen by the British as a terrorist and later as an ally of the Nazis, although in the early 1920s he had been perceived as an ally of Great Britain.

13 The AHC was founded in 1936 as a representative body, made up of representatives of the newly established political parties, in turn (in most cases) linked to the traditional elite. It was chaired by the *mufti*, Amin al-Husayni.

14 The *mufti* returned to the Middle East in 1946, when he arrived in Cairo. He was not to return to Jerusalem until 1966.

15 The number of Palestine Arab refugees in 1948–49 is disputed. UN figures estimated the number at approximately 726,000 (cf. Morris, 1990).

16 The 1948 war and the expulsion of Palestinians from Palestine are referred to as *nakba*.

17 Irgun and Stern were extremist movements using terror in their struggle against the British as well as against the Arab population.

18 *Fida*, or *feda*, in Arabic means to sacrifice or redeem, and *fedayeen* therefore refers to 'those who sacrifice', or fighters who risk their lives recklessly.

19 The All-Palestine Government continued to exist until 1959, but according to Migdal, it ceased for all practical purposes to operate in 1952 (Migdal, 1980a: 36).

20 In the 1956 Suez war, the core of al-Fateh leaders, students in Cairo who as Palestinian *fedayeen* fought alongside the Egyptian army against the British, French and Israeli armies, was born. The founders of al-Fateh had been active in the foundation of the General Union of Palestine Students (GUPS) – Yasir Arafat was the first President of the Student Union. In 1959, al-Fateh and its leaders began to publish and spread their ideas while residing in Kuwait. In 1965, the first public communiqué was published. It was also in 1965 that al-Fateh pursued its first military attack against Israel. Among the Palestinians, it is usually 1965 which is celebrated as the anniversary of al-Fateh and the 'revolution'. In the 1960s, al-Fateh was supported by Syria. al-Fateh has, however, to some extent been tormented by factionalism as well as plagued by the politics of patronage and manipulation by the Arab states. In 1983, a virtual civil war broke out in the Fateh ranks in Lebanon and the Fateh Uprising was formed, led by Abu Musa. Another dissident group is the Fateh Revolutionary Council, led by Sabri al-Banna, more widely known as Abu Nidal, which has the support of Iraq. It broke away from al-Fateh in 1974, criticising the mainstream's promotion of a political settlement.

21 al-Fateh's 'Seven Points' also make reference to the importance of, and its commitment to, Arab unity (Laqueur and Rubin, 1984: 372).

22 For overviews of the PLO see Gresh (1983), Cobban (1984), Nassar (1991) and Sayigh (1997).

23 The original Charter of 1964 was amended by the National Congress of the PLO in 1968.

24 It is not specified when the Zionist invasion is considered to have commenced, but it is interpreted as being either in 1881 with the 'first large wave of immigrants' (address to the UN General Assembly, 13 November 1974, by Yasir Arafat, quoted in Laqueur and Rubin, 1984: 504–18), 1917 – the year of the Balfour Declaration (cf. Lukacs, 1992: 292) – or 1948, when the state of Israel was established.

25 In the same way, Israel has denied the existence of a specific Palestinian nationhood, and has argued that the Palestine Arabs rather belong to a wider Arab community.

26 Although established in 1967, the PFLP did not join the PLO until 1970. In the 1970s, it was the second largest organisation within the PLO and the main competitor of al-Fateh.

27 The DFLP was formed as an offshoot of the PFLP in 1969; its original name was the Popular Democratic Front for the Liberation of Palestine (PDFLP). The PFLP has split many times. PFLP–General Command (PFLP–GC) broke away from PFLP in 1968, and has since been the *avant garde* of the rejectionist front. The PFLP Special Command has two branches, both of which split from the PFLP. In 1977, another breakaway group was formed, the Palestinian Liberation Front (PLF), which in turn has divided many times. The main group is led by Abu Abbas and has been considered close to Yasir Arafat and al-Fateh – at least until the infamous attack by the PLF against a Tel Aviv beach in 1990 which led to the disruption of the US–PLO dialogue. Abu Abbas resigned from the Executive Committee of the PLO in 1991. The DFLP split in 1991 over the peace process, with Fida in favour of the peace process and the DFLP against.

28 George Habash is a Greek Orthodox from Lydda who studied medicine at the American University of Beirut. DFLP Chairman Nayef Hawatmeh is a Christian from Jordan.
29 During this time, there was considerable disagreement between the various Palestinian–Arab organisations, mostly between the ANM and Fateh over the timing, scope and feasibility of launching armed attacks against Israel (Sayigh, 1997a: 104 ff.). The Arab states also had their say in the matter.
30 During 1968 and 1969, both Fateh and the DFLP criticised the PFLP strategy.
31 Sayigh (1997a: 157) mentions, for example, Syrian pressure, Israeli counter-insurgency campaigns, Israeli and Jordanian attempts to create a different leadership in the occupied territories and a Lebanese desire to quell guerrilla activity within its borders.
32 *Ghourba* means exile, and the root of the word also connotes 'stranger' or 'outsider'.
33 A rejectionist front was formed, consisting of the PFLP, the PFLP–GC, the Arab Liberation Front (ALF) and the Palestinian Popular Struggle Front (PPSF). Four years later, the Front had broken asunder, and al-Fateh again dominated the scene. The rejectionist Front enjoyed, however, a considerable amount of support, especially among the refugees (Cobban, 1984: 62).
34 al-Saiqa is the Palestinian branch of the Syrian Ba'ath Party. It challenged al-Fateh from 1976 onwards, being supported by the PFLP–GC (also Syrian-supported), the PPSF and, to some extent, the DFLP. The Iraqi Ba'ath Party also created its own Palestinian branch, the ALF, which has, however, been too marginal to exert much influence within the PLO.
35 See Sayigh (1994) for an account of deteriorating Shi'a–Palestinian relations in the 1980s, as well as an orally based history of the Battle of the Camps.
36 Statement by Jordanian Prime Minister Zaid al-Rifai on the Implementation of Jordan's Disengagement from the West Bank, 20 August 1988, in Lukacs (1992: 525). According to the document, Gazan Palestinians would also still be able to have their temporary Jordanian passports renewed.
37 In 1974, the Arab League recognised the PLO as the 'sole, legitimate representative of the Palestinian people'. In the same year, the PLO also gained observer status in the UN.
38 Abu Iyyad was one of the central Fateh Central Committee personalities and responsible for security. He was assassinated in 1991.
39 The original Arabic, *sulta*, can mean both state and authority.
40 al-Fateh, the Syrian-supported al-Saiqa and the (then) PDFLP came forward with the proposal, and the PFLP, the PFLP–GC and the ALF were against it. In the final vote, however, only four delegates voted against (e.g. Gresh, 1983).
41 In 1977, the Steadfastness and Confrontation Front was formed, consisting of the PLO, Libya, Syria, Algeria, Iraq and South Yemen, in order to oppose Anwar Sadat's peace initiative. The Six Point Programme was agreed by the Steadfastness Front. To the Palestinians, Sadat's peace initiative and the Camp David Accords represented a sell-out and betrayal of the Palestinian cause. Anti-Egyptian tendencies rose high in the Arab world at large, and a Palestinian–Egyptian rapprochement did not occur until the era of Hosni Mubarak, from the early 1980s.

From intifada
to self-government

After the Lebanon disaster, when the PLO lost geographical proximity to Palestine and the battleground, the Palestinian struggle was gradually moved from 'outside' to 'inside' – the West Bank and Gaza. Here, politics and everyday life were in direct entanglement with the occupation. At first, mobilisation occurred through the extension of existing grassroots organisations and a more direct factional involvement in such mobilisation and activities. However, West Bank and Gaza politics were mobilised according to different logics from those which the PLO had mastered. PLO state-building ambitions had been further institutionalised, as had clientelism and rentier politics.[1] However, armed struggle as an option had been shown to be increasingly futile, and there was a need for the mainstream PLO to find a way to participate in the peace process in the Middle East.

Israeli politics towards the occupied territories

The Israeli occupation in a way served to re-integrate the geographical entities of the West Bank and Gaza, now brought under one and the same rule. The policy of the Labour government during the first decade of the occupation (1967–77) to integrate the West Bank and the Gaza Strip with the Israeli economy turned the area into a market for Israeli produce as well as a source of low-paid, menial labour in Israel. Jewish settlements were established in the West Bank, largely motivated by security needs; Labour's perceptions of the occupied territories were guided by security considerations. Until 1973, the occupied territories experienced an economic boom (e.g. Migdal, 1980a: 46). Israel perceived itself as the 'enlightened conqueror' (Kimmerling, 1997: 231) and maintained a discourse about the 'benign occupation'. With the assumption of power by the Likud bloc in 1977, Israeli integration politics were to an increasing extent fostered by nationalist ideological motives, with grossly increased settlement activity, amounting to creeping annexation.[2] Although the Likud policy of annexation was deemed 'irreversible' by many (Benvenisti, 1986), the policy was not formally to annex the territories, fearing the demographic composition of such a state. Likud sought rather to manifest Israeli control and undermine all attempts at mobilisation of Palestinian nationalism.

The economic growth which marked the initial years of the occupation did not, however, result in investments which could lead to the progress of non-agricultural economic sectors. Investments were made in household consumption, with a considerable increase in consumer goods (e.g. Migdal, 1980a: 47). The economic development of the West Bank and Gaza was seriously hampered by the occupation as the occupied territories were drawn into nearly complete dependence on Israel. Palestinian imports from Israel constitute around 90 per cent of total exports, while exports to Israel constitute 70 per cent of total exports (World Bank, 1993, Vol. II: 27). This has created an exceedingly vulnerable Palestinian economy, subject to external factors and wide open to macroeconomic shocks. In the case of Gaza, dependence on the occupation amounted to 'de-development' (Roy, 1995a).

With the land alienation that increased following the Israeli occupation and the expropriation of land, the Palestinian peasantry was turned into a cheap labour force in Israel, working largely in the agricultural and construction sectors. Prior to the Gulf War in 1990–91, 35–40 per cent of the Palestinian labour force, or approximately 110,000 people, commuted each day to Israel to work.[3] A new social class had been created, the daily or weekly Palestinian guest worker – Israel's 'nomad industrial reserve army' – in Tel Aviv (the main receiver of Palestinian commuting labour) and other Israeli cities and towns (Portugali, 1993: 10). Since 1993, however, the number of Palestinian labourers in Israel has been falling. One of the strategies of the *intifada* was to withdraw Palestinian labour from the Israeli economy – a strategy which was flawed, since Palestinian workers had become dependent on Israeli wages to such an extent that they were not able to deliberately refrain from this opportunity. It was, rather, Israel's policies which served drastically to reduce labour opportunities in Israel. During the Gulf War, the Palestinians in the occupied territories were subject to a six-week curfew, preventing workers from showing up for work in Israel. In March 1993, after an increase in incidents of violence, the Israeli government directly linked its country's dependence on the Palestinian workforce to security and sealed the occupied territories for an 'indefinite time'. The resulting loss of income from working in Israel brought the West Bank and Gaza to the verge of collapse. This policy has been reinforced in relation to the peace process. After each terror attack against Israeli targets, the Israeli countermeasure has been to seal off the territories. Thus there has been a permanent closure since 1993 which is eased and tightened depending on Israeli perceptions of the day-to-day security situation (see Chapter 4).

Politically, Israel has tried to co-opt moderate Palestinian leaders in order to undermine the nationalist political leadership. Indirect rule was always the favoured policy. However, while Labour during its period of power (1967–77) had sought to find an intermediary body with some sort of legitimacy in the Palestinian population, such as the notables, realising the difficulties in curbing the influence of the PLO (Mishal and Aharoni, 1994: 18), Likud deserted that strategy and instead attempted to build up new forms of organisation in order to boost Israel's dominance. In the early 1980s, the Village Leagues were created as an intermediary between the occupying power and the Palestinian population (see Ma'oz, 1984; Tamari, 1984). However, 'The Village Leagues was a coalition of rural thugs and other marginal personalities who, unlike the notables, had no standing in the Palestinian community and therefore little chance to enhance social control' (Robinson, 1997a: 17). The Palestinian population saw the Village Leagues as a cluster of collaborators and traitors (Mishal and Aharoni, 1994: 19), and they were largely considered a failure. From 1981 onwards, the 'civil administration' under a military commander oversaw the West Bank and Gaza, using a mixture of laws from the Ottoman empire, the British Defence Emergency Regulations, the Jordanian rule of the West Bank and the Egyptian administration of the Gaza Strip, along with some 1,500 Israeli military orders, meticulously steering every aspect of life (e.g. Benvenisti, 1990; Jerusalem Media and Communication Centre (JMCC), 1993). Political factions and the PLO were outlawed, and there was a conscious strategy of 'divide and rule'. Attempts at making Israel's control pemanent through co-optation were coupled with Defence Minister Ariel Sharon's 'iron fist' policy, including the confrontation with the mayors elected in 1976 (see Ma'oz, 1984). The aim of this policy was, according to Menahem Milson, head of the civil administration, to 'uproot the political influence of the PLO' (Ma'oz, 1984: 198).

Palestinian politics prior to the *intifada*

The Palestinian political strategy pursued since 1967 was one of 'steadfastness', *sumud* in Arabic. *Sumud* was partly a result of the Jordanian decision not to cooperate with the Israeli occupation. It was a strategy closely related to the land and agriculture, as well as indigenousness. The ideal image of the Palestinian was the *fellah*, the peasant who stayed put on his land and refused to leave. It was a more passive strategy than that of the *fedayeen* and the exile; a strategy which was further nurtured after the humiliating evacuation of Beirut. It also constituted an important subtext to the Palestinian as fighter/*fedayeen*, in symbolising continuity and connections with the land, with peasantry and a rural life, the knotty olive tree being one of the main symbols. This strategy indicated that uprootedness was not absolute; the Palestinians were still *there*, on the land. Steadfastness was in its early phase not combined with social mobilisation or institution-building. In the late 1970s and 1980s, a more active *sumud* was developed by Palestinian students engaged in attempts at preservation of land relations as well as of culture. Solidarity movements nurtured the idea of a self-reliant society based on the Palestinian peasantry.[4] There was also a nurturing of Palestinian folk culture, mainly through the press, poetry, novels, music and public events. *Sumud* degenerated after the establishment of the *sumud* fund in the late 1970s, when the Arab states decided to support Palestinian steadfastness. Steadfastness money largely fed into the pockets of the already wealthy and *sumud* as a concept decreased in legitimacy (Tamari, 1991: 62 f.).

According to Mishal and Aharoni, the *sumud* idea was nourished by the PLO as a means of control of the West Bank and Gaza. Steadfastness was described by Arafat:

> The most important element in the Palestinian program is holding on to the land. Holding on to the land and not warfare alone. Warfare comes at a different level. If you only fight – that is a tragedy. If you fight and emigrate – that is a tragedy. The basis is that you hold on and fight. The important thing is that you hold on to the land and afterward – combat. (Yasir Arafat, quoted in Mishal and Aharoni, 1994: 13)

In 1973, the relative calm of the occupied territories was temporarily brought to an end. Until the October War, the Israeli politics of relative liberalism had reaped its harvest in the form of a relatively quiescent population. This was acknowledged by the PLO: 'The patterns of "coexistence, travel, and tourism in Israeli cities and settlements may even deprive our people of their revolutionary identity and of their ability to preserve a cohesive national character"' (Zuhayr Muhsin, quoted in Sayigh, 1997a: 345).

The combination of increased social mobility in the form of increased opportunities for education (most visibly in the West Bank), amplified land alienation and urbanisation, increasing contact with the occupying power in the form of labourers in the Israeli labour market and the mounting pressures of a growing and youthful population, together with the vacuum-like political situation, proved explosive in the mid 1980s as PLO fragmentation augmented frustrations. Political and socioeconomic grievances merged and there was a rise in resistance activities throughout the occupied territories.

> 'Illegal acts' such as stone-throwing and demonstrations rose from 953 in 1985 to 1,358 in 1986 and 2,982 in 1987, while armed attacks rose from 351 in 1983 to 870 in 1986. By 1985 an estimated 250,000 Palestinians had experienced interrogation or detention – 40 per cent of all adult males had been held for at least one night – since 1967, of whom 43,000 had received prison sentences in Gaza alone. In the next two years 103 Palestinians died, 668 were wounded, and 12,842 were

arrested in confrontations with Israeli forces, while Israeli military courts passed another 7,457 sentences for security offences. In short, the pattern and skills of revolt were already in place by the start of the *intifada*. (Sayigh, 1997a: 608)

Also towards the mid to late 1980s, Jordan advanced its role *vis-à-vis* the West Bank as well as Gaza in an understanding with Israel and as PLO–Jordanian relations had reached freezing point. Jordan promoted a development plan for the occupied territories in 1986, with the intention of improving its standing in the occupied territories, through, for example, providing Gaza with official aid. Gazan refugees in Jordan were also allowed Jordanian citizenship.

Although the West Bank and Gaza were brought together under one administration with the Israeli occupation, there are vast differences between the two in terms of history and political, economic and social processes. Such divisions were to some extent bridged with the *intifada* (Tamari, 1990: 27).

The West Bank

The political, economic and social configurations of the West Bank were to a large extent formed under Jordanian rule and Jordan continued to have an influence after the occupation. During Jordanian rule, the Jordan Communist Party, the ANM and the Muslim Brotherhood operated on both the West and the East Bank as oppositional forces. In 1957, under Prime Minister Nabulsi, a law was issued disbanding all political parties. A time of repression followed, particularly directed against the communists, who constituted the largest political party in Jordan at that time (Cohen, 1982: 38 ff.). The communists argued that the West Bank had its own homeland, or '*watan*', separate from Jordan, and objected to all attempts by King Abdallah to annex the West Bank in an 'imperialist undertaking' (Cohen, 1982: 71). The Muslim Brotherhood in Jordan had good contacts with the Hashemite regime, as opposed to the repression that was being felt in Nasser's Egypt. The idea was to establish an Islamic state, but Arab nationalism was also accepted. The Brotherhood was strongly anti-communist (Cohen, 1982: 71). When the PLO was formed, fears arose in Jordan over the challenge it implied to the country's claims of sovereignty over the West Bank. A PLO memorandum of discussions between the PLO and Jordan in 1965 revealed assurances that the PLO would not act so as to tear the West Bank away from the East Bank (cf. Mishal's quotation from the document in Mishal, 1978, 68, n. 40).

Fedayyen activities during the revolution never struck a strong chord in the West Bank. Military attacks remained low level. This was due both to demoralisation among the population and to Israeli politics in the first decade, including the 'open bridges' policy facilitating relations with Jordan (Sayigh, 1997a: 209). Following the occupation by Israel, the Jordanian administration continued to exert a significant influence on West Bank politics (e.g. Ma'oz,

1984). The traditional moderate elite, the West Bank mayors, in general favoured Jordanian rule rather than liberation. The revolution served as an enticement to the 'inside' (i.e. the West Bank and Gaza), however. Social processes in the form of increased education and the new employment opportunities in Israel gradually undermined the traditional elite. From the mid 1970s, widespread education and a more mobile labour force paved the way for mass-based political movements and grassroots organisations. Universities served as a ground for political action and organisations. Student movements, women's movements and trade unions[5] – the latter strongly influenced by the Communist Party – were established. Similar processes took place in Gaza. Health care institutions, development organisations, agricultural institutions and self-help organisations were also formed. The existence of numerous women's organisations, trade unions, human rights groups, cooperatives, social work organisations and so on in the West Bank and Gaza created a vibrant civil society (Taraki, 1990; Muslih, 1995; Robinson, 1997a) based on voluntary association. Non-governmental organisations and committees were vocal in expressing criticism of the PLO, even while adhering to it as a general umbrella. These civil organisations strove for large-scale social mobilisation and emphasised development issues, and in that regard challenged the PLO mode of politics. Although many of these initiatives have been crippled by the involvement of factional(ist) and *hamuleh* politics, and hence by intense competition, the number and scope of these activities have served as an institutional counterstructure to the occupying power in the absence of a real state.

New ideological currents gained in influence following the occupation, such as Marxism–Leninism and al-Fateh's 'Palestinianism' (e.g. Sahliyeh, 1988).[6] During the early 1970s, a call emerged from influential West Bankers to establish a 'Palestinian entity' in the occupied territories (cf. Ma'oz, 1984; Brand, 1988a). These political developments influenced the PLO's adoption of such a strategy in 1974. Palestinians in the occupied territories from early on leaned more towards a political solution than those in exile. The PCP,[7] for example, whose influence on the West Bank was considerable (not least through its strong role in labour and union activities), saw armed resistance as a dead end, since the *fedayeen* could never really challenge the heavily armed and strongly motivated Israeli army. The PCP advocated a Palestinian state in the occupied territories, alongside Israel, as did the DFLP (cf. Sahliyeh, 1988).

In 1973, the PNC decided to establish the PNF in the West Bank in order to integrate the PLO and the occupied territories (see Cobban, 1984; Ma'oz, 1984). This was the main point of reference of the emergence of a pro-PLO nationalist elite in the West Bank. The traditional elite had until then advocated pan-Arab hegemony through Jordanian control of the West Bank. Due to its superior organisational structure, the PCP became the leading group of the PNF, implying a cleavage between the Fateh-led PLO and the communist-dominated PNF in the West Bank (Cobban, 1984; Ma'oz, 1984). There was also concern in the PLO about a potential challenge from the PNF concerning control and leadership, while the PNF advocated a certain amount of autonomy in decision-making (Litvak, 1997: 175). After a number of deportations, the PNF was dismantled in 1974 (Cobban, 1984: 173; interview with Alfred Toubbasi, 14 November 1994).[8]

In the municipal elections of 1976, the pro-Jordanian elite was swept from municipal office and was replaced with nationalist, pro-PLO mayors. Although the new mayors were radically nationalist, Ma'oz underlines their pragmatism in seeking a 'realistic' relationship with both Jordan and Israel, which implied that several of the mayors criticised the PLO's 'unrealistic' approach and called for a Palestinian state alongside Israel (Ma'oz, 1984: 145). Since 1976, no elections have been held. The mayors were actively involved in the National Guidance Committee set up in 1978 as a response to the Camp David Accords. Sharp divisions between moderate and radical, leftist-leaning mayors were intensified by different approaches towards the Accords. The National Guidance Committee consisted of both West Bank and Gazan representatives of various organisations. Most mayors and members of municipal councils were fired in 1982 because of their refusal to cooperate with the newly installed Civil Administration. During Sharon's 'iron fist' policy, two of the mayors (Fahd Qawasma of Hebron and Muhammad Milhem of Halhul) were deported and two others (Bassam Shak'a of Nablus and Kamir Khalaf of Ramallah) were maimed in attacks by Jewish extremists (see Ma'oz, 1984). Since then, the towns have been run by Israel, with the exception of Bethlehem, whose mayor, Elias Freij, remained in office.[9] In 1982, the National Guidance Committee was banned.

Other modes of organisation are exemplified by the 'national institutions' in the occupied territories and Fateh's attempt to include various grassroots organisations in the Fateh structure (Litvak, 1997: 178 ff.). This strategy was boosted in the early 1980s when Fateh established its own organisations, foremost of which was the Shabiba, the Fateh youth movement for social action. Leaders of the national institutions were called the 'organisational leadership' (*qiyadat tanzimiyya*). This was another form of leadership, in terms of socioeconomic and sociocultural profile. The other factions also established their own organisations.

Demographically, the population of the West Bank and Gaza stood at 2.8 million at the end of 1997, according to the census carried out by the Palestinian Central Bureau of Statistics (PCBS; www.pcbs.org), established as part of the PNA (see Chapter 4). Demography is in a very real sense part of the Palestinian–Israeli conflict and the results of the PCBS census were described as 'inflated' by Israeli officials. According to the census, the population of the West Bank stood at 1.9 million (www.pcbs.org).

Gaza

The demographic structure of Gaza is completely different from that of the West Bank. According to the 1997 census, Gaza's population was 1 million. Gaza is thus one of the most densely populated areas in the world. In 1996, the population density of Gaza was 2,700 per square kilometre,[10] compared with 300 per square kilometre in the West Bank (PNA Ministry of Planning, 1996–97 Human Development File). Almost 64 per cent of the total Gazan population are registered refugees (www.pcbs.org). Population growth amounts to 6.1 per cent in Gaza (compared with 5.6 per cent in the West Bank) (www.pcbs.org), leading to a highly youthful population in both the West Bank and Gaza, with more than 50 per cent of the population under 15 years of age. Gaza has been hardest hit by the effects of a scarcity of labour opportunities for the ever grow-ing workforce. There is a sharp division between refugees and residents.

From an historical political perspective, Gaza has been marked by the Egyptian administration between 1948 and 1967 (with a four-month interrup-tion during the Israeli occupation in 1956). The Students' Union, whose base was in Cairo, in 1956 established an underground resistance movement in Gaza called the Popular Resistance. Ideologically, the Popular Resistance was a combination of sentiment from the Muslim Brotherhood and Ba'athism, competing with the leftist-oriented National Front, led by Haidar Abdel-Shafi. Both the Popular Resistance and National Front suffered from the harsh Israeli occupation, along with a subsequent Egyptian clampdown when Gaza was again returned to Egypt (Cobban, 1984: 180 f.).

During the early years of the revolution, Gaza was more actively involved in armed resistance than was the West Bank. Here, violence, confrontations and attacks made for a situation approaching an uprising (Sayigh, 1997a: 209). Fateh became the dominant organisation in the 1970s, although the PFLP also gained some influence. There have never been elective municipalities in Gaza, whether under British or Egyptian or Israeli rule. Politically, Gaza suffers from its isola-tion from the Arab world at large as well as from the West Bank. In the after-math of the Jordanian civil war, Israel escalated its confrontation in Gaza, and guerrilla attacks subsequently decreased (Sayigh, 1997a: 209). Mobilisa-tion in Gaza was put on hold and the centre of politicised activity moved to the West Bank. The destitution of Gaza, with its lack of basic natural resources and employment opportunities, adds to its image as a place of grievances.

Roy (1995a) argues that, in contrast to the relatively plural civil society in the West Bank, there is no such thing in Gaza. This is due to a number of interrelated factors, most importantly the Israeli occupation, the military legal system and the different degrees of repression which have characterised Israeli politics *vis-à-vis* the two entities. Opposition in the West Bank and Gaza has not been posed against a legitimate, internal power structure, but against an alien, imposed and illegitimate power. This in turn has caused severe problems for the civil organisations that do exist, 'continuously plagued by a host of problems, including political factionalism, tribalism, classism, and parochialism' (Roy, 1995b: 225).

It is thus no coincidence that it was in Jabalyia refugee camp in Gaza that the *intifada* was born. The immediate igniting spark was the killing of four Palestinian workers by an Israeli truck. Whether the incident was accidental or not is not of importance, since it was interpreted as a deliberate act. A disillusioned and frustrated younger generation, the members of which had grown up with the occupation and for whom military repression had become commonplace, no longer feared the Israeli army and authorities, indicating how class and national grievances had merged. They had lost patience with the diplomatic turns of the PLO and had no confidence in the ability or will of the Arab states to assist their cause. Previous tensions between the West Bank and Gaza were bridged by the *intifada* and its creation of greater cohesion.

The *intifada*

one of the most striking characteristics of the Palestinian national struggle has been the spontaneity of its uprisings, and the problematic relationship between these and the national leadership. (Sayigh, 1994: 5)

Palestinian resistance in the occupied territories reached a peak with the *intifada* (which means 'rising up and shaking off' in Arabic), its mass mobilisation and its thorough politicisation of the Palestinian population.[11] The uprising was a mass movement based on a combined strategy of 'limited violence' (such as stone-throwing and the use of Molotov cocktails), large-scale confrontations with the Israeli defence forces, mass demonstrations and civil disobedience. The latter included strikes, the closure of shops,[12] non-cooperation, in some areas (most notably the Christian West Bank town of Beit Sahour) refusal to pay taxes and a general attempt to withdraw from the structures of the occupation. The *intifada* denoted a form of people's empowerment. 'Victory gardens' were established in order to grow vegetables and fruit for self-sufficiency at the household level.

It is, of course, a truism to say that the *intifada* was a response to twenty years of occupation. The Lebanon experience and the forced evacuation of the PLO from Lebanon were one important reason for a relocation of the struggle to the inside. The PLO and Arafat had attempted to enforce the connections between the PLO and the occupied territories (Sayigh, 1994: 208), since the West Bank and Gaza were now the only areas from which the struggle could be moulded. However, the *intifada* was not the result of any conscious strategy by the PLO. The PLO was as surprised as any other actor in the Arab–Israeli conundrum over the turn of events which was written by the *intifada*.

The *intifada* broke out because we had reached a point where we couldn't take any more. The collective punishments, things were added and added. Things had to happen. Especially when the Palestinians were expelled from Lebanon. If the Palestinian issue was to stay alive, the only chance was here in the West Bank and Gaza. (Interview with Fateh activist, 16 November 1994)

Politically, the *intifada* implied that the population of the West Bank and Gaza was prepared to take matters into its own hands. There was renewed disappointment over the Arab states and the disinterest in the Palestinian cause at the Arab League summit in Amman in November 1987, when attention was focused on the Iran–Iraq war and the Palestinian question was not top priority.[13] The uprising was a sign that a younger generation in the occupied territories had lost faith in the PLO's ability to resolve the Palestinian dilemma through either military means or politics and diplomacy. The focal point of Palestinianism and Palestinian resistance was moved from the 'outside' to the 'inside'.

Institution-building and leadership organisation

Resistance was combined with increased institution-building. The institution-building of the 1980s, in the form of health care institutions, agricultural co-operatives, human rights organisations and solidarity networks, was channelled into the *intifada* and its deliberate attempts to withdraw from the structures of occupation. These mainly grassroots and civil society initiatives also led to a new middle class reaching positions of intermediate power, further challenging the role of the traditional elite and the urban notables. This middle class was 'larger, younger, better educated, from more modest class origins, and less urban than its notable counterpart' (Robinson, 1997a: 19). A large portion was professional, that is, teachers, physicians, lawyers, and so on. This mode of organisation provided a new role for the middle command, non-privileged young activists from rural areas and refugee camps.

The dominant form of political organisation during the *intifada* was the political committee, implying a new form of decision-making as well as organisation. Decisions previously taken at municipal or national level were now taken by popular committees. Local popular committees dealt with food storage and distribution, security, education, self-reliant agriculture, health care, and so on. Neighbourhood organisations and local committees played a prominent role in social and economic issues.[14] One variant was the militant strike forces (Robinson, 1997a: 94–6).

The UNLU, which directed the uprising in organisational and activist terms, created a unified and centralised leadership which to an extent bridged factionalist divisions. The UNLU consisted of local members of al-Fateh, the PFLP, the DFLP and the PCP and other, undefined, political forces. Most UNLU leaders were middle-command activists, often with a lower-class or refugee background.

The UNLU was a clandestine organisation and the actual figures rotated; that is, as soon as someone was arrested, he was replaced. However, by 1992–93, the UNLU had disintegrated and ceased to function effectively (Hunter, 1993: 269 f.).[15] While Litvak argues that the UNLU represented a loose and decentralised form of leadership (Litvak, 1997: 181), Heacock holds that it could be described as a centralist, Lenin-style organisation, in the sense of its, and its factions, 'guiding role' and in its position as an intermediate between the PLO and grassroots activism (Nassar and Heacock, 1990b: 198). Its leadership was composed of lower-middle-class and middle-class elements, many with a university degree. Many were drawn from student movements.

The traditional elite also made a step forward; this time, however, with 'new' leaders, that is, professionals and the intelligentsia (Jarbawi, 1990), rising to prominence. The Palestinian 'personalities', as they were called, constituted a combination of traditional leaders, in the form of business-people, landowners and *hamuleh* leaders, and 'new' leaders. This leadership was generally more moderate and pragmatist than the UNLU and *intifada* activists, and drew its legitimacy from its relationship with the PLO. Nationalists loyal to Fateh had already been nurtured as a form of intermediary leadership prior to the *intifada* (Jarbawi, 1990). The inclusion of the personalities in the Palestinian delegation to the peace negotiations in Madrid confirmed that the traditional elite had not yet played out its role. However, since they are regarded as not having 'fought' or 'struggled', they are often regarded with suspicion by rank and file activists.

Initially, the PLO had little influence in the *intifada*, although Khalil Wazir (Abu Jihad) soon began to explore the situation and to coordinate activities between the 'outside' and the 'inside'.[16] Abu Jihad sought to escalate the uprising, and also to make it a platform for himself to challenge Arafat (Sayigh, 1997a: 618). As early as January 1988 the leaflets began to contain references to the PLO as the leadership of the uprising (CNU03A).

The nationalism of the intifada

With the *intifada*, there was a change in the content and direction of Palestinianism, with a new focus on the West Bank and Gaza as the bases for a Palestinian state. The goal of the uprising in the occupied territories was to bring an end to Israeli occupation and to establish a Palestinian state in the West Bank and Gaza. The *intifada* led to the resolute acceptance of a two-state solution – a process which commenced in 1974 and provided the PLO leadership with an opportunity to promote its drive for a share in the peace talks. The PNC Declaration of Independence in November 1988 and the acceptance of UN Resolutions 242 and 338[17] were an immediate response to this development. Although the specific borders of the declared state of Palestine were not defined, this could be understood as *de facto* recognition of Israel. This is also the way in which the PLO has portrayed the decision.

Although mainstream Palestinian nationalism had thus accepted the two-state solution as the goal, the ultimate objective of the PFLP and other minority organisations was still the liberation of all Palestine in accordance with the 1968 Charter. On the one hand, the PFLP accepted the *intifada* strategy and was included in the UNLU. Despite the PFLP's abstention from voting at the 18th PNC, the PFLP in the occupied territories did not express a negative stand-point on the PLO decision. On the other hand, the PFLP was strongly against the peace negotiations, and eventually the DOP.

THE 'LAND', THE 'PEOPLE' AND THE 'STRUGGLE'

In the UNLU leaflets, the main source of *intifada* discourse, there were calls for an independent Palestinian state under the leadership of the PLO. 'Liberation' was not referred to as frequently. Instead, the slogans of the *intifada* were the rights of 'return, self-determination and an independent state'. The 'state' entered official nationalist discourse in a more explicit way than previously. The Palestinian Declaration of Independence states that:

> Palestine, the land of the three monotheistic faiths, is where the Palestinian Arab people was born, on which it grew, developed and excelled. The Palestinian people was never separated from or diminished in its integral bonds with Palestine. Thus the Palestinian Arab people ensured for itself an everlasting union between itself, its land and its history.
>
> Resolute through that history, the Palestinian Arab people forged its national identity, rising even to unimagined levels in its defence, as invasion, the design of others, and the appeal special to Palestine's ancient and luminous place on that eminence where powers and civilisations are joined . . . All this intervened thereby to deprive the people of its political independence. Yet the undying connection between Palestine and its people secured for the land its character, and for the people its national genius. (in Lukacs, 1992: 411)

The Palestinian Declaration of Independence thus devotes itself to the same kind of nationalist discourse as the Palestinian National Charter, although it is more clearly and explicitly 'Palestinianist'. The land is the clear base of Palestinian identity. The union between the land of Palestine and the people is 'ancient' and 'everlasting'. It is an organic, romantic view of the nation and of the relationship between 'land' and 'people'. This essentialism has almost biological connotations, as if the people grew from the land. Celebrations of 'Land Day' (*yom al-ard*) on 30 March can here serve as an example of the importance of the land and the emotions connected with it in *intifada* discourse: 'In the memory of the 14th unforgettable Land Day and in opposing the politics of extension of the cancerous settlements which the colonial government of Israel has proceeded . . . during this week we shall cultivate the land and develop it, especially the land threatened by confiscation' (UNLU55). In cultivating the land, the Palestinians showed that it could not be taken away. Although not a prioritised strategy, *sumud* continued to have a bearing upon nationalist discourse.

'STRUGGLE' IN A NEW DISGUISE: CULT OF THE HERO, CULT OF THE BLOOD

The uprising had far-reaching consequences in raising Palestinian self-esteem and dignity. Psychologically and emotionally, the *intifada* meant a new form of daring activism and pride. 'The *intifada* is a sacred thing' (interview with former Fateh activist, 2 October 1994), and the action of the *intifada* was worshipped in its entanglement with Palestinian identity. This was also evident in a glorification of martyrs and worship of *intifada* heroes. 'And I think it was very lovely, because there was a risk in it, and it was not bad. [. . .] It was my duty, and I loved it, because you were doing something you believed in' (interview with former Fateh activist, 12 January 1995).

The *intifada* represented pride, dignity and glory through militant activism, which signified struggle and resistance. In the above quotation, the risks inherent in the struggle are themselves glorified, the danger itself represents thrill, it was 'lovely'. In the *bayanat*, the *intifada* was depicted as our 'honourable and glorious uprising'. The uprising, the action, the process in itself was worshipped in the narcissistic political self-love of nationalism (cf. Anderson, 1991).

In the Declaration of Independence, the aspects of struggle and sacrifice in Palestinian identity are evident:

> And in generation after generation, the Palestinian Arab people gave of itself unsparingly in the valiant battle for liberation and homeland. For what has been the unbroken chain of our people's rebellions but the heroic embodiment of our will for national independence? And so the people was sustained in the struggle to stay and to prevail. (Lukacs, 1992: 411)

The 'people gave of itself', sacrificed for the sake of the land. The 'struggle' supported and confirmed the people. Further:

> Occupation, massacres and dispersion achieved no gain in the unabated Palestinian consciousness of self and political identity, as Palestinians went forward with their destiny, undeterred and unbowed. And from out of the long years of trial in ever mounting struggle, the Palestinian political identity emerged further consolidated and confirmed. [. . .] And so Palestinian resistance was clarified and raised into the forefront of Arab and world awareness, as the struggle of the Palestinian Arab people achieved unique prominence among the world's liberation movements in the modern era. (Lukacs, 1992: 412)

The struggle as part of Palestinian identity is repeatedly emphasised and the Palestinian people is equated to the liberation – the Palestinians are what they are to achieve. All the wrong done to the Palestinians have not discouraged them. Despite all their sufferings, the Palestinians move ahead unabated, forwards, progressing towards their glorious future. Connotations to Arabism are significantly downplayed compared with the PLO Charter, although Palestinians are described as the *avant garde* of the Arab world.

Intifada came to mean the ultimate struggle, in the same way as the revolution before it had meant all-encompassing struggle. In the late 1980s *intifada* replaced *al-thawra* as the main concept of struggle, symbolising an harmonious blend between the 'outside' and the 'inside', as well as a unique possibility to imagine struggle as a continuous, evolutionary phenomenon. There was a 'symbiosis between our revolution and our courageous masses' (CNU01A).

Both the revolution and the uprising were depicted as natural, evolutionary, unstoppable processes, their heat and strength symbolised by glowing lava. *Intifada* means a feverish shudder, shake or tremble, like shaking the dust off something. Both *intifada* and *thawra* signify violent, sudden movements and activities. In UNLU leaflets, the *intifada* was often described as the eruption of a 'volcano' (e.g. CNU03A). The 'earth was trembling under the feet of the occupier' (CNU03B); the *intifada* was an 'earthquake of the land' (CNU03B).

> Those generations – the children of the revolution and of the Palestine Liberation Organisation – rose to demonstrate the dynamism and continuity of the revolution, detonating the land under the feet of its occupiers and proving that our people's reserves of resistance are inexhaustible and their faith is too deep to uproot.
>
> Thus did the struggle of the children of the RPGs outside our homeland and the struggle of the children of the sacred stones inside it blend into a single revolutionary melody. (Palestine National Council, political communiqué, 1988; Lukacs: 415)

Generations follow upon generations in the above quotation from the PNC's political communiqué of November 1988; the 'children of the sacred stones' followed upon the 'RPG children' in a cyclical development of the nation and its struggle. The people are unstoppable, 'inexhaustible', and cannot be uprooted. They will stay on the land and make the land 'detonate' 'under the feet' of the occupier. The land itself exploded under their feet in the attempt of shaking the occupation off; that is, the land itself refused the occupation (CNU03B).

Sacrifice and suffering were also referred to. The uprising was in solidarity with the 'blood of our martyrs' (CNU01A): 'In the spirit and in the blood we sacrifice our life for you, oh martyr. In the spirit and in the blood we sacrifice our life for you, oh Palestine' (CNU02B). Martyrs were always to be cherished and certain days were devoted to honouring them and visiting their families. Symbolic funeral processions were held and death for the nation was cherished. Funerals became large-scale nationalist demonstrations and manifestations. As underlined by Anderson (1991), to die for the nation was a cherished thing in nationalist discourse. Agents of the nation were expected to die for its preservation, but it would be no ordinary death, but something solemnly acknowledged by the producers of nationalism.[18]

National calendars often structure time in relation to death. The *intifada* produced its own calendar of memory and celebrations. The day when the uprising is supposed to have started, 9 December, became a day of celebration and a general strike day. Indeed, the ninth of every month was held as a day in memory of the outbreak of the *intifada*. These dates also clearly show how nationalism is internally contested. The Islamist movements, and especially Islamic Jihad, proclaimed their own celebration day on the sixth day of every month, as they claimed the sixth was the actual initiation of the uprising. Here, a struggle of symbolic power was enacted. Another day was added to the national calendar during the *intifada*, the Day of Independence (*yom al-istiqlal*), 15 November, which was also widely celebrated. Both days of remembrance initially carried popularised meanings, but when in the mid-1990s autonomy had replaced the struggle and formal nationalism had taken over, symbols previously of great importance lost some of their meaning, since they no longer symbolised struggle.

To extend this point a little, a typical Palestinian national calendar appears as follows, oscillating between traumas and achievements:

19 November 1935	Izz al-Din al-Qassem killed
1936–39	Great Revolt
9 April 1948	Deir Yasin massacre
15 May 1948	The *nakba*
1 January 1965	Birth of the revolution
7 June 1967	Israeli occupation of East Jerusalem
21 March 1968	Battle of Karameh
28 October 1974	PLO acknowledged by Arab Summit
13 November 1974	Arafat in the UN General Assembly for the first time
30 March 1976	Land Day, six killed as Israeli troops fired on Palestinians protesting against land expropriations in Nazareth
12 August 1976	Tal el-Zataar, massacre in refugee camp in Lebanon
16–18 September 1982	Sabra and Shateela massacre
9 December 1987	The *intifada* began

16 April 1988	Abu Jihad killed in Tunis
15 November 1988	Declaration of Independence at the 19th PNC meeting in Algiers
13 September 1993	DOP signed in Washington
25 February 1994	Hebron massacre, twenty-nine Palestinians killed
4 May 1994	Gaza–Jericho Agreement
1 July 1994	The 'homecoming': Arafat returned to Palestine
28 September 1995	Oslo II Agreement
20 January 1996	Presidential and Legislative Council elections
September 1996	Gunfight between IDF and Palestinian police
January 1997	Hebron Agreement

Not all of these days are of equal importance, but what they do signify is the way in which Palestinian nationalism structures time in relation to events which can be placed into the two categories of 'struggle'/resistance/pride and 'suffering'/death/martyrdom/sacrifice. Nationalist calendars are ways of organising a chaotic existence as well as giving meaning to events. Through memorising catastrophes and triumphs, the meaning of events is repeated and provides information content to the politics of identity. Days commemorated annually include the 'birthday' of the revolution, Land Day, Sabra and Shateela, and the assassination of Abu Jihad, whose impact on the occupied territories was fundamental. 'We will acknowledge the arrival of the Black September, the September of Sabra and Shateela and the slaughtering of Palestinians . . . with eyes of tears. . . . This month we distinguish the memory of the martyrs whose blood was drawn on the road of the struggle until the liberation and national independence' (UNLU45). 'Struggle' is also remembered and re-created in this way, as at the yearly celebration of the 'birth of the revolution' on 1 January: 'Our Palestinian people gathers in the beginning of this month in the memory of the sweet Palestinian revolution which inaugurated the road of struggle of the Palestinian people with the explosion of the legendary fighting rifle . . . and [manifested] its presence on the map of the world' (UNLU91).

THE *INTIFADA* AND 'SELF'

The *intifada* therefore had immense implications for Palestinian identity and self-definition. When it comes to self-description, the people were described as 'heroic', 'brave', 'courageous' and 'glorious'. A typical passage reads:

> Masses of our courageous Palestinian people! Heroes of the blood, the victory and the stones! You who write the songs of love, return and a halt to the injury and departure! New disciples of al-Qassem, the redemption and the sacrifice! Artisans of the glorious history! You who wrote Palestine in the alleys on the terraces of the houses! (CNU03B)

The people were a people of 'martyrs', and Sheikh Izz al-Din al-Qassem was referred to by both the UNLU and the Islamists (CNU02B). al-Qassem and the Great Revolt of 1936 represented the start of the struggle. al-Qassem was in a sense a 'revolutionary father', he was the origin of the revolution and the 'struggling' aspect of Palestinian identity. Another such historical hero was 'Abd al-Qadir al-Husayni, who was killed in the battle for the Qastel, outside Jerusalem, in 1948.[19] *Intifada* leaflets elevated and paid homage to the 'hero', the 'fighter':

> A thousand thousand salutations, endless honor and glory, exaltation and eternal life to you our people's martyrs, heroes of the uprising, who saturate the soil of the beloved homeland with rivers of your spilt blood, hoist the banners of freedom and independence, and with your pure shed blood pave the way to victory and the independent state under the leadership of the great and powerful PLO. (UNLU3)

The *intifada* discourse indulged in adoration of the hero, the martyr and a blood cult.

> We will die upright and we will not surrender! They shall not pass! The uprising will triumph! [. . .]
>
> O heroes of the victorious uprising, the uprising continues dipped in pure and immaculate blood, day after day, watering the soil of our precious homeland, registering cardinal achievements and being strengthened step by step through little triumphs that accumulate, one on top of the other, layer after layer, to foment the great and magnificent victories that will build the independent Palestinian state. (UNLU12)

Blood symbolises both sacrifice and nationalist purity. Martyrs were singled out as very particular carriers of Palestinian identity in the sense that martyrdom in an obvious way signified both 'struggle' and 'suffering'; that is, they had taken action and died while in struggle. Other groups singled out through the same mechanism were the 'wounded', the 'detained' and the deported (e.g. UNLU3).

To be put in prison was a form of sacrifice for the national cause. It was not as honourable as being martyred, but it belonged to the same category of manifesting 'struggle' and commitment. Prisons were a special locus, a space where suffering was activated among those who had struggled. When being interviewed, most male activists structured their life histories through two things: education and participation in the struggle. Almost matter-of-factly, but also with pride, respondents placed themselves within the struggle through beginning their story by saying how many years they had spent in prison.

Representations of Israel and Zionism were harsh in the *bayanat* (Mishal and Aharoni, 1994; Mishal, 1997: 203). The UNLU leaflets were, however, careful to nominate Israel and Zionism as the main enemy rather than 'Jews', echoing the PLO's portrayal of the enemy. The *intifada* (like the PLO) in fact produced a much more benign and less exclusivist 'other' discourse than is usually portrayed in world media. However, Israeli policies *vis-à-vis* the *intifada* were frequently equated with Nazism. Detention camps were 'Nazi camps'; Sharon, Peres and Rabin were referred to as 'fascist dwarfs' (UNLU16); Rabin was a 'shedder of blood' (UNLU11) and a 'terrorist' (UNLU25). Despite these gruesome characterisations, the UNLU leaflets did not contain descriptions of Israelis or 'Jewishness'. Negative stereotypes were thus not reproduced on the level of ethnic/national categories. Neither were such stereotypes used in ascriptions of identities to a certain population. Instead, they were specifically directed to the Israeli government and its policies:

> They are repeating the acts of the Nazis and the fascists by obligating the wearing of an identity tag, in order to differentiate between us and the Zionist laborers at places of work, and by their attempts to compel our workers and our people in the steadfast Gaza Strip, the strip of heroism and defiance, to accept a special identification card which enables its bearers to go to their places of work. (UNLU41)

The UNLU also directed itself in positive terms to 'progressive and democratic forces and the Jewish peace forces that support our people's national rights' (UNLU21), again indicating that the *intifada* leadership did not consciously contribute to ethnicist stereotyping. In addition, there were warnings directed towards the Israeli political leadership not to underestimate the capacity for struggle of the Palestinian hero: 'Are you aware that the solution to the stone problem and so forth will only come when you remove yourselves from our land and recognize our legitimate national rights, self-determination, and an independent state, and not by talking nonsense, going on the rampage, and exercising oppression?' (UNLU25)

The uprising redefined societal structures and roles. Gender roles were, for example, changed as women became more articulate and politicised and increasingly evident in demonstrations and political events. Women's movements became articulated on gender issues for the first time. A new and more dynamic image of women was fostered (Jawwad, 1990: 69). In the revolutionary period of the 1960s, women were 'men's sisters', 'martyrs,' mothers' and 'factories for men' (Jad, 1990: 137). Now, women were more visible as activists. Later, in the early 1990s, Hanan Ashrawi came to epitomise the Palestinian woman as a leading political figure.

At the same time, however, Palestinian women were pulled in the opposite direction with the retreat to more traditional values and also by the national(ist) discourse itself. National struggle and liberation were to be a continued priority as opposed to women's emancipation. This was also manifest in the fact that the women's movement was still divided, each organisation connected with one of the four dominant political organisations (al-Fateh, the PFLP, the DFLP and the PPP). In the women's movement, gender issues have always been subordinated to nationalist political discourse. In the mid 1990s, self-criticism was often raised, regretting the fact that women's organisations have over the years been devoted to nationalist politics, leaving gender issues aside for the future in accordance with PLO/Fateh ideology that national liberation comes first. 'Our primary goal is to liberate our country and maybe after that we will talk about women's issues. Because we cannot talk about the liberation of women if the men are not liberated' (interview with woman activist, Fateh, 16 November 1994).

Initially, the *intifada* served as a catalyst for a more active women's role in the struggle. Women's visible and active role was nurtured and glorified by the factions. International Women's Day in 1988 was a massive manifestation, and became a symbol for a popular nationalism which was all-embracing for the first years of the *intifada*. In leaflets, there were calls for participation in the women's day (e.g. UNLU35). It has since, however, declined in symbolism, as did most other days of popular/nationalist manifestations.

Concepts of Palestine, the land, as a woman were also common during the *intifada*: 'Rejoice, oh Palestine, for your knights who arrive in the sun, ten thousand heroes and others who dress you in a wedding dress. And the bridegroom he is the martyr in Jabalyia and Nablus and Kfar Ni'ma in the legendary South'. (CNU04A).

'Palestine the land' was thus a woman to be rescued by 'the Palestinian, the martyr', who was the knight and the bridegroom. The land was the object which was nurtured and cherished, while the active Palestinian, who set out to rescue the land and who gave his life for it, was a man. A marriage was to occur between the land and the people. Sometimes the Palestinian woman was still the 'mother of martyrs'. 'Thousand salutes to the Palestinian mother who gives birth for Palestine, who observes sit-ins and demonstrates for Palestine!' (CNU04H). The territory of Palestine was thus represented as a 'mother' of Palestinian martyrs; the reproductive role of the woman was still her function in the nationalist struggle. The politicisation of women's reproductive capacity also has other implications, such as the gendered division of labour in representations of identity. While men represent the struggle, women represent the suffering. Women's contribution to the nation and the cause is represented by their sacrifice of sons being martyred.

Gender relations were also affected by the increased role of Hamas, capitalising on the appearance of women. Women's dress code has become a visible hallmark of the movement. Hamas has made an issue of making women wear the *hijab*, the traditional headscarf. Unveiled women have been subjected to violent harassment (e.g. Legrain, 1991b: 84). The veil became a symbol not only of increased religiousness, and of the augmented role of Hamas, but of a serious and strict, disciplined form of nationalism. It symbolised that women were following the modest way of life of the uprising; that is, there were to be no gaiety, no social gatherings, no celebrations. The *intifada* was a time of disciplined struggle and suffering; it was an era of seriousness, symbolising that there was no reason for joy as long as the occupation continued. Sincerity and strictness represented nationalism. The secularist movements were slow in responding to Hamas capitalising on women's appearance as a symbol of their version of Palestinianism, leading to criticism from Palestinian women's movements. 'Women who fought the imposition of the veil said that they became "martyrs of the veil"' (interview with Dr Eileen Kuttab, 7 November 1994), communicating that they were also 'martyrs' and therefore just as nationalist.

> Article 17: The Muslim woman has a role in the battle for liberation which is no less than the role of the man, for she is the factory of men. Her role in directing generations and training them is a big role. The enemies have realized her role: they think that if they are able to direct her and raise her the way they want, far from Islam, then they have won the battle. (Maqdsi, 1993: 127)

In Hamas ideology, the role of women as producing men – 'she is the factory of men' – was even more explicit than within UNLU discourse. The role of women was in reproduction, in producing men, the real subjects and agents of struggle. Modernity and women's emancipation were perceived as part of the enemy's strategy in the struggle against Islam and national liberation. The role of women was as childbearers, as those who nurtured and brought up children. This is also to be seen in relation to the demographic aspect of the Palestinian–Israeli conflict, frequently expressed in terms of demographic numbers. On both sides, the question of women's fertility is politicised, and this politicisation has now been taken over by the Islamists.

Women as bearers of children thus play an ideological role as a symbol and an image of producing 'fighters'. In the Declaration of Independence, the role of women is described: 'We render special tribute to that brave Palestinian Woman, guardian of sustenance and Life, keeper of our people's perennial flame' (Lukacs: 414). Women's symbolic role in the nationalist movement focuses upon the role of the family; as mothers they suffer the martyrdom and imprisonment of their sons, and at sit-ins and demonstrations related to the prisoner issue, women constitute the bulk of participants. Women became defenders of the nation in the sense that they were given the role of guarding against the intrusion of negative social values, of corruption, of moral degradation, of Western cultural invasion.

End of the intifada

By 1990, it had become increasingly clear that the uprising found itself in a deadlock. This was partly due to growing sentiments of exhaustion in Palestinian society. The most intense and all-embracing part of the *intifada* had in fact lasted no more than two years. 'We got tired from the *intifada*. I feel like that myself. I don't want to do anything like that again. Almost all houses have something, someone lost or injured or imprisoned' (interview with woman Fateh activist, 16 November 1994). Economically, it was the Palestinians who suffered most from the measures of general strikes, the closure of shops and the attempt to withdraw from Israeli structures. Politically, the Israeli reaction to the uprising was harsh, with the use of military repression and collective punishment. Measures included curfews, border closures, demolition of houses, administrative detention and sheer military violence.[20] Although violence and military repression had always been part of Israel's strategy, the human rights situation deteriorated from the commencement of the *intifada*, with the harsh use of an 'iron fist' policy in attempting to crush the uprising. This was despite several acknowledgements by Defence Minister Yitzhak Rabin (the architect of the 'iron fist' policy) and top security echelons that the *intifada* was a political problem which needed a political solution.

Although the *intifada* in the initial period used only limited violence, explicitly abstaining from the use of firearms and knives, violence increased from 1990–91. The mass-based uprising went from a civil character of low-scale violence to an escalating involvement of gangs using larger-scale, more intense violence, and the *intifada* militarised. Although it still represented identity, pride and dignity, there was in the mid 1990s some soul-searching and self-criticism. 'Our good *intifada*, it was the first two years. After that it began to go down' (interview with Fateh activist, 12 January 1995).

To a large extent the decline of the *intifada* was due to PLO involvement (Litvak, 1997; Robinson, 1997a; Sayigh, 1997a). Robinson (1997a) argues convincingly that the PLO failed sufficiently to support and make political use of the *intifada*, since it feared the competition of the new West Bank/Gaza elite. In fact, the spontaneity of the uprising lasted no longer than to March 1990, when the UNLU ceased to act autonomously (*ibid*.: 88 f.) and was replaced by well-known 'personalities' (Robinson, 1997a: 99). With the uprising, Arafat had increased his position as the only real leader of the Palestinians. His wrestling to power and use of funding served on the one hand to promote state-building aspirations and, on the other, to undermine the emerging new elite on the 'inside'. It also, however, entailed the fragmentation of the Fateh movement in the occupied territories (Sayigh, 1997a: 635). This was in line with Arafat's mode of operating so as to discourage alternative centres of power. It was not only Fateh leaders on the 'outside' who sought to subjugate the internal process to their control; the PFLP and DFLP were equally concerned about losing control of the 'inside' (Sayigh, 1997a: 636). This interpretation is also in agreement with how many factional representatives and *intifada* activists explain the demise of the uprising:

> [The outside leadership] feared their role as maximum leaders and decided with their own elements here in the occupied territories to . . . interfere directly, to force their presence, their role and to destroy it, because the *intifada* represented a threat, a clear, direct, serious threat to the existing hierarchical leadership of the PLO in Tunis. (Interview with Riad Malki, 7 October 1994)

After 1990, the PLO to an increasing extent used the old elite and 'prominent personalities' in order to counter initiatives by the younger elite (Robinson, 1997a: 89).

Internal divisions and intra-violence in the form of collaborator killings increased after 1990. One particular function of the UNLU and the popular committees was to settle conflicts and deal with crime. The moralistic, serious and disciplined kind of nationalism represented by the *intifada* was reflected in its system of justice. Mediation committees drew on the experience of the *hamuleh* system, but comprised the nationalist *intifada* leaders rather than the *hamuleh*. Many times, members of mediation committees were also involved in violent strike forces (Robinson, 1997a: 112 f.). The kind of 'justice' meted out to collaborators, but also to 'drug dealers' and 'prostitutes', all outcasts in Palestinian society, was often harsh, and towards the latter part of the *intifada* collaborator killings became brutal, uncontrolled and arbitrary (Rigby, 1997; Robinson, 1997a). While, in the early phase of the uprising, collaborators were invited to 'return' to societal norms and morals, towards the end alleged collaborators were openly killed by the military wings of the factions in, for example, the casbah of Nablus, the city which has become most infamous for these procedures. 'There was a drive to purify society, to rid the Palestinian community of "unclean" elements' (Robinson, 1997a: 126). Between 1989 and 1993, some 150 to 200 collaborators were killed yearly in the 'murderous purge' (Rigby, 1997: 54). Explanation for this may be found in the mounting revolutionary zeal and the factionalisation which rendered the *intifada* increasingly militarised. In this process, the category of 'collaborator' was enlarged so as to include anyone who 'undermined the national struggle', a highly arbitrary category (Rigby, 1997: 55).

Collaborators represented a 'grey zone' category; being Palestinians but having betrayed their cause, being not Israeli, but collaborating with the enemy. To have order in the Palestinian garden, or home, they needed to be wiped out. 'They lost themselves' is the expression used by some Fateh activists. 'They are inside our people and at the same time they are enemies,' 'they must be killed' (interview with Fateh activists, 2 October 1994). Collaborators as a category are partly boundary-transcending, making them a particular threat. They are (or were) Palestinians, but they cooperate with the Israelis against their fellow Palestinians – they are not 'real' Palestinians; their Palestinian-ness can be questioned, they are stripped of a Palestinian identity in the eyes of the community. They represent a 'grey zone' of being neither real Palestinians nor Israelis. In that sense they also represent a 'stickiness', using Bauman's (1989) terminology, since they are not real Palestinians but are at the same time hard to define and separate from the rest of society. Through the collaborators, the enemy had infiltrated the 'inside' (cf. Bauman, 1989: 97 f.).

From 1990 the *intifada* had to respond to escalating external pressure. In 1990, a new Likud government came to power in Israel, following a period of coalition government. Also in 1990, after a PLF attack against a beach close to Tel Aviv, conducted by the Abu Abbas group, the USA decided to close the dialogue it had opened in 1989 with the PLO. As the Soviet Union and Eastern bloc collapsed, the Palestinians lost important allies,[21] further forcing them to rethink their strategies.

THE GULF WAR

In Palestinian ranks, the Gulf War of 1990–91 incited a temporary upswing for the idea of an Arab solution. In the initial phase of the Iraqi occupation of Kuwait, the PLO distanced itself from the Iraqi position, but with the increased American military build-up, attitudes shifted in favour of Saddam Hussein, who challenged US interests and military strength.[22] The PLO advocated an 'Arab solution' and abstained from voting in the Arab League decision of August 1990. The atmosphere in the West Bank and Gaza during the Gulf War was one of feverish expectation. The Scud missiles fired by Iraq represented a flexing of muscles; it was perceived as though an Arab state was finally threatening the air power of Israel. People gathered on the roofs to witness the new vulnerability of Israel. This should be related to the Palestinian inferiority complex – finally, Israel was being placed in the vulnerable position.

The PLO position angered the Gulf states, which expelled Palestinian migrants on a mass basis, freezing PLO and Palestinian assets in banks and cancelling disbursement of financial assistance to the PLO and the occupied territories. Large parts of the Palestinian population in Kuwait – as in other Gulf states – were deported, arrested, abused or killed as a sort of punishment for the PLO and Palestinian sympathy for the Iraqi side in the war.[23] The PLO position was also due to its drawing closer to Iraq since the mid 1980s and its increasing frustration with dwindling financial support from the Gulf countries. The economic setback for the Palestinians as a result of the Gulf War was very significant, indeed nearly disastrous (cf. Roy, 1991). The PLO, in a speech by Abu Mazen, later apologised for its politics during the Gulf War (cf. Mahmoud Abbas, 1993).

The Gulf War left the Palestinians politically and economically weaker than they had been for many years. Palestinian support for Iraq had serious consequences. The Palestinians lost support and credibility among the international public as well as among Israeli leftists.

Islamism as counter-discourse

The solemnity and chastity of the *intifada* went hand in hand with an increased salience of political Islam in Palestinian society, providing a new and challenging definition of Palestinian nationalism and identity.

Islamism played a central role in the formative years of national identity, through its institutional elite variant as well as in the radicalised form manifested by Sheikh Izz-al-Din al-Qassem. Although the Muslim Brotherhood and other Islamist organisations had been formed in Palestine during World War II, and although the Muslim Brotherhood participated against Israel in the 1948 war and was a main political force during the Jordanian era, Islamism in Palestine became stronger only after the 1967 war and the humiliating Arab defeat. An Islamist view of the Arab–Israeli conflict gained credence.

> The Arab nation has not been able to unify its vision of the Palestinian struggle. At times, it has been considered a question of dignity or nationality; at other times, of stolen land and property, the struggle of dispossessed people, or one bound by the cables of occupation; at still other times, it is considered as a part of the game of nations. While Islam does not contradict any of these perceptions, it does not consider any or all of these reasons as the *accurate understanding of the conflict . . . It is a struggle between truth, represented by Islam, and falsehood, represented by total disbelief, by Zionism and its supporters: Crusaderism and atheism.* (Ghanima, quoted in Haddad, 1992: 268, emphasis added)

The conflict was increasingly regarded by some groups as a conflict between Muslims, on the one hand, and Jews and their Western Christian supporters on the other. Partly, this was a response to the failure of secular Arab nationalism, but it was also the result of perceived threat against Muslim identity. The Islamic reawakening was a mechanism of defence. Further, it was a strategy utilised in order to gain support for the struggle against Israel from the larger Muslim world (Haddad, 1992: 268). It was also a response to the 'Judaisation of Palestine', expressed in Israeli claims of historical rights to the territory based on religion, as well as to the rise of ultra-nationalist, religious Jewish organisations and the perceived 'Judeo-Christian'/'Zionist/Crusader' 'conspiracy against Islam'.[24] In the first decade of the occupation, however, this Islamism represented only a small minority of the West Bank/Gaza population. It was a largely powerless and non-confrontational movement focusing on education and the Islamisation of culture, values, symbols and lifestyles.

Hamas

Hamas sprang from the Muslim Brotherhood (Ikhwan al-Muslimun), which was formed in Egypt in 1929. Its Palestinian branch was established in Jerusalem in 1946. During the 1950s, the Muslim Brotherhood adopted a non-confrontational approach towards the Jordanian regime and supported King Husayn in his confrontations with communists, Arabists and Nasserists. In Gaza the situation was different, and the relationships between the Brotherhood and the Egyptian regimes were less stable. Education and preaching were important aspects of the movement, which established Islamic educational institutions throughout the territories. Although the Muslim Brotherhood did participate in, for example, the 1948 fighting and advocated *jihad* as a main strategy, it lost some of its fighting spirit during the first decades of occupation. In the West Bank, the Muslim Brotherhood suffered from its separation from the East Bank and stepped down from its earlier political visibility (Milton-Edwards, 1996: 86). In Gaza, the Brothers concentrated on internal politics and the process of Islamisation of Palestine, and pursued a non-confrontational strategy *vis-à-vis* Israel. There was a conscious decision not to join the Palestinian movement in resistance against Israel (Milton-Edwards, 1996: 92).

Thus although an Islamist interpretation of the conflict with Israel acquired increased salience, the main embodiment of Islamist politics did not embrace an activist struggling approach. It was, rather, internal politics which constituted the main focus for Hamas. From 1976 onwards, tension between the Islamists and the secularists reached unprecedented levels. Islamist tendencies became increasingly politicised and gained influence and legitimacy (Milton-Edwards, 1996: 103). This newborn militancy was directed against the PLO and 'un-Islamic' tendencies in society rather than against Israel. The main enemy was the communists.[25] Israel's actions during the era of the Muslim Brotherhood served to strengthen the base of the Brotherhood, since it was left largely unobstructed in its work. There were even direct links between Hamas and the Israeli government. Not until May 1989 did Israel launch a campaign to arrest Hamas leaders. Hamas was declared illegal in September 1989. Since then, Israel has tried to destroy the Hamas movement.[26]

Hamas as an organisation in its own right was formed in February 1988, a few months after the *intifada* broke out. Its main leaders were Sheikh Ahmed Ismail Yasin, who was a Muslim Brother, and Dr Abd al-Aziz al-Rantisi, a teacher at the Islamic University of Gaza.[27] Sheikh Yasin had earlier favoured the pragmatic Muslim Brotherhood approach, but Hamas broke with this tradition and advocated a more militant line. This was in all essential respects a response to the *intifada* and its approach of confrontation, as well as the activism of Islamic Jihad prior to and during the early phase of the *intifada*. Now, through Hamas, the Muslim Brotherhood for the first time actively confronted the occupation.

Institution-building by the Muslim Brotherhood provided Hamas with a social base for its work. Its connections with the Islamic Congress and its economic influence – through the *waqf* (the religious endowment), the Islamic Congress is a considerable owner of land and real estate – made Hamas an ever more potent challenge to the PLO as well as Israel. Control over mosques – a powerful means of communication – also gave Hamas a considerable advantage over the secular groups in the struggle over political discourse. After Hamas's establishment, the organisation hastened to take control over a large number of mosques, particularly in the Gaza Strip (Milton-Edwards, 1996: 149). Hamas succeeded in establishing a strong organisation in a short time.

Like other Islamic movements in the Muslim world, Hamas has been active and efficient in establishing social welfare structures. Extensive institution-building and networking in the form of schools, mosques, health clinics, kindergartens, charities, sports clubs, choirs and computer centres provided an effective recruitment base. Hamas has, for example, established '*zakat* committees' for the needy, to which Muslims are supposed voluntarily to donate 7 per cent of their income (Roy, 1993: 29; Milton-Edwards, 1996: 127).[28] An Islamic Centre (al-Mujamma' al-Islami) was established in Gaza in 1973, which gained control over a large number of Gazan mosques. The centre also provides social and educational services. Much of the relative success of Hamas is due to its active approach in educational matters, such as the establishment of Koranic schools. The Islamic University in Gaza is a Hamas stronghold.

In opinion polls carried out by the CPRS between January 1994 and March 1995, in answer to the question 'Which of the following factions do you support?', Hamas received around 15 per cent and Islamic Jihad between 3 and 4 per cent. During the *intifada*, elections for chambers of commerce, student council elections and so on indicated that Hamas's support was considerably greater, sometimes reaching 35–40 per cent in certain districts. Legrain states that there is an over-representation of men and a slight under-representation of refugee camp dwellers in the membership of Hamas. It is, by and large, a student movement, with its greatest support from a young, male student body (Legrain, 1994). Furthermore, Hamas has more followers in the north and the south than in the central West Bank (Legrain, 1991a: 85, 1994; Abu-Amr, 1994: 21; CPRS polls, January 1994–March 1995).

Although Islamism is a movement which has risen to prominence in impoverished societies, it is not a movement of the poor in those societies. It is, rather, an ideology and movement for the educated middle class; it is perceived as an alternative to the obstructions of upward social mobility, rather than an expression of impoverishment. As in most processes of politicisation and mobilisation, the intelligentsia – students, teachers, technicians – plays a crucial role.

Islamic Jihad

Islamic Jihad (al-Jihad al-Islami) is also a splinter group of the Muslim Brotherhood.[29] It originated in Egypt in the mid 1960s, and emerged in the occupied territories in the early 1980s. According to Milton-Edwards, four different Islamic Jihad groups existed in the 1980s: Islamic Jihad (Shqaqi-Auda faction), Islamic Jihad Jerusalem Brigade, Islamic Jihad Battalions and Islamic Jihad Palestine (Milton-Edwards, 1996: 116; see also Legrain, 1990: 76). Of these the Shqaqi-Auda faction is the largest and the one most often referred to.

Islamic Jihad had a more action-oriented profile than the Muslim Brotherhood. From early on it advocated armed struggle against Israel. The organisation holds that only dramatic and immediate action can bring change. Islamic Jihad categorically rejects Israel and its right to exist (Abu-Amr, 1994: xvii). The organisation maintains strict discipline and secrecy (Abu-Amr, 1994: 95), and regards itself as a revolutionary vanguard.

Prior to the *intifada*, Islamic Jihad had launched a spectacular military campaign throughout the Gaza Strip, including attacks against Israeli taxi drivers, an escape from Gaza central prison and the killing of an Israeli police officer (Milton-Edwards, 1996: 121 f.). In a clash between Islamic Jihad activists and Shin Bet in the autumn of 1987, four activists were killed and immediately declared martyrs, giving rise to a wave of demonstrations (Milton-Edwards, 1996: 121 f.). In relation to the igniting spark of the *intifada*, it was in fact Islamic Jihad which was the first organisation to produce a leaflet paying tribute to the uprising:

> Bravo to the passionate, bravo to the men of freedom, bravo to the honourable, bravo to the defenders of the homeland and our people, bravo to those in the veins of whom the blood of rejection and revolution pulsates, bravo to all voices rising in the sky repeating: Death to Israel! Bravo to all the arms cursing the Satan of Satans: Israel! . . . Bravo to those who observe our existence and our identity and our traits, bravo to those who win for us a sip of freedom and a moment of the honour which is known by our dear nobles! (JHD01)

The very activist-oriented approach of Islamic Jihad is reflected in the leaflet, saluting the 'passionate men of freedom', who actually *act*, who do something in order to 'win for us a sip of freedom'. Victory can be achieved only if there is willingness to act, to sacrifice and to endure. Israel here has satanic proportions and Israel should 'die'. In fact, this could be seen as a continuation and modification of Fateh's revolutionary nationalism, focusing on the act as a main constituent of Palestinian nationalism.

With the establishment of Hamas, Islamic Jihad lost much of its previous influence. In addition, it suffered from the harsh Israeli repression at the start of the *intifada*, which made it more difficult for the organisation to operate within the occupied territories. Relations between the Muslim Brotherhood and Islamic Jihad have been competitive at times and clashes occurred in Gaza in the late 1980s (Abu-Amr, 1994: 46). The Muslim Brotherhood is described by Islamic Jihad as having chosen the 'path of belief' rather than the 'path of *jihad*'. 'The uniqueness of the Islamic Jihad movement lies in forging a dialectical relationship between the path of *jihad* and the path of belief. In this sense, the Islamic Jihad blends religion and nationalism in its endeavour to annihilate Israel, combat Zionism, and establish an Islamic state in Palestine' (Abu-Amr, 1994: 103; cf. Milton-Edwards, 1996). The differences between Hamas and Islamic Jihad relate to the priority given to the issue of Palestine. Islamic Jihad places Palestine in the 'first room' of supremacy, while the Muslim Brotherhood believes that Islam is more important than Palestine. Islamic Jihad also equates the call for a revolution made by al-Qassem which sparked the Great Revolt of 1936 with the adventurous activities carried out by Islamic Jihad prior to the *intifada*, which it believes led to the *intifada* (Abu-Amr, 1994: 100).

Islamic Jihad was at its most popular when it was a new force. This support showed an over-representation of non-refugees (Legrain, 1994: 417). Two or three months after the *intifada* broke out, Islamic Jihad was virtually destroyed, but re-emerged at the end of 1988 in the form of periodic communiqués, symbolic monthly strikes and the organisation of commando operations launched from outside the occupied territories. The deportation of over 400 Islamist activists in December 1992 boosted Jihad's credibility (Legrain, 1994: 419).

The Islamist movements and Palestinian nationalism

In the Hamas Charter, the importance of unity of the Islamic *umma* is stressed repeatedly and Hamas is described as an 'international movement' (Article 29 of the Covenant). One of the most important themes in Islamic political discourse is whether the liberation of Palestine is to come 'first' or whether Palestinian society should first undergo an Islamic transformation. This debate is strikingly similar to the discourse of the 1950s and 1960s; that is, whether Palestinian liberation or Arabic unity should come first. In Palestinian nationalism there has thus been a constant dichotomisation between particular Palestinian nationalism (*wataniyya*) and wider notions, such as the Arabic *qawm* or the Islamic *umma*. To the Brethren, Islam was more important than Palestine, and the Muslim Brotherhood made no claims on Palestine as such. Nationalism was considered a mistake, and it was also a mistake to confine the direction of the struggle to Palestine – it should extend to embrace the struggle of Muslims in all parts of the world (Abu-Amr, 1994: 23 f.). With the establishment of Hamas, a sharp change occurred in the movement, which now embraced the concept of nationalism (cf. Milton-Edwards, 1996).

> As effective participation in the struggle for national liberation was seen by the vast majority of Palestinians as constituting a necessary condition for the acquisition of political legitimacy, Palestinian Islamism had no other choice but to appropriate the foundation of the legitimacy of its national rival – patriotism. Fighting Israel was the only way for the Muslim Brothers legitimately to enter the political arena while preserving their religious preoccupations. In Palestine, pietist Islamism had to transform itself into a 'revolutionary Islamism', in order to be able to pursue its course of 'Islamisation from below'. (Legrain, 1994: 425)

Hamas discourse denoted a clear territorialisation of Islamism. 'Palestine' became a non-negotiable value. '[T]he homeland is cherished and everything that keeps us from it, including our lives, is cheap. So just think if we are talking about Palestine, the land where Muhammad ascended to Heaven, the land of the prophets and miracles' (Hamas94). The prominence of Palestine is related to religious symbolism and the importance of Palestine in Islam. 'Homeland' and religiousness are fused. Because of its blessedness, the homeland is bestowed with a higher sacred value than all other spaces or geographies on Earth. To ascribe sanctitude to the homeland is to render it a value which cannot be replaced. This assignment implies a hierarchisation of territories/ spatial locations in the world. In Hamas leaflets, the land is often envisaged as *al-ard al-isra al-ma'araj* – the land of Muhammad's midnight journey to the Seven Heavens (e.g. Hamas94): '1. Palestine from the sea to the river is Islamic land, and it is impossible to yield one inch of it to the enemy' (Hamas49). Islamism in this context may be depicted as a nationalism which draws on religious values and idioms as the bases for the 'imagined community'. This politico-cultural discourse is comparable to the nationalism of the 1940s–60s, striving to keep foreign invaders and 'penetrators' in the form of colonial powers at bay. The main contribution of Hamas and Islamic Jihad to political ideology is their redefinition of the 'nation' and their combining of modern state theory with a search for perceived authenticity, tradition and indigenousness.

> Article Twelve: If other nationalisms have material, humanistic, and geographical ties, then the Islamic Resistance Movement's nationalism has all of that, and more important, divine reasons providing it with life and spirit where it is connected with the originator of the spirit and lifegiver, raising in the heavens the divine Banner to connect earth and heaven with a strong bond. (Maqdsi, 1993: 125)

According to Hamas's Charter, the organisation represents a spiritual nationalism, representing the aspiration of a fulfilment of immaterial values. Moral, ethical considerations make Hamas's variant of nationalism stand out.

Hamas and Islamic Jihad represent a morally superior option; a kind of moral process of purification. Through a retreat and commitment to Islamic values, Palestinian society was to regain its dignity and self-esteem.

> Article Nine: The Islamic Resistance Movement evolved in a time where the lack of the Islamic Spirit has brought about distorted judgement and absurd comprehension. Values have deteriorated, the plague of the evil folk and oppression and darkness have become rampant, cowards have become ferocious . . . The nation of truth is absent and the nation of evil has been established; as long as Islam does not take its rightful place in the world arena everything will continue to change for the worse. (Maqdsi, 1993: 125)

As Islam has 'waned away', there is a stage of confusion and obscurity. The absence of Islam has left the world in chaos and disorder. Only through a return to Islam can dignity and order be recaptured. Part of Islamic revivalism has been a 'purification process' of nationalism, including a campaign against drug dealers and criminality.

The only way to liberate Palestine is through Islam: 'there is only one way to Palestine, and that is Islam, as a doctrine, movement and holy war. The proof lies in the failure of other approaches which faltered in spite of big sacrifices' (*Al-Haqiqa al-Gha'iba*, n.d.). Despite the efforts of the secular nationalists, all attempts had failed and it was therefore time to try new approaches. Hamas declared:

> Article Twelve: Nationalism (Wataniyya), from the point of view of the Islamic Resistance Movement, is part and parcel of religious ideology. There is not a higher peak in nationalism or depth in devotion than Jihad when an enemy lands on the Muslim territories. (Maqdsi, 1993: 125)

This quotation reveals the simultaneous political and cultural discourse provided by Hamas. Here, we should note the rich religious symbolism. When the unbeliever/enemy lands on holy Islamic land, this represents a process of 'pollution' and 'defilement'. The land is polluted when the enemy 'invades' it. This causes disorder and a mixture of peoples and cultures which should by all means be avoided. Hence this is also a discourse on 'belongingness' and on the making of 'social boundaries'. Boundary discourses are also discourses on purity, on keeping the inside 'clean' and unmixed and not letting the enemy trespass across the boundary.

In Hamas discourse, there is an ambivalent attitude towards the categories of 'Israel' and 'Jewishness'. On the one hand, and on the level of rhetoric, there is clearly a racist discourse (cf. Milton-Edwards, 1996). Jews were described as 'dirty' and as polluting the land (e.g. Hamas100, 7 July 1993, from the archives of the Arab Studies Society).

> O our children: the Jews – brothers of the apes, assassins of the prophets, bloodsuckers, warmongers – are murdering you, depriving you of life after having plundered your homeland and your homes. Only Islam can break the Jews and destroy their dream. Therefore: proclaim to them: Allah is great, Allah is greater than their army, Allah is greater than their airplanes and their weapons. When you struggle

with them, take into account to request one of two bounties: martyrdom, or victory over them and their defeat. (Hamas, No. 1)

This discourse differs sharply from that of the secular UNLU, which refrained from such racist remarks. On the other hand, there is also an Islamic tradition of tolerance through the *dhimmi* system, which is also prevalent in Hamas ideology (cf. Chapter 4).

The conflict with Israel was described as one of belief, and hence it could only be interpreted in terms of right or wrong. It was an existential issue. The ideology of Hamas leaves it opposed to all forms of peace negotiation. In the Hamas Charter of August 1988, it is stated:

> Article Eleven: The Islamic Resistance Movement [firmly] believes that the land of Palestine is an Islamic *Waqf* upon all Muslim generations till the day of Resurrection. It is not right to give it up or any part of it. Neither a single Arab state nor all the Arab states, neither a King nor a leader, nor all the kings or leaders, nor any organisation – Palestinian or Arab – have such authority.
>
> Article Thirteen: [. . .] Those conferences are nothing but a form of enforcing the rule of the unbelievers in the land of Muslims. And when have unbelievers justly treated the believers? (Maqdsi, 1993: 126)

Since the struggle over Palestine is a struggle between believers and unbelievers, there is thus no use in negotiating. No compromise solutions can be accepted (HMS01). Territory belongs to Allah and no worldly government has any right to negotiate divine land. To sell the land is blasphemy: 'No to the negotiations with the enemy! No to the surrender of one inch of the Palestinian land! The road to liberation is the road of jihad!' (Hamas37, 3 March 1989, in *Filastin al-Muslima*, Issue No. 3, March 1989). Hamas also resented the political initiative by the PLO in November 1988: 'In whose name are you condemning to failure the uprising and delivering a death blow to the achievements of the exemplary and *jihadic* achievements?! Which of the martyrs authorized you?! Which of the wounded solicited you?! Which of the widows has approached you in supplication?!' (Hamas Special Leaflet). Political initiatives designated deviations from the struggle as main representations of Palestinianism. Hamas addressed itself to the PNC:

> We all hope that you will stand behind the aspirations of your people, for the people chose the way . . . the way of jihad, honor, and sacrifice, finding that for the sake of Allah and the liberation of Palestine [. . .]. In this stand we see the hope and aspiration of our people everywhere to arouse in you the spirit of the struggle, the spirit of the outbreak of the revolution in 1965. We call on you to take under your wing the spirit of the children of the stones and the continuation of the armed struggle, no matter what the cost . . . Our people is still possessed with the same readiness to make sacrifice after sacrifice, and it expresses this through this blessed uprising which has been recorded as a phenomenon unprecedented in history. (Hamas Special Leaflet)

Initiatives for peaceful negotiations were portrayed as aberrations from the armed struggle launched in 1965. Hamas here used a discourse and images originating in Fateh narrative in order to place the current disparities in perspective and to find a communicative base.

RELATIONS WITH THE PLO

The Muslim Brotherhood has been suspicious of the PLO and in particular of the leftist and communist groups. Communism is perceived as blasphemy and lacking in moral value and obligations (Abu-Amr, 1994: 28). Nevertheless, owing to the battle for public sympathy, it is between Fateh and the Brethren/Hamas that the most severe confrontations have taken place. According to Legrain, the early communiqués of Hamas did not even mention the PLO; 'it does not exist' (Legrain, 1990: 181).

Hamas and Islamic Jihad chose to remain outside the UNLU as well as the PLO.[30] During the *intifada*, Hamas competed with the secular nationalist leadership of the UNLU through organising its own bills, communiqués and strike days, although there was also a certain amount of coordination.

Both Hamas and Islamic Jihad believe that the main wrongdoing is the PLO's deviation from the Islamic path:

> We Islamists neither hate nor reject these organizations, groups, and political parties, nor oppose them because they are carrying arms against the Zionist foe, but because they are not carrying Islam, nor ruling by the Koran . . . We want those organizations and groups to discard all the anti-Islamic ideas, doctrines, programs, and slogans . . . We want them to be committed to Islam, to the Koran and the Sunna, in word and deed, in everything, small and large, and to adopt the Islamic doctrine and carry weapons simultaneously. However, and regrettably, we note that these organizations have categorically rejected, and still reject commitment to Islam, from their inception until today. They have adopted constitutions, principles, charters, and man-made doctrines which have no relationship to Islam. Based on that, we will not accept, and our Muslim people will not accept, and our *umma* will not accept the leadership of these organizations. (*Al-Jihad fi Filastin: Farida Shar'iyya wa-darura Bashariyya*)

The PLO is criticised for having deviated from the path of God. In addition, it is perceived as a creation of the Arab states:

> Article Twenty-Seven: The Palestine Liberation Organisation is closest of the close to the Islamic Resistance Movement, in that it is the father, the brother, the relative, or friend; and does the Muslim offend his father, his brother, his relative or his friend? Our nation is one, plight is one, destiny is one and our enemy is the same, being affected by the situation that surrounded the formation of the organisation (PLO) and the chaotic ideologies that overwhelm the Arab world due to the ideological invasion that befell the Arab world since the defeat of the Crusades and the ongoing consolidation of orientalism, missionary work, and imperialism. The

organisation (PLO) adopted the idea of a secular state, and as such we considered it. Secularist ideology is in total contradiction to religious ideologies, and it is upon ideology that positions, actions, and decisions are made. [. . .] When the Palestine Liberation Organisation adopts Islam as its system of life, we will be its soldiers and the firewood of its fire which will burn the enemies. (Maqdsi, 1993: 130 f.)

The relationship with the PLO is described as one of a family. The PLO is '[a] father, [a] brother, [a] relative, [a] friend', reminding us that nationalism is an ideology of kinship and extended family relations. The PLO and Hamas share the same enemy and the same destiny. The dispute between them may be perceived as a family quarrel, originating in the fact that the PLO has been misguided by the 'ideological invasion' which commenced with the Christian Crusades. Once the PLO is guided back to the right track, Hamas will be the soldiers of the PLO and the family will be reunited. Hamas submits itself to the authority – the 'fathership' – of the PLO, and is prepared to make sacrifices; to become 'soldiers' of the PLO.

Hamas's radical refusal to negotiate the Palestinian cause has not spared the movement from the ambiguities of pragmatic political behaviour. Dr Mahmoud Zahhar, spokesperson of Hamas in Gaza, in 1988 put forward a proposal indicating a readiness for a two-state solution (Abu-Amr, 1994: 76). Spiritual leader Sheikh Yasin has become known as a pragmatist; in 1989 he expressed support for a Palestinian state and negotiations with Israel and abstained from demanding the expulsion of Israel (Sayigh, 1997: 650 f.). He also stated that he would be willing to join a Palestinian delegation in negotiations with Israel. Dr Zahhar asked that Hamas be allotted one-third of the seats of any Palestinian delegation that was to negotiate with the Israelis. Although these overtures were repudiated by the movement in a later communiqué, they reflect the ambivalence in the Islamist camp regarding the most effective way to achieve leadership of the Palestinian resistance. During the spring of 1990, Hamas decided to request integration in PNC under certain conditions, such as 40–50 per cent of the seats of the PNC to be allocated to Hamas (Sayigh, 1997a: 651).

The increased role of Hamas was further emphasised in December 1992, when there was accelerated activity in the form of murders and kidnappings by Hamas members. When the organisation succeeded in kidnapping an Israeli soldier, who was later killed, the Israeli government decided to deport 412 Palestinians, allegedly members of Hamas and Islamic Jihad, to Lebanon.[31] Sheikh Bitawi told Hisham Ahmed: 'To be away from the homeland was the most difficult trial to endure' (Ahmed, 1994: 30) and 'The sheer fact of uprooting a person from his land, home, family and job and to throw him in a no man's land is the worst a human being can face. Imprisonment compared to deportation can be considered a picnic' (Ahmed, 1994: 80). The 1992 deportations carried the whole symbolic discourse of uprootedness, dispossession, suffering and sacrifice. They increased the standing of the Islamists in Palestinian society, since the deportees were evidence of suffering and steadfastness and therefore of Palestinianism. The image projected with the help of the international media was one of a righteous, deeply religious, committed and steadfast community of men in the snowy Lebanese mountains who organised their lives and pursued their prayers in the cold.

Islamic movements and the struggle

Hamas's literature is filled with references to *jihad*, the goal of which is the liberation of Palestine rather than the establishment of an Islamic state in all Muslim countries (Milton-Edwards, 1996: 190 f.). To the Islamists, struggle is encompassed by the notion of *jihad*. Three concepts of struggle therefore embody Palestinian national/political identity: *thawra, intifada* and *jihad*.

According to the Hamas Charter, the motto of the Islamic resistance movement is the following: 'Allah is its goal, the Messenger is its leader, and the Quran its constitution. *Jihad* is its methodology, and Death for the sake of Allah is its most coveted desire' (Maqdsi, 1993: 124). Further, Hamas says, 'There is no solution to the Palestinian Problem except by Jihad' (Maqdsi, 1993: 126). Death and suffering have a special meaning in this context. To be killed in action proves one's ultimate commitment to the nation. To become a martyr (*shahid*) is, however, a higher goal in itself, and the belief in the continuation of life in paradise is a powerful motivation for sacrificing one's life while carrying out attacks against Jews and Israelis.

> We can know who is martyr because all the people has [respect for him]. For example, I give you one person, like Hani Abed.[32] This is the martyr, [someone] who can find his place in society, not for one week, two weeks, three weeks, but for ever. Until now, we remember the first sacrificed, the first companion, the first friend of the Prophet, they are living with us until now, they are alive, this is the martyr. He is alive all the time, not in our dreams, but in our lives. It's not enough to have a picture of him. No, he is present in our minds. This is the martyr. (Interview with Islamic Jihad sympathiser, 19 January 1995)

A martyr was someone who sacrificed, and Islam required sacrifice. Because the martyr had sacrificed, he was respected by all of society, regardless of faction. A martyr had eternal life, 'he is alive all the time', and through this guarantee of everlasting life, in the minds of many, he would become somebody.[33] The martyr/*shahid* concept was in the 1990s strongly flavoured by Islamist discourse, although the cult of martyrdom has been central in Palestinian discourse since the 'era of revolution'. Nationalist martyrdom during the revolution was also influenced by Islamist discourse and there was a belief that a martyr for Palestine ascends to heaven in the same way as a martyr for Islam (Peteet, 1991: 106). Islamism added a new dimension to the Palestinian as struggling hero. In the aftermath of the Hebron massacre in February 1994, both Hamas and

Islamic Jihad resorted to the use of suicide bombs on Israeli public civilian buses and against military checkpoints. Suicide bombs could be interpreted as a way of communicating; as a way of communicating a *capability*, that one is able to act, to produce a threat to the dominant Israeli Jews and that Israeli Jews are vulnerable. Violence consists of symbolic actions and rituals which communicate a message (cf. Fanon (1968), on the idea of the cleansing capacity of revolutionary violence).

> It is necessary that the Jews understand that in spite of their chains, their prisons and detention camps, in spite of the endurances which our people endure in the shadow of the criminal occupation, in spite of the streams of blood which are drawn off every day, in spite of the wounds, our people is more enabled than them in the endurance and firmness in front of their injustice and their arrogance. Until they know that the politics of violence will only meet with more violence on behalf of our sons and our young who love the gardens of eternity more than they love the life here manifested by our enemy. (HMS01)

Islamism also provided the martyrs with the promise of reward in the form of life hereafter. 'This promise of paradise cannot be made by the PLO. Only Hamas and Islamic Jihad offer a true "martyrs'" reward' (Milton-Edwards, 1996: 191). Through becoming a *shahid* you would be guaranteed everlasting life. The readiness to die was also related to the denotations of the 'martyr' concept, turning the assailant into a hero, making headlines in the global media drama. Through perceptions of a continuation of life, there were beliefs of becoming *someone*, through acts which would make you remembered. If you could not become somebody in the 'living life', then you could make sure that your name would be among the selected few martyrs, someone who was eulogised, praised, honoured, someone whose family is invited for sweet coffee, rather than bitter. Suicide also communicates control. In this context, it represents the power to cause grief and disorder in Israel.

> Equip yourselves with stones, sticks, axes, and knives. Go up to the roofs, little children as well as adults, and call 'Allah is great', and remember the words of Allah: 'Fight them! Allah will chastise them at your hands, and He will lay them low and give you victory over them, and He will heal the breasts of folk who are believers'.[34] (Hamas2)

Blood and its forfeit are as important to Hamas as they are in PLO discourse.

NOTES

1 On rentier political economies, see Beblawi and Luciani (1987). By this is meant that economies are based more on externally generated capital than on tax revenues. The concept has been elaborated mostly with regard to the oil-producing economies, but is also extended to imply economies dependent on aid.
2 In 1997, settlers on the West Bank numbered 160,000 (Aronson, 1997: 127).

3 *Jerusalem Post*, 26 October 1990. For an overview of the labour situation in the West Bank and Gaza, see Øvensen (1994), and for a detailed account of Gaza, see Roy (1995a).

4 The image of the soil and its cultivators is an oft-repeated theme in folk nationalisms. Also in cultures where agriculture no longer serves the most important role, folk tales are centred around the keepers of the land (cf. also Eriksen 1993: 101 ff.).

5 See Hiltermann (1990a, b, 1991) for an account of the role of trade unions in the national movement in the occupied territories. Labour unions were active in the West Bank and Gaza prior to the occupation. Following the occupation in 1967, unions were allowed to operate in the West Bank but were banned in Gaza. Unions in Gaza were allowed to reopen in 1980, but were not allowed to hold elections. Each of the four main political factions (al-Fateh, the PFLP, the PCP and the DFLP) initially supported their own union branches, but were united in 1990. In 1992, the unions were again divided, and have since been hampered by factionalism, as well as subordinated to the overall national(ist) cause. Hiltermann nevertheless maintains that the significance of the unions has been major. Since the Declaration of Principles (DOP), of 13 September 1993, divisions have been emerging between the returnees who used to represent the Palestinian labour unions in exile and the 'inside' leadership.

6 In an opinion poll carried out among Palestinians in the occupied territories in 1986, 93.5 per cent of those interviewed (1,024 respondents in the West Bank and Gaza) considered the PLO to be the 'sole and legitimate representative of the Palestinian people'. Yasir Arafat was considered the preferred Palestinian leader by 78.8 per cent, while George Habash, in second place, was deemed the preferred leader by 5.6 per cent. The poll was carried out by Mohammad Shadid and was sponsored by the Palestinian Jerusalem-based newspaper *al-Fajr* and the Australian Broadcasting Company (Shadid and Seltzer, 1988; cf. also Lesch and Tessler, 1989b; Sahliyeh, 1988).

7 The PCP was during this time divided into the Jordanian Communist Party in the West Bank and the Palestinian Communist Organisation in Gaza. In 1990, following developments in the then Soviet Union and Eastern Europe, and after lengthy internal debate, the PCP changed its name to the Palestine People's Party.

8 Alfred Toubbasi was one of the founders of the PNF. He was deported from the West Bank on 22 November 1974 and allowed to return in the summer of 1994. 'They took us all night and [at] half past eight in the morning, the car stopped and they took us down from the car. They took the blindfold from our eyes and we saw the mountains of Lebanon in front of us. And they said: "Go this way and this way and this way and don't look back. Don't walk outside of this small lane, there are mines here and there." So we went and after half an hour walking, the Lebanese army came and that was it' (interview with Alfred Toubbasi, 14 November 1994).

9 Freij later became Minister of Tourism in the PNA. He died in 1997.

10 An increase of 1,000 people per square kilometre in less than ten years (cf. Benvenisti and Khayat, 1988: 109).

11 There is a vast literature on the *intifada*; see, for example, Lockman and Beinin (1989), McDowall (1989), Peretz (1990), Schiff and Ya'ari (1990), Nassar and Heacock (1990a), Brynen (1991), Hunter (1993) and Robinson (1997a).

12 The commercial strike implied an active role in the politics of resistance by the merchants and thus by the urban middle class. Most merchants supported the *intifada* leadership and willingly closed their shops (Tamari, 1990). There were also, however, cases of coercion, when masked youths warned shopkeepers to shut their shops (Schiff and Ya'ari, 1990; Hunter, 1993).

13 Yasir Arafat was the only participant who was not met at the airport by King Husayn, a sign of the frosty relations between Jordan and the PLO in the late 1980s.

14 In retrospect, some argue that the experience of the popular committees was in fact highly varied, and that it was only in a few places that they had any staying power as an organisational structure (e.g. interview with Saleh Abdel Jawwad, 31 January 1995). Tamari (1991: 68) argues that the role of the popular committees has been overestimated.

15 In the aftermath of the Hebron massacre in February 1994, when twenty-nine Palestinians were killed by Baruch Goldstein, a Jewish settler from the extremist Kach organisation, the UNLU was re-established for a short period.

16 Abu Jihad belonged to the original Fateh leadership and was in command of the 'inside', developing a detailed knowledge of the West Bank and Gaza. Generally known as a pragmatist in PLO circles, he was assassinated in April 1988, in his home in Tunis, by Israeli Mossad agents.

17 UN Resolution 242 (dating from 1967) calls for the withdrawal of 'Israeli armed forces from territories of recent conflict' and Resolution 338 – designed in the aftermath of the 1973 October War – calls for the implementation of Resolution 242 and for negotiations between the parties in order to achieve peace. The PLO did not previously recognise the resolutions because the Palestinians are not mentioned or referred to, other than as the 'refugee problem'. There is no reference to, or recognition of, a Palestinian 'people' or 'nation' (cf. the resolutions in Laqueur and Rubin, 1984).

18 Anderson (1991) notes the importance of the tomb of the unknown soldier. Many nations have special days in memory of their fallen war heroes, exemplified by Israel's highly solemn memorial day of fallen soldiers, where the whole 'nation' comes to a standstill.

19 'Abd al-Qadir al-Husayni was the nephew of the *mufti*, and was considered his ablest commander, commander of the Arab irregulars in the Jerusalem area. He was also the father of Feysal Husayni. A third nationalist founding father was Ghassan Kanafani, a writer and poet who belonged to the PFLP and was killed in a car explosion in Beirut in 1972. These three nationalist ancestors are important in the way that they exhibit the different phases of the Palestinian struggle. al-Qassem was the originator, in a way the first struggling martyr. Husayni was the result of the catastrophe, while Kanafani was killed during the revolution. Abu Jihad is a fourth martyr, killed during the *intifada*, although not a son of it.

20 See Shalev (1991) for an overview of Israeli politics *vis-à-vis* the *intifada*.

21 For an analysis of the relationship between the Soviet Union and the PLO, see Golan (1980, 1997).

22 Although the PLO initially declared itself to be against the Iraqi invasion of Kuwait, and although its position was not unambiguous, in *intifada* leaflets, the 'Iraqi brothers' were given support and the American military build-up in the Gulf and later military aggression were seen as an occupation of holy land (cf. UNLU61).

23 It should be noted that the Palestinian community in Kuwait made a point of expressing support for the Kuwaiti regime in times of threat (Brand, 1988a: 125), and a large number of the Palestinians in Kuwait did support the Kuwaiti regime during the Gulf War. The expulsion of Palestinian labour should also be seen in light of the attempts to decrease Arab labour in these countries at large.

24 Abu-Amr (1994: 6), however, shows that the membership of the Muslim Brotherhood in the West Bank declined after 1967, and argues that Islamic tendencies were weakened. On the other hand, he argues that the Muslim Brotherhood used the wars of 1967 and 1973 to increase religious sentiment (Abu-Amr 1994: 11). He also argues that the occupation in one way enhanced religiousness, since the occupation threatened 'Palestinian Arab and Islamic identities' (Abu-Amr 1994: 12).

25 One example of Hamas antagonism against the left was the torching of the Red Crescent office in Gaza in the early 1980s. Head of the Red Crescent society was Heidar Abdel Shafi, who has been considered left-leaning (Milton-Edwards, 1996: 106 ff.).

26 Milton-Edwards shows how Israel's policy of non-interference in the life of the Muslim Brotherhood turned into encouragement. In 1978, Israel's civil administration in Gaza encouraged the registration of the Mujama, the Islamic Centre as a charitable society (Milton-Edwards, 1996: 105). In 1989, Hamas spokesperson Mahmoud Zahhar met Israeli Defence Minister Yitzhak Rabin (Milton-Edwards 1996: 151).

27 Yasin's family settled in a refugee camp in Gaza during the war of 1948 (Abu-Amr, 1994: 64). Sheikh Yasin was sentenced to fifteen years in prison in 1989 for violent acts against Israel. Demands for his release were made continuously. In September 1997 after a scandalous and failed Israeli assassination attempt on Khaled Masha'al, a leading Hamas personality residing in Jordan, a furious King Husayn managed to secure Sheikh Yasin's release. After a brief stop in Jordan, he returned to Gaza. al-Rantisi was among those deported from the West Bank and Gaza to southern Lebanon in December 1992 (see below), and he soon became the main spokesperson for the deportees. He returned a year later, was held in detention for two years and released in 1997.

28 The compulsory *zakat* is 2.5 per cent.

29 The founding fathers of Islamic Jihad were Fathi Shqaqi, a pharmacist from Rafah, and Abd al-Aziz al-'Auda, a lecturer at the Islamic University in Gaza and the faction's spiritual leader. Shqaqi's family fled from the Ramla district to a refugee camp in Rafah in Gaza. He was deported in 1988 (Abu-Amr, 1994: 93 f.) and was based in Damascus until his assassination in Malta in October 1995. 'Auda also originated from a refugee family. His family was settled in Beersheba and fled to Jabaliya camp in 1948 (Abu-Amr, 1994: 94).

30 It is not clear whether Islamic Jihad was associated with the UNLU during the first part of the *intifada*. Some observers say Islamic Jihad joined the UNLU in the initial phase but left in early 1988 (see Legrain, 1990: 180 and n. 16: 189). Abu-Amr argues that Islamic Jihad did not position itself against the UNLU and that there was some coordination between the two (Abu-Amr, 1994: 115). Islamic Jihad activists and leaders claim that there was no such coordination (interview with Islamic Jihad leaders, 24 November 1994 and 19 January, 1995).

31 Lebanon refused, however, to accept the Palestinian deportees, who were stranded in Marj al-Zuhur camp in the no man's land between Israel and the Israeli security zone in southern Lebanon. Half the deportees were allowed to return to the West Bank and Gaza in September 1993, while the remainder returned in December 1993, a year after the original decision.

32 Assassinated when trying to enter his booby-trapped car on 2 November 1994.

33 As, for example, the eulogy over Hani Abed in Saftawi (1994).

34 Surah of Repentence (9), 14.

4

State-building and the peace process

The peace process initiated by the Madrid Conference,[1] set up as a US response to Arab commitments in the Gulf War of 1991, failed to achieve any tangible results. The Israeli and Palestinian delegations met ten times between October 1991 and May 1993. Although the Palestinian delegation received instructions from the PLO, the actual negotiators were not members of the PLO but prominent 'political personalities' from the West Bank and Gaza, excluding Jerusalem. Israel refused to meet the PLO and East Jerusalem Palestinians as it was forbidden by Israeli law to have any contact with the PLO (hence the make-up of the Palestinian negotiation team). Negotiations were surrounded by media hype and rarely touched on substantial issues. Procedure took the upper hand. The Israeli Prime Minister, Yitzhak Shamir, later admitted that his intention was to drag the negotiations out so as to create new *faits accomplis*, and that there was no Israeli interest in a 'land for peace' deal. For the mainstream PLO, the peace process was an opportunity to recover from a weakened position. However, it had since 1973 been seeking a role in the peace process, and its entry into negotiations with Israel was not only a result of its early 1990s predicament.

In the occupied territories, as negotiations did not lead to any tangible results, as the PLO had reached a financial drain also affecting the West Bank and Gaza, and as politics had become ever more fragmented, the political atmosphere was one of apathy and despair (Roy, 1993). An intense debate within the PLO, concerning internal politics, mismanagement and other detrimental effects of the neo-patrimonial system, had also come the fore (Sayigh, 1997a: 658).

When Labour won the Israeli elections in 1992, they found it evident that the current negotiation structures were untenable. Prior to that, initiatives had been made by the Labour Party and the Palestinians for a different type of negotiation process, realised in the secret Oslo talks.[2] Here, Israeli and PLO officials eventually met face to face in small-scale, streamlined negotiation teams, directly mandated by Israel's Prime Minister, Yitzhak Rabin, and the PLO Chairman, Yasir Arafat. The negotiations, initially thought of as a 'back channel' to feed into the official Washington talks, led to the DOP, preceded by mutual recognition. The atmosphere in the West Bank and Gaza immediately altered to one of electrified anticipation.

The DOP was not a peace agreement, but a statement that the parties wanted to solve their long-term conflict, and provided a scheme for doing so. 'This was not peace, but a mutual expression of peaceful intentions' (Butenschøn, 1998: 17). The scheme was a staged process in which self-government for Gaza and Jericho was a first step.[3] Permanent status negotiations were to be based on UN Resolutions 242 and 338, the West Bank and Gaza were to be seen as an integral unit, and the most thorny issues (Jerusalem, refugees, settlers, borders and security) were left for permanent status negotiations, which were, however, to begin no later than three years after the initiation of self-rule. The interim period was to last for a maximum of five years, i.e. until 7 May 1999. At the PLO Central Council in October 1993, sixty-three delegates voted in favour of the DOP, with nine abstentions. The PFLP and DFLP, as well as other oppositional factions, started to boycott PLO meetings after the signing of the DOP (*Journal of Palestine Studies*, 1994a: 172). The Oslo process was preceded by a number of initiatives in the late 1980s and early 1990s, and in fact the actual outcome of the Norway negotiations drew to a large extent on all the proposals since the Camp David Accords, including the Shamir–Rabin plan of 1989, which was also based on elections and an interim government. The important difference from all previous proposals was that the DOP was the only one to include the PLO.

The implementation of the plan for autonomy implied a withdrawal of Israeli troops, to be replaced as a first step by a Palestinian police force controlling Gaza and Jericho. Discussions on the implementation of the DOP – which also drew up a time frame for the implementation of the schedule – were difficult and interrupted by the Hebron massacre of February 1994, which led to a temporary Palestinian withdrawal from the negotiations. The killing of at least twenty-nine Palestinians by a lone settler extremist threw the Palestinian population in the occupied territories into an atmosphere of despair and outrage. The UNLU briefly re-entered the political stage, producing a special call for a 'week of wrath' against the 'forces of occupation and the settlers'. The 'Gaza–Jericho first' solution was criticised and continued negotiations were described as implying 'surrender' and 'scorn of the blood of the martyrs' (UNLU special call). The Palestinian 'street' perceived events as yet more proof of their vulnerability and of Israel's unwillingness actually to obtain peace and act against settlers. In the aftermath of the Hebron massacre, the Palestinians tried to lift forward the settlements as perhaps the main obstacle to a further agreement. In April, Hamas's armed wing, the Izz al-Din al-Qassem Brigade, took responsibility for terrorist activities, 'revenge attacks' for Hebron, against Israeli civilians.[4] The Hebron massacre also caused outrage in Israel.[5]

The details of the self-government proposal were hammered out in the Cairo Accords of 4 May 1994. The concept of self-government – first formalised in the Camp David Accords – in all previous proposals seen as anathema to the PLO – was thus accepted as the 'first step' in a longer process. Administrative functions in the form of education, health, social affairs, culture, tourism and taxation were handed over to the PNA in the first phase. Negotiations on Jerusalem, refugees, water, borders and settlements were to begin as soon as possible after the implementation of the first step, that is, Gaza–Jericho first, but no later than three years afterwards.

The Interim Agreement of 28 September 1995 expanded Palestinian self-rule to the West Bank, beginning with the six major cities, excluding Hebron (a separate deal on Hebron was reached in January 1997 under the Israeli Likud government). The Agreement divides the territory of the West Bank into different zones. Palestinian authority extends in a full sense (which in turn means severely restricted autonomy) only over the 'A area', that is, the six major towns, comprising 3 per cent of the total area of the West Bank. The B area comprises approximately 450 villages, 27 per cent of the territory, where Israelis and Palestinians have a divided security responsibility. The bulk of the West Bank is C area, 70 per cent of the territory, still in the sole control of Israel, implying a fragmentation of territory, strangulating Palestinian towns and villages, and opening up for oppositional critique that a 'Bantustanisation' of Palestine is occurring (Bishara, 1995; Said, 1995, 1998; Butenschøn, 1998).[6] Further administrative functions have also been transferred under the Interim Agreement, such as agriculture, labour, electricity, the postal service and local government.

In the negotiations, the goal of the Palestinians of a Palestinian state was rejected by Israel until the mid 1990s. In the spring of 1996, however, the Labour Party, as a response to the PLO Executive Committee's change of the PLO Charter in April 1996,[7] removed the paragraph in its party platform opposing a Palestinian state. The Oslo Agreement was based on an understanding between the PLO and Labour Party that a Palestinian state of some sort was the only realistic outcome of the process, although dependent on the performance of the PNA in safeguarding Israeli security (Kimmerling, 1997: 236). According to many observers, there has been a similar, although slower and more reluctant, shift in Likud discourse in the process of coming to terms with the concept of a Palestinian state. Likud uses the terms 'state-minus' or 'autonomy-plus' to indicate the restrictions that must, according to this point of view, necessarily be imposed upon such an entity. Israel's Prime Minister, Benyamin Netanyahu, referred to Andorra and Puerto Rico as possible types of political status that could be accepted (Heller, 1997: 10 f.).[8] However, the real and undeniable impact of the Oslo process was not whether the historical land of Palestine was to be divided, but rather how much and on what terms.

State-building

With self-rule, state-building rapidly intensified.[9] The self-government that has been extended to the Palestinians is limited indeed (cf. Butenschøn, 1998), given its distinction between 'people' and 'territory' (cf. de Jong, 1998). Nevertheless, the Agreements created a *de facto* if not *de jure* allowance for intensified Palestinian state-making (cf. Chase, 1997; Frisch, 1997a, b; Heller, 1997; Rigby, 1997; Sayigh, 1997a), given that the PLO now gained control over population, territory (however limited and divided), presence at international borders, and control over internal functions usually in the hands of a state bureaucracy such as education, administration, taxation (cf. Finer (1975) on the role of the taxation system), social welfare, and so on. The Palestinian political structure also adopted a presidency, police and passports, all material and symbolic aspects of statehood. Whatever the outcome of the (currently crisis-ridden) peace process, the interim period implies that the Palestinians have entered a phase of state-building. In fact, there already exists a 'semi-independent' (Heller, 1997: 9) or quasi-state, in turn a logical outcome of PLO state-building in exile. With the DOP, statism has deepened as legitimation has occurred in the territorialisation of the state-in-exile.

Despite the indisputable shortcomings of the peace process, one fact remains:

> One unique circumstance is that although not sovereign or independent, and indeed although bound by myriad restrictions imposed by the agreements with the Israelis, the new Palestinian Authority has more power over more of its people in more of Palestine than any Palestinian agency has had in the twentieth century. (Khalidi, 1997: 203)

However, the state-building project is to an increasing extent characterised by 'authoritarianism in decision-making, the anti-institutional personalisation of power, and the pervasiveness of violence in the system' (Robinson, 1997a: 175; cf. also Frisch, 1997 a, b; Hilal, 1998), involving a personalised political system circling around a charismatic neo-patriarchal leader (Frisch, 1997a, b). Debate rages over the mismanagement of public resources, a judicial system crippled by institutional weakness and legal confusion, interference by the executive in the judiciary, militarisation and human rights abuses. The regime could be labelled semi-authoritarian, with personalisation circling around Yasir Arafat allowing patronage relations and weakened institutions. This also has its legacy in PLO statism. However, this project has also provided a new debate on democracy, governance, the internal relations of individual rights and group rights, human rights, accountability and the rule of law, and so on, as two institution-building logics collide.

The establishment of the PNA, and hence part of the PLO, on Palestinian soil also meant a restructuring of the 'outside–inside' relationship, with the exterior again taking the upper hand (Litvak, 1997; Robinson, 1997a), moving the logic of state-building as a companion of the revolution inside, which then found itself on a collision course with another logic of state-building.

Institution-building and political structure

One ingredient of the DOP was the elections to a Palestinian Council. The elections to the Legislative Council and the Presidency in January 1996 marked the introduction of an entirely novel phenomenon and institution in Palestinian political life. The PLC differs from the PNC in a highly important regard: 'The elected PLC obtains its legitimacy from the exercise of popular will based on the universal adult franchise' (Hilal, 1998: 122), rather than a revolutionist logic in which decisions were made by consensus, as the ideology and requirements of struggle for liberation demanded a centralist-style leadership.

Although as a first experience the elections must be deemed generally fair, Palestinian observers noted several irregularities. The electoral system[10] meant that some of the candidates could make it to the Council through mobilising their extended families, and through support networks provided by the *hamuleh* system. Frisch (1997a: 353) argues that the election campaign was 'dominated by hamuleh politics'. However, according to an exit poll conducted by the CPRS, the most important quality when electing a candidate was 'being a fighter/activist'. Twenty-eight per cent of the population thought that this was the most important quality, closely followed by being 'religious', held to be the most important by 24 per cent (CPRS exit poll, 20 January 1996). Thus different patterns of electing candidates coexisted. Although the election led to Fateh dominance, and although PNA candidates for the most part were elected, a significant number of fighters and independent nationalists also managed to get elected, in fact obstructing Arafat policies of relegating the *intifada* elite to lower positions. This includes people who were kept away from the official Fateh list (e.g. Husam Khader[11]) and people who were advised by the Chairman not to stand (such as Salah Ta'amari[12]).

As part of the Oslo Accords, the elections came about through negotiations with an external actor rather than being a response to internal bargaining and a conscious decision to embark upon a transition towards democracy.[13] In addition, it has been argued that the elections did not serve as a cornerstone for building a democratic state, but rather served as an instrument to create a new legitimacy for Arafat, since the Oslo process had crushed the old 'Palestinian consensus' (Shkaki, 1996b; Robinson, 1997a: 195). To a large section of the Palestinian political spectrum, those factors rendered the elections illegitimate. All opposition factions boycotted the elections (for a discussion, see Hilal, 1998: 127 ff.). Discussions on the elections focused on whether they would legitimise the agreements and hence Israel's continued superiority over the occupied territories (the opposition), or whether they would underline the Palestinian popular will of self-determination (supporters). After intense debate, in mid December 1995 Hamas ruled out the possibility of participating in the elections, following a division between the 'inside' and the 'outside' leaderships, the latter being strongly opposed to Hamas participation. A number of prominent Hamas members and sympathisers, however, entered the elections on other lists, such as Imad Falouji from Gaza, who entered under the title of 'independent Fateh'.

The PFLP and DFLP also discussed whether or not to participate. Whereas the internal leadership favoured taking part in the political process, the outside leadership opposed it, and they gained the upper hand. 'Inside' leaders even travelled to Damascus to try and influence the decision, but to no avail. Several PFLP and DFLP leaders in the inside were critical of this decision (interviews, autumn 1997). Some PFLP members, however, stood as independents. According to the PFLP, rather than elections in the West Bank and Gaza only, elections should have been held to the PNC and include all Palestinians as the electorate, that is, including the diaspora.

The first parliamentary elections were highly symbolic. The importance of the event was shown in the high voter turnout of 88 per cent in Gaza and 73 per cent in the West Bank, implying that the opposition's call for a boycott did not strike a chord among the Palestinian electorate.

THE EXECUTIVE

Following the elections, there has been a formal division of the interim government into three branches: the Executive, headed by the President, the Legislature and the judiciary. Although the Executive Authority was initially deemed to be elected by the Legislative Council, with the possible exception of 20 per cent of the ministers, who could be appointed directly by the President, this rule was not followed.[14] However, to a large extent the Authority still reflects strategies of co-optation and a delicate balance between different interests, including between clan and faction, between 'inside' and 'outside', between clan and clan, between regional locations, and between (former) landowners and PLO bureaucrats. The Cabinet is primarily made up of a combination of representatives of the large families from the traditional elite, urban notables and PLO bureaucrats, together with a few West Bank/Gazan professionals and civil intelligentsia. There is ample evidence that the politics of the PNA and the lack of an institutionalised judicial system have worked so as to revive the *hamuleh* structures, weakened during the decades of civil society mobilisation and *intifada*.[15] The PNA has even established an Office of the President for Tribal Affairs to regulate problems occurring between families.

The Executive Authority is thus made up of a combination of family elites and PLO elites, effectively leaving the inside strugglers outside the central power. There is a real conflict of interest between the Executive and Legislative

Council, concerning legislation and government accountability. Mistrust and lack of cooperation characterise the relationship. Given the Executive's tendency to neglect the law-makers, government is posed against parliament. The Executive has refrained from ratifying laws and resolutions that have been passed by the Council. Most seriously, the Basic Law had not been passed by the Authority, despite three readings in the Council. According to many, the Executive is deliberately trying to marginalise the Legislative Council (interviews with PLC members, autumn 1997). The lack of a constitutional framework complicates the relationship between the two branches of power.

The staff of the ministries and departments are still appointed by the President, meaning that deputies and directors-general do not always follow the same line as the minister. The results of the politics of appointments have been multiplicity and difficulties in cooperation. A controversy in the Ministry of Agriculture over the licensing of Israeli citrus products, for example, proved impossible to solve, since the Deputy Minister was appointed by Arafat personally and was thus more powerful than the Minister himself (see *Palestine Report*, 24 October 1997). The Authority developed a large and inefficient bureaucracy, with people being appointed in order to provide a power base for Arafat. There is a 'patronage system provided by the burgeoning state bureaucracy' (Robinson, 1997b: 48). The total number of Palestinians employed by the PNA is over 60,000, including approximately 40,000 police and security personnel (Robinson, 1997b: 48). Including the families of those employed by the PNA, over a quarter of Gazans are 'directly dependent on the PNA for their livelihood' (Robinson, 1997b: 49). According to some reports, a not insignificant number of personnel collect salaries without even showing up at their offices – a policy which has also followed the revolution. The PNA claims that the largesse of the public sector is the result of employment policies intended to alleviate the consequences of Israeli border closures.

This patronage system has its bases in the PLO political logic, which compensated for the lack of territorially based institutions as bases of legitimacy. The much talked about 'Corruption Report' on an investigation conducted by a committee of the Legislative Council in 1997 should be seen in terms of a deterritorialised revolutionary movement being territorialised. In addition, the main problems that the report pointed at (in fact, there were three reports, the initial one by the General Control Office in the Finance Ministry) could be summarised as improper accounting structures, mismanagement and rash spending.

According to Robinson (1997a, b), the personalisation of politics is part of the strategy of undermining the *intifada* elite, which is a major goal of Arafat and the PLO. However, patronage politics is a more enduring feature of PLO-style state-building and needs also to be seen in the perspective of lack of statehood and the need for legitimacy.

THE LEGISLATIVE COUNCIL

The eighty-eight-member Council has met with a number of problems in asserting itself as an integrated body of Palestinian political life. In a self-evaluation report, Council members established that there has been a high degree of confusion in the work of the Council. Also, the Council suffers from a lack of experience and a lack of sufficient infrastructure. There are also tensions between the Council and the Executive Authority. The Council mentions the Authority's 'block on the official media, preventing it from reporting on the Council's work'[16] as well as the Authority's refusal 'to abide by the council's decisions or even to give its opinion of the council's decisions' as serious impediments in its work (PLC, 1997: 160). One of the main factors behind this state of affairs is that the PLC was created after the establishment of the Executive (Hilal, 1998: 123).

The problems of the Council, which originate to some extent from within the Council itself, have to do with lack of experience and Fateh domination. In addition, the PLC is heavily biased towards the middle class and towards non-refugees. Only one-ninth of PLC members are camp residents (Hilal, 1998: 135). 'Technocrats and bureaucrats comprise over 60 per cent of the membership of the PLC. Business-people formed 8 per cent of the Council, and those in private institutions some 6 per cent. The rest (a quarter of the PLC), are individuals who were active in the *intifada* and in the national movement' (Hilal, 1998: 136). Five women candidates made it to the Council. Difficulties other than those in the Palestinian domain are Israeli obstacles, such as closures between the West Bank and Gaza or between cities in the West Bank. A degree of pluralism is evident in the Council's debates and there are continual attempts to strengthen its legislative and oversight capacity.

POLICE AND SECURITY

Within the context of the agreements, the PNA was to be responsible for internal security. External, or Israeli, security was one of the trickiest issues of the negotiations and continued to be thorny in the wake of large-scale military attacks by the Islamist movements. The result has been a militarisation of Palestinian politics and society (Frisch, 1997b; Usher, 1998).

According to Article IV, 3 of the Interim Agreement of September 1995, the number of Palestinian policemen would amount to 30,000, of whom 18,000 were to be stationed in Gaza and 12,000 in the West Bank. Former guerrillas and activists were now to protect the Israelis from attacks by the Palestinian opposition. Israeli security needs required the Palestinian police force to take action, using repressive power against its own population.[17] The PNA was thus caught in a dilemma, being pressured from both Israel – its partner in the negotiations and in the DOP and Gaza/Jericho – and its own populace. Security cooperation between the two former enemy armies represented a drastic and sudden change in institutions and values. Every suicide attack committed by the Islamist movements underlined the fact that the previously well defined boundary between friend and enemy had become exceedingly blurred. No longer did the entirety of the Palestinian movement fight the same struggle, as mainstream nationalism allied itself with Israel while radical forces were still claiming their right to fight a legitimate struggle against an illegitimate occupation.

Repression by the authorities has involved mass arrests, the closure of universities and other civil infrastructure and charity organisations, physical abuse, torture, and restrictions of basic rights and freedoms. Fifteen Palestinians have died while in custody, in a number of cases torture is clearly the cause of death (e.g. Amnesty International, 1996; *Jerusalem Report*, 21 August 1997). In February 1995, in relation to the Beit Lid attack, a state security court was set up based on the Egyptian military law of 1962, implying arbitrary and summary trials without due process. The courts are severely criticised by many observers. The death penalty has been introduced and death sentences have been implemented. The institutionalisation of the judicial system remains low, leading to the failure of the rule of law.

The existence of the police and security apparatus implies that there is now a structure with a 'legitimate use of violence', to use Weber's (1947) famous definition of a state. The Palestinian police and security apparatus is, however, greatly oversized. According to the Interim Agreement, the repressive apparatus could comprise 30,000 personnel. Today, no one seems to know the exact figure, but between 35,000 and 40,000 is a common estimate, meaning that the ratio of policemen to citizens is one of the highest in the world. It is also the largest segment of a large PNA bureaucracy. The security forces are also divided among themselves and the exact number of different security forces is uncertain. Fragmentation serves as one ingredient in a 'divide and rule' strategy, where the individual branches report solely and directly to Arafat, and where different branches compete with each other, preventing the formation of a strong and united body which could enter politics (cf. Robinson, 1997a; Usher, 1998). The security apparatus entered the political system prior to the establishment of government and even prior to the arrival of Yasir Arafat and the returning PLO structure, indicating that the foundation of the political system is security. This is not surprising, given what has earlier been concluded about struggle as a foundation for national identity as well as Israel's security concerns in the negotiations.

Revolution versus state-building

The transformation from an anti-colonial liberation nationalism, basing its legitimacy in the notions of 'revolution' and 'struggle' for what is 'right', to state-building and the raising of institutional capacity and administration is clearly no smooth process.

> This is a different challenge than the struggle with Israel. Part of its difficulty lies in the fact that this type of transition entails a move beyond black-and-white issues into an engagement with the contradictory currents within a nationalist movement, which are deliberately obscured during a struggle with an outside adversary. (Chase, 1997: 8)

In a way, the current period of interim solution and transformation contradicts everything which the PLO used to represent, although the mainstream PLO argues that the current process is the necessary step towards statehood. Although PLO institution-building reached statist characters, legitimacy was attributed not to the system but to an ideology, an idea. The revolutionary, rejectionist, rebellious political culture that was fostered and nurtured by twenty-seven years of occupation, by the PLO official nationalist discourse and by the popular nationalist discourse of the *intifada* thus creates difficulties for the newly established Authority in implementing its policies and building the future state. A Fateh member expressed it thus:

> The Palestinian mentality is a rejectionalist mentality. This is the *first time when people are to accept things*, so the problem is with the led people. Because they reject authority. The problem is with the people to be led. They have not been trained to be led, because to be led is a colonial structure. And the people are trained to object, to reject, to not accept authority, because all the time through history the authority was [an] oppressive one, and now you have to prove that you are not that, you are an authority of the people, for the people, and to the people. (Interview with PNA official and member of Fateh, 14 September 1994)

For the first time, the Palestinian population was to be *for* an authority, to support a system of rule. Since the politicisation of Palestinian society has been oriented towards rejection and opposition, it was not easy to redirect this society to being 'for' something. With the establishment of the PNA, there was for the first time a Palestinian government in Palestine. Still, the winning of legitimacy for this new system was not without its complications. Salim Tamari argues that the *intifada* created a youth culture, a 'defiant culture', which posed itself against traditional structures of authority and patriarchy. A more egalitarian, populist culture was thereby nurtured. A rebellious society which was difficult to control and suppress had been created. Moreover, a daily discipline of work and education was lacking due to the higher priority given to political activities and to opposing existing structures of authority and control (Salim Tamari, lecture at Birzeit University, 4 August 1994).

A member of Fateh and PNA official phrased it thus:

> Just imagine a situation where just a month ago we were telling people, it is revolutionary, patriotic, nationalistic, a national duty not to pay taxes. And now

we are telling, we the same people, telling the same people, things that are very contradictory. We are telling them it's nationalistic, patriotic, revolutionary, a national duty to pay taxes. So we have to reorient the mentality of the people by 180 degrees from 1 to 100. (Interview with PNA official and member of Fateh, 14 September 1994)

The reproduction of Palestinian nationalist discourse thus took a new and different form, with official nationalism actually being able to draw concretely on the symbols of statehood, and the goal of establishing a state in the future drawing nearer. Yet this process was not straightforward. Previously, the nationalist discourse had centred around liberation, struggle and opposing imposed structures. With the establishment of the PNA, the Palestinian leadership had for the first time to re-create a nationalism centring around positive concepts of building and restructuring, without being able to communicate the benefits of this system effectively. One notion used is 'national reconstruction' (Shkaki, 1996b). 'Our great people are entering a new stage in the struggle, which needs greater efforts and the contribution of every Palestinian with all his capabilities, to build our national Palestinian authority and ensure the victory of our just aims' (PLO Executive Committee, Statement on Israeli–Palestinian DOP, Tunis, 12 September 1993). 'Struggle' is thus dressed in new clothes and is in the process of picking up a new meaning, that is, 'building'.

State-building: 'this is a country to be made'

The PNA and its sympathisers stressed the transitional character of the period of self-government and underlined that the Gaza–Jericho first arrangements should merely be seen as the first step in a longer process, the goal of which was to establish an 'independent Palestinian state in the West Bank and the Gaza Strip with East Jerusalem as its capital' – this became the main PLO slogan of the 1980s. Self-government was thus a continuation of the previous struggle. The process of establishing the Palestinian state was portrayed as irreversible. 'In 1989, I was saying that within five years' time, we have a passport. This year we have a passport. In the celebrations of the year 2000, the celebrations in Jerusalem will be [held] between Israel and a Palestinian state' (interview with PNA minister and member of Fateh, 12 October 1994). This determinism was partly a result of pressing circumstances; a way to enhance legitimacy in a confusing situation. Official nationalist discourse also drew on the notion of building something which was not there; to start from scratch was a perception which was strong in the PNA and among Fateh supporters of the Authority and the agreements. The point about standing at a brand new situation, a starting point in history indicates the importance of imagining time in a certain way. '*This is a country to be made*. It's a state-building, it's a nation-building, it's institution-building . . . it's a matter of putting things together from point zero' (interview with PNA official and member of Fateh, 14 September 1994, emphasis added). Representatives of official nationalism emphasised the state-building character, that it was a matter of the creation of a state and a nation. An active process of creating the state was envisioned: 'We are to emerge from the ashes,' said one PNA official (interview, 14 September 1994).

The agreements: 'the best of the worse'; 'minimum of the minimum'

Although an absolute majority of the Palestinian population has since the signing of the DOP supported the peace process, even during the most daunting times, to most Palestinians, the agreements with Israel are also problematic.[18] The main opinion is that the agreements do not represent the fulfilment of Palestinian national(ist) aspirations, but reflect what it was possible to achieve under the circumstances (cf. Jørund Lønning, 1998: 170). Official nationalism denoted a change from 'politics of resistance' to 'politics of realism' – the Palestinian movement now had to accept what was feasible. The only realistic option was perceived as diplomacy. In explaining this change, there were frequent comparisons with the past and its 'missed opportunities'. The peace process and the DOP ought also to be seen as a logical outcome of the political process of the PLO, commencing with the efforts to be included in a Middle East process in 1973 and followed closely by the 1974 PNC decision. The agreements signed with Israel were seen as a first step from which the Palestinians could negotiate a better position.

> At least we started. I don't say that we gained all that we want. But politics is usually the art of the possible, not the impossible or the slogans . . . Before Arafat made this courageous step, we made many political mistakes, we missed many golden opportunities. But at least we started. (Interview with PNA minister, independent, 2 November 1994)

> I think that one of our tragedies [is] that the Palestinians most of the time [have been] saying no, we didn't say yes. But finally, we said yes. (Interview with Fateh activist, 23 October 1994)

In the quotations above, there is also a sense of self-criticism; that is, in the past, the Palestinians had missed opportunities through politics of negation (cf. Khalidi, 1997). And when resistance was impossible, Palestinian politics had to change fundamentally to adopt politics of diplomacy and negotiation. It was not as though the PLO rejected such strategies – they had been part of PLO politics since 1974 – but in terms of the domains of identity, struggle had continued to dominate. PLO politics have never cast Palestinian identity in terms of 'accepting' politics. In relation to the peace process, no longer was Palestinian politics merely an issue of resistance, but the agreements constituted 'reality' and must be used as the frame of reference for Palestinian politics; they were perceived as a *fait accompli*, impossible to fight or resist. In Palestinianist discourse, the agreements were also determined by superpower politics out of the control of the Palestinians.

> The Oslo agreement is not our dream, it is according to the new order after the Gulf War, and we accepted this agreement from a weak position. And this is the only alternative, this is the only option for our future, but this is not our dream, and this is not a fair agreement. (Interview with PNA minister, 30 March 1995)

> The Oslo agreement is the minimum of the minimum that the Palestinians want, and the minimum of the Palestinian rights. But the Palestinians learned that they must be realistic. The agreement is not what the Palestinians want, but what the world wants. (Interview with PNA official and member of Fateh, 4 December 1994)

These statements reveal the difficulties in seeing the agreements in terms of black or white. The agreements were also to be understood in the light of Palestinian weakness; Palestinians had to accept 'what the world wanted'.

Furthermore, since there was now a Palestinian authority, problems and difficulties could not all be blamed on Israel. Issues were being blurred and becoming more complicated as the Palestinian cause was changing. The struggle now also revolved around what *kind* of internal structures were to be established. Previously, the 'hows' of self-determination belonged to an abstract, mystified sphere of 'after the revolution/liberation'. Democracy, political pluralism, human rights, legal institution-building and the rule of civic law were all concepts and structures that entered Palestinian political debate in a very real sense, as the exceedingly confused situation of hard to define 'less occupation' and 'more Palestinian rule/power' created confusion and frustrated expectations. 'The biggest part is of course Israeli [obstacles] . . . The other part is concerning us; changing from a revolutionary thinking and administration to a state, and the [fact] that we are coming to a completely destroyed infrastructure' (interview with PNA minister and member of Fateh, 12 October 1994).

Fateh: state-building party and internal opposition

The peace process has revealed deep splits and divisions between the various sections of Palestinian political life. Although the Fateh movement is the backbone of the PNA and supports the peace process, the movement is divided internally. Many observers argue that there has been a deliberate depoliticisation of the Fateh movement in PNA politics (Frisch, 1997a, b; Robinson, 1997a), and that the PNA is in effect a one-party regime (Hilal, 1998: 133).

One issue is embitterment among the younger cadres of *intifada* activists who were left without a role in the new structure. Fateh opposition in the West Bank and Gaza is sometimes expressed in those terms, that the people who waged the 'real' struggle, who suffered from imprisonment and injuries and who sacrificed in the struggle should be part of the decision-making process. 'Struggle' had for years represented a kind of life, an existential base, and what could activists do now, having lost important years of education during the *intifada*, with unemployment reaching unprecedented levels? The peace process is seen by many rank and file activists as an elite project from which the lower strata and the real strugglers are alienated and excluded, with key positions in the Authority and security services given to the 'outside' former Fateh cadres and bureaucrats.

Fateh is no longer an underground movement fighting for liberation, but a semi-open 'movement'/organisation with 'on the ground' offices, the Fateh Higher Committee in the West Bank with Marwan Barghouti, a charismatic reformist returnee as the General Secretary, and the Fateh Higher Committee in the Gaza Strip. Primary elections in the Fateh movement in Ramallah revealed high support for street activists and *intifada* fighters, leading to a halt in the elections, which were initially planned for the whole region. In the national elections, several Fateh leaders chose to stand on a different list or were not allowed to stand on the Fateh list. The PLC today is largely dominated by Fateh, but Fateh representatives do not act as a monolithic bloc within the Council. Some of the Fateh members of parliament are highly critical of the Executive and sometimes behave as if in opposition to the Authority. The lack of oppositional faction representatives in parliament makes this group exceedingly important in terms of the internal political debate. According to CPRS data, all PLO factions except Fateh have lost support since the beginning of self-rule, and Fateh received 38.5 per cent of popular support in a December 1997 poll (CPRS, Poll No. 31). In a CPRS poll in March 1998, Fateh had increased its support to 46 per cent (CPRS, Public Opinion Poll No. 32, 5–8 March 1998), only to decline to 39.8 per cent in November 1998 (CPRS, Public Opinion Poll No. 37, 12–14 November 1998). One tendency is increasing political frustration expressed in 'support of none' of the political factions, meaning that the percentage of people saying that they would not support any of the factions rose from 13.8 per cent in 1995 (CPRS, Public Opinion Poll No. 21, 7–10 December 1995) to 31.6 per cent in 1998 (CPRS, Public Opinion Poll No. 37, 12–14 November 1998). According to these results, Fateh is, then, by far the largest party in Palestinian politics. Further, it has not suffered from its role as state-bearing party to any noteworthy degree, nor has it paid any consequences of the stalemated peace process. From the opposition, there is a great deal of suspicion regarding Fateh's heavy dominance:

> [Arafat] wanted to have the tribe around him, he wanted to have the movement, the party. And he said, well, I am at risk. You are threatened, Hamas is going to take positions. So, are we in the same family? Am I your leader? Blah, blah, blah. They took to the streets. They asked him to pay the consequences, and they couldn't get a lot from him. Arafat wants to have a group around him, . . . technocrats, and

corrupted people, by media-name, if you like. This is how he likes to work. This is how he prefers to work. Let's say a normal fighter within Fateh ranks, who spent twenty years in prison or ten years, who was deported, etc. etc. Arafat might have difficulties with him, but with a man like Nabil Shaath, like Jamil Tarifi, he has no difficulties. (Interview with DFLP sympathiser, 6 October 1997)

The Fateh movement in the interim period thus represents a dichotomy. It is the state-building party, but also contains many frustrated, opposing and critical voices and discourses. Fateh also suffers from Arafat's strategy of co-optation and coercion in his attempts to streamline the movement. Robinson (1997a) argues that Arafat has struggled to reconstitute the Fateh cadre system, removing uncomfortable former activists and replacing them with loyalists. The appointment of Zakaria al-Agha as head of Fateh in Gaza led to the resignation of many Fateh activists. The killing of Fateh leader As'ad Saftawi in Gaza in 1993 is, according to Robinson, 'widely believed' to have been ordered by Arafat (1997a: 180). However, Arafat's attempts to control the movement do not necessarily imply that Fateh is completely controllable.

The mentality of the President is that he is the leader of the revolution still inside, he wants to deal with everything according to his own ideas and we believe that this is not a good way to do it, here on our land. Maybe we can understand it in Beirut. I can't say we accept it, but we can understand it at that time, but we will never accept it here, on our land. Our people want the freedom, democracy and their human rights and till now, we are very sorry to say that we don't have it. (Interview with PLC member, Fateh, 20 October 1997)

In fact I always speak to those who are the Islamic opposition or from the left-wing opposition. I tell them that you are not doing your job fine. You are supposed to be more tough in your opposition than us, but I feel in the Council that we are the opposition, not you. (Interview with PLC member, Fateh, 21 October 1997)

Although Fateh is the backbone of the political system, the PNA also depends on support parties, such as Fida, with a leftist, democratic and nationalist agenda but with miniscule support among the Palestinian population. (The PPP can be characterised as loyal opposition.) In fact, on the popular level, they hardly exist.[19]

To younger Fateh activists, or former activists, Arafat has lost a certain amount of his legitimacy as the incarnation of Palestine. The symbolism is that, through signing, Arafat gave up on 'struggling', and accordingly his position as the leading symbol of Palestine was diminished. Furthermore, the agreement had led to Gaza being a 'big prison', a common metaphor used to describe the situation, with closures excluding an increasing number of Palestinians from entering Israel for work. Simultaneously, Israel had 'opened the gate' to the Arab world in terms of increased political/diplomatic relations and economic exchange. While the Palestinians perceived themselves to be further marginalised and alienated, Israeli–Arab relations were increasingly open and all-encompassing, through increased negotiations, meetings and discussions of future regional cooperation.[20] It should be emphasised that the young male activists of the *intifada* – the *shabab* – have for long been vehicles of social change in Palestinian society. They are at the core of resistance in the West Bank and Gaza, and their potential role cannot be easily dismissed. That is to say, their discontent in the wake of the establishment of self-rule should be taken seriously. In this stratum, there is now a well-grounded political culture of opposition and rejection, and their grievances may well serve as a catalyst for social unrest.

The leftist opposition

The leftist opposition (the PFLP and DFLP) took a stance against the peace process, suggesting a counter-narrative to the era of autonomy. Both the PFLP and DFLP now find themselves in political crisis in the aftermath of the Oslo process. While in the 1960s and 1970s the PFLP in particular was the main challenger to al-Fateh, both the PFLP and DFLP now have difficulty in coming to terms with the new reality and in formulating a credible agenda of opposition, at least in the 'inside'. The leftist opposition is today marginal in terms of popular support in the West Bank and Gaza. In relation to the agreements with Israel, support for the PFLP had declined to 3.5 per cent by December 1997 (CPRS Poll No. 31, 22–30 December 1997). The DFLP is hardly existing, supported by a mere 1 per cent (*ibid.*). The decline in leftist appeal started in the late 1980s (Sayigh, 1997a: 644 f.). In the outside, however, they have retained their influence.

According to the PFLP and DFLP, the agreements had 'nothing to do with real peace', since they dealt only with parts of the Palestinian population, that is, the West Bank and Gaza (interview with PFLP activist, 1995). Both the land and the population were fragmented by the agreements and this could not serve as a satisfactory solution to a nationalist conflict. Another reason for disagreement was that self-rule was for the population and not the land. The disconnection of territory/space/land and people/population is what construes Palestinian nationalism, and hence the goal of that ideology is to resurrect this linkage.

> We are talking about territoriality, a united territory, a united people, one people, one territory, and one form of rights, one territory, one people and one form of rights. Obvious, direct ones. Independence is independence, sovereignty is sovereignty, self-determination is self-determination. It can't be camouflaged by something else. You cannot tell me that, well, you can run education and health, and then you say, well, but you have to remember that this is sovereignty, that this is independence. No, this is not independence. This is to run education and to run health. We have to abandon the times of poetry. We have to feel and sense facts. If I run education, I run education. Period. (Interview with DFLP sympathiser, 28 September 1994)

There was also discontent with the downplaying of the UN resolutions. The DOP states that the final solution should be built upon UN Resolutions 242 and 338 – talking about withdrawal from occupied territories,[21] and in the Palestinian view implying a complete Israeli relinquishing of the West Bank, Gaza and East Jerusalem. The PFLP and DFLP argued that those resolutions had effectively been bypassed, since a solution could, according to the agreements, be based on whatever the parties agreed upon, which implied too loose a commitment to international resolutions.

> First of all, the agreement provides us with something that we, the Palestinians, never asked [for], never requested, [which] was never part of our political dictionary: autonomy. It doesn't even exist in the Palestinian language, not only the political language, but the Arabic language. People have started to say 'autonomia' as a new concept. So people who fought for the last forty-two years in different ways, who sacrificed their lives, who lost their beloved ones, they did it for independence. They never thought that they did this in order to get autonomy. Now, that's deception. Autonomy tries to take advantage of the sacrifices, of the sufferings of the people in order to legitimise itself. It lacks legitimacy, it's alien to our people. I can see it as a first step only if the accord says that this is just the first step towards independence. And the Palestinians don't have the ability, or the strength, or the power, or the imagination, or the wisdom, the experience, the qualified persons, the luck to work through these conditions to improve them to something else. (Interview with PFLP sympathiser, 7 October 1994)

To sign an agreement on autonomy was reminiscent of the ultimate humiliation. Autonomy was a deception, considering the long Palestinian struggle; to accept autonomy was to lure the people. Rather than state-building, a 'Bantustanisation' was occurring. The failing link was perceived as the weakness of the current Palestinian leadership and Israel's strength, leaving the balance of power in Israel's favour. In fact, according to the leftist opposition, the agreements boiled down to a Zionist conspiracy: 'Oslo is not an agreement, it is a conspiracy in the dark by people who didn't have the legitimacy to do it' (interview with PFLP sympathiser, 29 October 1994). The politics of Netanyahu later fed into this analysis, and to many implied that the critics had been right all along – all that Israel was ever willing to concede was autonomy for a divided and miniscule part of the remnants of Palestine. To the leftist opposition, the agreements signified surrender, and to capitulate was to give up the most important part of political Palestinian-ness. Palestinian identity, defined by its struggle, could never be connected with defeat. To go from goals of statehood to autonomy implied far-reaching concessions, on the brink of treason.

That the issue of refugees was left for permanent status negotiations was another symbol of loss and surrender. Palestinian struggle and suffering had for decades been centred around the politics of exile and longing, and the right to return to one's home. Their deep disappointment should also be interpreted against the background that the PFLP and DFLP had now been left out of political decision-making and influence.

According to the leftist opposition, negotiations had to be firmly based on UN Resolutions 242 and 338, implying a considerable change since the era of revolution when these resolutions were opposed on the grounds that they were unfair to the Palestinians.[22] Today they are perceived as the most just framework for any kind of negotiation. In other fora, the PFLP and DFLP have called for an international conference within the UN framework; negotiations should take place under the UN umbrella and the goal must be to implement the UN resolutions. Meanwhile, the struggle should continue against the occupation, with 'all means', that is, including military means: 'We Palestinians have the right to face the oppressors. We have the right to fight the Israeli occupation, by all means that we have [a] possibility to use. Why to renounce a right, a natural right of a nation?' (interview with DFLP sympathiser, 21 September 1994). As also emphasised by supporters of the process, to struggle against occupation was a legitimate and inherent right, which should not be compromised. Struggle and negotiations could coexist. 'Armed struggle' was still a possibility, a means of struggle, but not the main road. Gradually, new solutions were brought forward, taking the Marxist forces further away from rejectionism.

The long-term solution: 'a democratic state in all of Palestine'

Concerning the solution to the Palestinian–Israeli conflict and the long-term goal of the PFLP and DFLP, the ideological goal was still 'a democratic state in all of Palestine',[23] although this notion carried different connotations than it had twenty years previously. Disagreement existed over opinions of an independent state versus a democratic state. Both factions have accepted a state in the West Bank and Gaza as a first step, however.

> There are many options, and we are open to other options, whether to the East or to the West, but first of all independence. We need to feel that we are equal to everybody in the area. To Jordanians, to Israelis, to anybody in the world, and then we are ready to cooperate . . . unless we achieve this, there will be no stability, because if you have one single Palestinian that is unsatisfied, he will create troubles. (Interview with DFLP sympathiser, 28 September 1994)

Like Fateh and official nationalism, this DFLP personality stated that the Palestinians would not be satisfied unless an independent state was established. If the Palestinians were not satisfied, they were capable of creating instability, which was something of a warning to both the Israelis and the PNA.

The ideal solution was perceived as 'one secular, democratic state for them and for us' (interview with DFLP sympathiser, 21 September 1994); one country, one state without borders, and with democracy prevailing. At the same time, the ideal solution was not realistic, because of what was perceived as exclusivist Israeli claims upon the land. However, there still existed a 'dream Palestine' to be remembered and idealised. Furthermore, and for the same reasons, neither was the West Bank/Gaza option deemed realistic. Although a little extreme, the following quotation could serve as an example of leftist discourse:

> It is not important for me, its name. If its name is still Israel, it is not important. If it is Israel, if it is Palestine, if it is Israpalestine, if it is Paleisrael. If [there was a change in the law], I would not be as a Jerusalem Palestinian – this is a dangerous thing that I will tell you, and I am brave to tell it – I would not be against to be [an] Israeli citizen, and to ask all Palestinians in the West Bank to be Israeli citizens. Because at that time, there would be no problem, because Israel would not be a Jewish state. It's one land, it can't be divided.
>
> There must still be a time so that they [can] be convinced of this idea. Through this time, there will be struggle. We will make bitterness to them and they will make bitterness to us. This bitterness is a precondition to reach the idea that I am telling you. Because the balance of power is with Israel, and they are the occupiers and we are without our national symbols, it seems that there will be [a] transitional period in which we have to struggle for our symbols as Palestinians so as to have some balance and this balance will lead to the solution of integration. (Interview with PFLP sympathiser, 27 September 1994)

The idea of one democratic state for all reflects the civic-ness of PFLP and DFLP nationalism. The time was not, however, ripe for the dream of one state to become a reality. There was a 'need of bitterness', of suffering and violence, in order for both Palestinians and Israelis to be convinced of the appropriateness of this solution. This represented the old paradox in PFLP discourse. On the one hand, the PFLP delineated a civic variant of Palestinian nationalism, that democratic principles and not ethnic, national or religious ones should structure the state system to be. The 'one state for all' slogan seems to be the least chauvinistic of all proposals. On the other hand, military violence was needed in order to make people understand this. In order for people to be willing to live together under the same political/legal framework, force was needed, underlining the revolutionary side of the PFLP. Furthermore, the two-state solution was a step towards the democratic state. Only if the Palestinians were given their national symbols, realised in a state, could there be a balance between Israel and the Palestinians, and only in that way could the 'one state' solution be implemented. Equality was to be gained through statehood. The goal of the 'democratic state' was not simply to be seen as a political ambition, but as part of existential identity.

Islamism

Based on its ideological rejection of the peace negotiations, to Hamas the Madrid process symbolised 'surrender' (Hamas78) and was based on fragmentation caused by a Zionist–American alliance (Hamas83). The DOP was illegitimate and treacherous (Hamas105). In connection with the peace talks, a short-lived alliance was forged between the Marxist–Leninist, a-religious PFLP and DFLP – with many Christian leaders – and the ultra-religious, Islamic Hamas. Due to the immense ideological divergences between the two sides, this alliance did not survive.

In practice, several Hamas leaders are pragmatic, leaving the door open for a dialogue with Israel and cooperation with the PNA (cf. Chapter 3). In April 1994, *Palestine Report* described a peace initiative from Hamas, implying a 'conditional peace'. Ahmed (1994: 114) describes this position as 'deliberately ambiguous'. Further, 'It is clear that Hamas is torn between its ideological stance towards the peace process and the constraints of the current situation on the other' (Ahmed, 1994: 114). Or, as Abu-Amr puts it, 'the current situation is too overwhelming' (interview, 22 July 1994). In the period covered by this study, Hamas ruled out the possibility of participating in the PNA or in any elections for a Palestinian Council under the conditions and circumstances of the DOP and the Cairo Agreement. It did, however, express a willingness to participate in, and called for, municipal elections. There were on and off negotiations between Hamas and the PNA; PNA strategy being to co-opt Hamas in the new political framework. Severe tensions were, however, most seriously underlined by the November 1994 fighting, when thirteen Islamists were gunned down by PNA police in Gaza. Hamas also placed the PNA in a difficult situation, given that it not only maintained the level of violence against Israel but escalated it, introducing a new, deadly military strategy – bombing of civilian targets in the midst of Israel carried out by young men willing to kill themselves together with a number of Israelis. This new strategy was most probably not the immediate outcome of the peace process, but of the development of Hamas's strategic planning after the expulsion to Lebanon in December 1992. However, the new terror coincided with the implementation of the peace process. Hamas considered its role to be that of a liberation and resistance movement against the occupation, and now also took over the vacuum created by the PLO's final step into the camp of diplomacy. The first attacks in 1994 were revenge attacks against the Hebron massacre, but from then on it was sometimes difficult to find a precise motive for the attacks. In October 1994,[24] a bomb exploded on Dizengoff Street in the middle of Tel Aviv, killing twenty-one people. In January 1995, Islamic Jihad took responsibility for an attack against soldiers waiting for a bus in Beit Lid, close to Netanya. Twenty-two people were killed. In August 1995, another bus exploded in Jerusalem.

After the Interim Agreement, there was increased dubiety concerning the position of Hamas. Although Hamas decided not to participate in the 1996 elections, several people affiliated to the organisation stood and made it to parliament. A few months later, in February/March 1996, Hamas's military branch took responsibility for the most devastating series of terror attacks ever to be carried out by the Islamist movement. Four bombs exploded in the course of eight days in the midst of Jerusalem, Tel Aviv and Ashkelon, and over sixty people were killed. The bombs illuminated severe divisions within the movement and several leading Hamas personalities condemned the attacks. Among the Palestinian population, there was widespread condemnation of the bombings and Hamas lost considerable popular support. In September/October 1996, Hamas's support was down to 8 per cent, the lowest in any CPRS Poll (CPRS, Public Opinion Poll No. 24, 26 September–17 October 1996). The attacks of 1996 also revealed the deep split within Hamas between the traditional leadership and younger activists, between the 'inside' and 'outside' leaderships, and between the political and military wings. Through the mix of repression and cooptation which has been pursued by Arafat's regime (see Robinson, 1997a, b), Hamas has been partially weakened as a political alternative. Also, when, in May 1996, Netanyahu won the elections in Israel, it was clear that Hamas's bombs had been fundamental in determining the election results, pushing the Israeli public further into fear and anxiety. Following those incidents, Hamas became temporarily more quiescent, abiding by Authority policies for a year. In September 1997, it had still not recovered and the suicide bombs at Mahane Yehuda market and Ben Yehuda pedestrian street in the middle of Jerusalem of July and September 1997[25] failed to have a positive impact upon the Palestinian populace, with 9 per cent supporting Hamas (CPRS Opinion Poll No. 29, 18–20 September 1997). Not until the autumn/winter of 1997 did support for Hamas rise again. In December 1997, it stood at 11.6 per cent of the population (CPRS, Opinion Poll No. 31, 22–30 December 1997), probably due to the release of Hamas spiritual leader Sheikh Ahmed Yasin, who was released after Israeli security forces attempted to assassinate Hamas leader Khaled Masha'al in Jordan. King Husayn was infuriated over the Israeli violation and his strong demands led to the immediate release of Sheikh Yasin, who had been imprisoned since 1989. He was first sent to Jordan for medical treatment, and Yasir Arafat visited him there. His return was widely celebrated in the West Bank and Gaza. However, its impact for Arafat was problematic, first because Yasin was released without his involvement, but rather with Israel, Jordan and Hamas as the core players, relegating Arafat to a 'walk on' part; and second because the symbolic power of the release of an imprisoned spiritual leader stole some radiance from Arafat as the incarnation of Palestine. Thus the only real forces in Palestinian political life today are Fateh and Hamas. In March

1998, however, support for the latter seemed to have again declined to 9 per cent (CPRS Opinion Poll No. 32, 5–8 March 1998).

The agreements: 'we are the true owners of Palestine'

From an ideological point of view, the DOP and the subsequent agreements were depicted by Hamas and Islamic Jihad as treason: 'We consider this to be a great historic act of treason and a dangerous one which will begin the dissolution of this leadership which has sold the struggle, sold the blood and sold the rights of the Palestinian people' (Sheikh Hamameh in Ahmed, 1994: 110). 'And the aim, the sole aim of the Madrid conference and then Oslo and Cairo was to make the Israeli occupation legal, to legitimise the Israeli occupation, to force the Israeli state to be part of the Islamic world or the Middle Eastern world' (interview with Hamas sympathiser, 16 November 1994). Thus the aim of the peace process, as formulated by the Oslo and Cairo Agreements, was, according to Islamist discourse, to force the Israeli state upon the political structure of an Islamically defined Middle East. Therefore, the agreements were not perceived as altering the situation of the occupation, but served to create its legitimacy.

The concept of land is paramount in this discourse. The agreements did not ensure Palestinian sovereignty over what was rightfully theirs. To sign an agreement disconnecting the links between the land and people, believed to be organically linked, was considered more or less impossible. The agreements were seen as serving Israeli economic interests and as leaving the Palestinians without independence and with a large section of the population still in exile. Not only was the intention to open up the Arabic and Islamic world to the Israeli economy, but the agreements represented an Israeli success in establishing Greater Israel. The notion of 'gates' and 'doors' that were opened symbolised that Israel had now been able to 'enter' the Middle East, where it did not really belong (interview with Islamic Jihad representative, 24 November 1994). 'Doors' and 'gates' which were opened or closed represented mechanisms of exclusion and inclusion. That boundaries became more flexible represented a danger and a menace. Flexibility of boundaries might lead to an invasion of the disharmony existing outside the boundary to the inside. At the same time as Israel was getting 'closer' and managing to penetrate inside the boundary, the agreements were seen as giving Israel sole control over both borders and boundaries.

> We refuse autonomy, because this is not actually representing the facts in the area. We are the true owners of Palestine, the Jews have no rights to establish their state at the expense of the Palestinians, and autonomy means that we are going to recognise Israel as the true owner of the land, and we [would be] a national minority in Israeli society. (Interview with Hamas leader, 11 January 1995)

To Hamas, the issue was about righteous ownership: the land belonged to the Muslims and could not be negotiated. To accept autonomy was incongruent with what was *right*. Right did not stem only from the idea that Palestinians were the people of the land, but from Palestine being the land of God. In conformity with mainstream nationalism, as well as leftist oppositional discourse, Islamists saw the struggle against the occupation as a 'right'. The difference was that, since Palestine was considered *waqf* and all of Islamic Palestine, including today's Israel, was considered 'occupied', right was drawn not only from international legality but also from religion. If autonomy were to be accepted, one would be admitting that Israel has rights too. Ownership of the land was religiously defined and divine. Compromises on what was God-given became almost absurd. Islamic Jihad was, in this regard, even more inconciliatory and dogmatist: 'The right could not be divided. There is one right, this is all the right. Not more than that and not less than this. And I will [continue] until I achieve my goals, or I will die. This is our way, and this is our right. We will continue' (interview with Islamic Jihad sympathiser, 19 January 1995). '*The right cannot be divided, there is one right, this is all the right.*' Two peoples could not have the same right in the same land. The perceived virtue of the cause leaves two options: to struggle or to die.

The long-term solution: 'we have to get rid of Israel from this area'

Turning to the issue of the preferred solution of the Islamic movements, statements were ambiguous and unclear. The official position was that all of Palestine was *waqf*:

> It is still our land. It's our land. Nobody can deny this. No moral bases, no political bases, no historical bases give the Israelis the right to establish their state on our land. It's our land.
>
> Q: Are there any conditions under which Hamas could accept a two-state solution?
>
> A: No. No. This is not a political issue. It is an Islamic issue. So we are not here representing our views, we are representing our religion. (Interview with Hamas leader, 11 January 1995)

The Islamic movements had in a way taken over the discourse of Arabism, which used to argue that the penetration of the great powers artificially divided an organic unity. Only, now the unity was described as Islamic rather than Arab or Arabic. Palestine was a 'property' which belonged to 'us' – Muslim Palestinians. A two-state solution was out of the question, not so much because of political opinions or attitudes, but because of religion. Religious values were non-negotiable. Religious nationalism was in possession of a powerful image, that is, God-given rightfulness. In Hamas discourse, there was, however, room for a more accommodationist agenda, as in statements by Islamist leaders that a two-state solution could be accepted at least as an intermediate solution and given the fulfilment of certain conditions, such as the dismantling of the settlements (e.g. interview with Sheikh Imad Bitawi, 7 May 1995).

> And we find Israel in this area as an occupying country, representing the head of the crisis of the Western civilisation . . . So we have to get rid of Israel from this area, because Palestine is Arabic and Islamic land, and those who are strangers they represent a dangerous challenge to our civilisation, and our religion and the future of our generation. So we don't accept its existence in the area at all. (Interview with Islamic Jihad leader, 24 November 1994)

Israel represented Western imperial civilisation, and Islamic civilisation was imagined as a counterforce against Western civilisation. Although Israel represented 'strangers', geographically Israel had transcended a physical border, and was therefore perilous.

The liberation of parts of Palestine could, however, be a step towards achieving the goal of an Islamic state (interview with Islamic Jihad sympathiser, 19 January 1995). This was reminiscent of PLO discourse in the 1970s, with the 1974 decision that Palestine could be liberated in stages. But the ambiguity in Islamist discourse remained, since there was a lack of clarity on visions, strategies and goals. 'Liberation' and 'establishment of an Islamic state' were rather vague and abstract ideas. Whether 'liberation of any Palestinian land' was a first step or could be accepted as an end goal, because Israel was so strong, was not clear.

> We accept that there is a government in Palestine and beside it the government of Israel for now. But in the future, we don't accept that . . . To avoid problems between the peoples in this country, we accept two governments in this country, to avoid problems, to avoid fightings between the people. (Interview with Islamist sympathiser, 7 May 1995)

An Israeli state next to a Palestinian state might in fact be accepted by political Hamas, but on the level of rhetoric and dogma it would be dangerous or impossible to abandon ideology right away, given the fact that Hamas's support had been gained from its emphasis on struggle and liberation.

Reformism

In the wake of the self-government agreements, a fourth political trend became more explicit in Palestinian politics, aside from mainstream Fateh nationalism and leftist and Islamist oppositional nationalism. This tendency, albeit still loose in its contours and with no clear common organisational focus, concentrated on internal politics and democracy. A common denominator for political figures associated with this line of thought was that they accepted negotiations with Israel, but argued that current circumstances were much too unfavourable to the Palestinians. This stream consisted of at least two parts: (1) the PPP, which was the only faction which could be said to represent the reformist approach; and (2) individual independents with no organisational focus. The one person most obviously connected with this line of thinking was Heidar Abdel Shafi, head of the Palestinian delegation to Madrid and Washington. Abdel Shafi was in the spring of 1995 the leading figure in establishing the Movement for Building Democracy in Palestinian Society. The goal of the movement was to foster a democratic culture in Palestinian society and to critically examine the negotiation process (interview with Heidar Abdel-Shafi, 29 March 1995). In 1998 it appeared that this line of thought had broadened. The organisational focus of the trend was the NGOs.

The agreements: 'they will retain authority'

Reformism supported peace negotiations with Israel, but believed that balance of power structures made it virtually impossible to come out with an agreement beneficial to the Palestinians unless certain conditions were first met. Those conditions had to do with both Israel and the Palestinians. Concerning Israel, there must, for example, be a total freeze in settlement activities, and concerning the Palestinians, they 'should put their house in order' and agree on the 'red lines' before negotiating any further (interview with independent political personality, 28 August 1994). If there was no common understanding, any agreement with Israel would only further weaken the Palestinian movement. This trend was critical of the agreements signed by the PLO, but perceived it easier to accept 'Oslo' than 'Cairo'. 'Oslo', however, still implied too many concessions on the part of the Palestinians, and was perceived as too vague actually to achieve an improvement in the political plight of the Palestinians. Scepticism was rather on the level of strategy. In addition, this line was, unlike that of the opposition, in perfect agreement with the Madrid process and the Washington negotiations. A large part of this political clique belonged to the former delegation and thus had a more immediate interest in that process than the Oslo Agreement negotiated by the PLO, or parts of the PLO.

> From the beginning we neglected to make use of our inner potential. We simply depended more on external factors, [the] support of the Arab world, support of the socialist world, from the Third World, so we neglected our own innate potential. The Palestinian leadership failed to make benefit of the *intifada* by failing to provide the needed organisation for all this. (Interview with independent, 28 August 1994)

Reformism to a large extent blamed the PLO and the Palestinian leadership for failure in the negotiating process. The person cited above spoke about the 'inner potential' of the Palestinians to foster change, pointing to the *intifada* as the utmost example of Palestinian inner potential. The Palestinian leadership failed to create the largest possible unity for an agreement. There was an implicit critique of the secrecy of the negotiations taking place in Norway and leading to the DOP, since the secrecy implied that Palestinians had no chance to debate the agreements or to agree on the 'red line'. Disunity was seen as a result of the leadership accepting agreements before reaching a national consensus.

Also, the DOP was a poor agreement because it did not acknowledge appropriate Palestinian claims to the land. Compromises in the agreement rather gave Israel the upper hand in giving land, without regard to the 'rightful' Palestinian ownership of the land. Palestinian willingness to compromise and trust in the Israeli negotiators were described as a retreat from Palestinian-ness in the form of resistance; it represented a reverse step from Palestinian pride, while the Israelis were permitted to act as superiors. This was equated with humiliation, and was the same argument found in the oppositional camps, although phrased differently:

> It's moving into a sort of dictation rather than negotiations. It starts with Israeli proposals and it ends with agreements that are extremely similar to Israeli initial proposals, so Israel is . . . making use of the weakness of the PLO, and making use of the lack of democratic decision-making process of the PLO. . . . And we envisage this Cairo Agreement as a step towards reorganising the occupation rather than as a step towards ending the occupation. (Interview with PPP personality, 5 October 1994)

Similarly to leftist and Islamist opposition, the PPP perceived the negotiations not as true negotiations between equal partners, but as strongly flavoured by the balance of power, allowing Israel to dictate the agenda. There was an additional emphasis on the weakness of the leadership. Israel was seen as imposing its will upon a much weaker negotiation partner. Like the opposition, the PPP argued that the Cairo Agreement implied a 'reorganisation of the occupation'.

The vagueness of the DOP could have been used in a more beneficial way, but was not:

> We started a new system of negotiation, 'sign first and negotiate later', so [the Oslo Agreement] had potential to go either way. And what you do with it is what counts. Unfortunately, what was done with it was to allow Israel to maximise its gains and minimise its losses; it allowed the process to adopt Israeli priorities, and maintain Israeli control and domination; it adopted the whole system of fragmentation, functional approach and it placed the Palestinian side as on probation. They have to demonstrate to the Israelis that they can deliver and Israel is in sole control of the process. (Interview with independent political personality, 24 February 1995)

Israel's putting the Palestinians to a test was seen as degrading. The staged process where the Palestinians were to prove to the world that they were worthy of the elevation to self-rule, as well as the Israeli Labour government's continual requirements of measures from the PNA against 'Islamist extremism', fed into the discourse of Israelis as strong, vigorous and calculating.

Some independents, although highly critical of the Authority, were equally critical of the opposition, and considered the oppositional rejection unrealistic. The agreements constituted a reality which could not be changed, and rejectionism was in fact playing into the hands of the Authority, since no alternative policies were presented.

Reformism, or civic nationalism, provided a form of democratic, 'loyal' opposition to the Agreement. They did not suggest a radical alternative, but represented a new agenda in Palestinian politics, consisting of calls for democracy, accountability, transparency, and so on, and a view towards strengthening civil society as a counterstructure towards the state-builders. Similarly to official nationalism, this trend apprehended the new era as state-building and defined its role within this process as to strengthen civil society. This discourse also represented a new formula for action. It was no longer 'liberation'/struggle or negotiations/the peace process which were to be the strategies, but internal democracy. Internal politics and democracy would be a way to alter power positions and the external situation, since the agreements could be cancelled through the use of democratic politics. Analysing this, one should bear in mind that although several of the proponents of this tendency belonged to at least a former leftist discourse, the PPP was a marginal organisation with influence merely among an intellectual elite.

NOTES

1 Although a majority of the PNC was in favour of the Madrid Conference at the 20th PNC meeting in September 1991, there was no consensus. The PFLP, the DFLP, the PFLP–GC and the PLF, as well as the al-Fateh Revolutionary Council, were against the peace process and self-government during an interim period. The factions which supported the agreement were al-Fateh, the ALF Temporary Command, the PDU/Fida and the PPSF. The establishment of Fida was the result of a split within the DFLP. Fida was led by Yasir Abd Rabbuh (later Minister of Culture and Information in the PNA), a long-time ally of Yasir Arafat, and criticised the negative stance taken by the DFLP. The PFLP later (during the autumn of 1991) suspended its membership of the Executive Committee of the PLO.

2 These insights and initiatives coincided with increased Norwegian interest and personal efforts by Terje Rød Larsen and Mona Juul, who were instrumental in setting up the Oslo 'back channel', the secret negotiations in Norway (Abbas, 1995; Corbin, 1994; Aggestam and Jönsson, 1997).

3 Egyptian President Anwar Sadat had already suggested a 'Gaza first' proposal in 1980.

4 The first attack was a car bomb, which exploded at a bus stop in Afula on 6 April, killing eight people, including the bomber, and wounding forty-four. A week later, on 13 April, coinciding with Israeli independence day (again highlighting the importance of time and remembrance in the discourse of the Palestinian–Israeli conflict), a bomb exploded in a suicide attack on a bus in Hadera, killing six, including the bomber (*Journal of Palestine Studies*, 1994b: 166 ff.).

5 In a speech to the Knesset, Prime Minister Yitzhak Rabin said: 'You are not part of the community of Israel . . . You are not partners in the Zionist enterprise. You are a foreign implant . . . a shame on Zionism and an embarrassment to Judaism' (*Journal of Palestine Studies*, 1994b: 157).

6 According to the Wye River Memorandum signed by Israel and the PLO on 23 October 1998, Israel is to transfer 1 per cent of the current C area to the A area, and 14.2 per cent from Area B to Area A, meaning that the PNA will be in full control of 18 per cent of the West Bank. In addition, 12 per cent of Area C is to be turned into Area B. By early December 1998, Israel had not yet ratified the agreement.

7 Arguably the most important part of the Oslo process was the mutual recognition in two letters by Yitzhak Rabin and Yasir Arafat exchanged four days prior to the signing of the DOP. The formalisation of PLO recognition of Israel was accompanied by a letter from Chairman Arafat to Prime Minister Rabin affirming that 'those articles of the Palestinian Covenant which deny Israel's right to exist and the provisions of the Covenant which are inconsistent with the commitments of this letter are now inoperative and no longer valid' (PLO Chairman . . . , 1993: 114–15). The PNC was not called upon to take this crucial discussion of the Covenant until April 1996. At this meeting, the PLO specified the paragraphs in the Charter which were null and void. However, the Charter has still not been redrafted, making this issue a perpetual thorn in Palestinian–Israeli relations. When Prime Minister Netanyahu consistently made a redraft a requirement for further progress in the peace process. In December 1998, in the presence of US President Bill Clinton, and as a result of the Wye River Agreement from October 1998, Palestinian leaders from the PNC, the PLC, as well as other national figures, voted on a show of hands at Arafat's call to annul those articles in the Charter.

8 See Hattis-Rolef (1997) for analyses of how Labour and Likud thinking about a Palestinian state has evolved.

9 Salim Tamari aptly phrased it: previously, the Palestinians constituted a 'nation without a state'. Following the establishment of self-government, it is a 'state without sovereignty', or an 'embryonic state-formation in a colonial set-up' (conversation with the author, 27 June 1995).

10 The election system chosen was a majority system in districts rather than a proportional representation system, which may have encouraged a 'localised' voting pattern rather than a national pattern. The majority system also implied a hindrance for the opposition to participate, since they were disadvantaged by this system. Some of the smaller parties' candidates who failed to gain a seat in fact achieved more than 5 per cent of the vote. For example, Zahira Kamal from Fida won 10.6 per cent of the vote in the Jerusalem constituency but did not get a seat, while Ahmed al-Zughair from Fateh won 10.9 per cent and achieved a seat in the PLC (Hilal, 1998: 133 and n. 6: 144). A proportional system would have allowed a more plural legislative assembly.

11 A Fateh activist from Balata refugee camp in Nablus, a member of the Executive Committee of GUPS, who was deported on 11 December 1987 and returned in 1994.

12 Or As'ad Qader, a Fateh member and military commander who spent almost thirty years in exile, winning a seat in the PLC in the Bethlehem district.

13 On transitions, see Rustow (1970), Diamond, Linz and Lipset (1990), Shain and Linz (1995) and Potter *et al.* (1997).

14 If Feisal Husseini's Ministry without Portfolio is included there were twenty-three ministries between 1996 and 1998. Nine of the ministers (if we count Yasser Abbed Rabboh twice since he is Minister of Culture and Minister of Information) have been appointed, which constitutes 39 per cent of the total.

15 See Usher (1997), Frisch (1997a) and Robinson (1997a). According to Robinson, this is a longer-term process in the sense that the old elite was able to recapture some lost influence with the help of both Israel and the PLO in the latter phase of the *intifada* (Robinson, 1997a: 90–3).

16 A private TV station broadcast live legislative sessions to the dismay of the Authority. First, the station was jammed and then, in the spring of 1997, its initiator, Dao'ud Kuttab, was imprisoned.

17 This has not, however, led to public distrust of the police and security forces. According to a CPRS poll in June 1998, 77.7 per cent of the West Bank and Gaza population evaluated the performance of the police and security forces as 'good' or 'very good' (CPRS Poll No. 33, 3–6 June 1998).

18 CPRS polls indicated a large amount of support in the immediate aftermath of the signing of the DOP: in September 1993, 64.9 per cent supported the deal; 27.9 per cent opposed it and 6.6 per cent defined themselves as hesitant. Euphoria reached peak levels when the Palestinians celebrated, dancing in the streets and handing out olive branches to Israeli soldiers. Support then declined with the Hebron massacre and delays in reaching the first agreement on implementation, only to increase again with the signing of the Gaza–Jericho Agreement. In March 1995, when discussions about negotiations on the implementation of the second step came to the fore, support reached the highest level ever: 66.6 per cent, with 21.4 per cent against and 12 per cent with no opinion. In December 1996, after seven months of Netanyahu rule and two months after violent clashes between Palestinian police and the IDF, 78.7 per cent of the population still supported the peace process (CPRS Poll No. 25, December 1996). In November 1997, 68.3 per cent defined themselves as supporters of the peace process and 28.2 per cent as opponents (CPRS Poll No. 30, November 1997). In March 1998, 67 per cent of respondents continued to support the Oslo process, while 29 per cent were opposed to it (CPRS, Public Opinion Poll No. 32, 5–7 March 1998).

19 In June 1998, the PPP received 1.5 per cent of popular support, and Fida 0.6 per cent (CPRS Poll No. 34 25–27 June 1998). In a BirZeit survey, Fida received less than 1 per cent and the PPP 2.1 per cent of the vote.

20 As part of the multilateral negotiations on economic development, regional summit conferences were held, beginning in Casablanca in 1994, and followed by Amman in 1995 and Cairo in 1996. After Netanyahu's election, things took a reverse trend and only a few Arab states attended the fourth economic summit in Doha, Qatar, in 1997. The climate between Israel and Egypt as well as Jordan cooled considerably, with President Mubarak and King Husayn openly displaying their distrust of Israel's Prime Minister.

21 Arabic and Israeli interpretations disagree on whether it is from 'occupied territories', as in the English version of the text, or 'the occupied territories', as in the Arabic and French versions.

22 The resolutions were considered unfair, since they did not speak about the Palestinian 'people', but referred to Palestinians only as 'refugees'.

23 Although the DFLP was in fact the first PLO organisation (in 1973) to advocate a two-state solution.

24 This was shortly after an attack against a pedestrian street in West Jerusalem and the kidnapping of Nahson Wachsmann, an Israeli soldier, who was killed together with the kidnappers in a rescue attempt by Israeli security forces. The autumn of 1994 was thus a flurry of Hamas activity.

25 There was also a bomb at a café in Tel Aviv in March 1997. The circumstances surrounding that attack were, however, unclear.

5

Palestinian identity:
a border construction

Denial

Dispersal has given rise to the Palestinian narrative as the 'wanderer of the Earth' and an identity which experiences deniance: 'We are thrown from one airport to another airport and no one wants to accept us' (interview with PPP leader, 4 September 1994). Homelessness and insecurity constitute main representations of Palestinian identity. Dispossession and uprootedness amplify feelings of being deserted and at the mercy of stronger forces. Dislocation is symbolised through such metaphors as 'in any airport you find Palestinians'. This insecurity and desertedness capture the Palestinian identity which is denied at every 'airport'; at every international border, the Palestinians are reminded of the legal uselessness of their identity. Insecurity also, however, provides an incitement to action, fighting and resistance.

> The quintessential Palestinian experience, which illustrates some of the most basic issues raised by Palestinian identity, takes place at a border, an airport, a check-point: in short, at any one of those modern barriers where identities are checked and verified. What happens to Palestinians at those crossing points brings home to them how much they share in common as a people. For it is at these borders and barriers that the six million Palestinians are singled out for 'special treatment', and are forcefully reminded of their identity: of who they are, and why they are differ-ent than others. [. . .] As a result, at each of these barriers which most others take for granted, every Palestinian is exposed to the possibility of harassment, exclusion and sometimes worse simply because of his or her identity. (Khalidi, 1997: 1 f.)

Palestinian difference and commonality are created at such borders and cross-ing points. It is here that the particularity of not belonging to any one state becomes painfully clear. The Palestinian 'pilgrimage' (cf. Anderson, 1991) is thus the denial and humiliation which constitute the Palestinian experience in meeting 'others'. Homelessness and lack of valid identity documents lead to humiliating experiences. 'I am nobody. I want to be somebody,' said a DFLP sympathiser when discussing the *laissez-passer* travel documents, in which the nationality of the Palestinians is classified as 'Jordanian' and the documents are issued by Israel. To identify oneself, whether at an Israeli military checkpoint in the West Bank, at the Eretz checkpoint separating Gaza from Israel, at the Allenby bridge or in any international airport, is connected with separation, exclusion and humiliation. 'The fact that all Palestinians are subject to these special indignities, and thus are all subject to an almost unique postmodern condition of shared anxiety at the frontier, the checkpoint and the crossing point proves that they are a people, if nothing else does' (Khalidi, 1997: 5).[1]

The state

A second key structure of Palestinian identity is its relation to the *future*, to the very objectives of nationalism. This is the opposite of denial. It is with the realisation of the independent Palestinian state that the Palestinian identity is also to become realised. Palestinian identity is not yet complete; it is an unfulfilled national identity, and Palestinian identity is sometimes expressed in those terms: 'to have'.

> To have a state, a land and a passport to go through, because they stop the Palestinians everywhere. To have a country. To have *watan*, a homeland, to be able to go everywhere. And to be related to somewhere and not all the time being kicked out from everywhere. (Interview with Fateh activist, 16 November 1994)

> To feel that I have my own roots in Palestine, to have my own passport, to feel like the British feel in Britain, the Americans feel in America, to be Palestinian [means] that we have our homeland, we can build our homeland, all our children will live like all the children in the world. (Interview with Fateh representative, 18 September 1994)

Embedded in Palestinian identity is the endeavour to obtain elevation to statehood, to become like others, to have what others have, 'to have a passport', to be able to have your identity firmly written into a document which cannot then be questioned. A formal, official recognition of the national identity of the Palestinians which is internationally confirmed or carries international significance is desired. To be a Palestinian is realised in achieving this state, the land, the homeland, the *watan*, indicating the degree to which Palestinian identity is ambivalent, represented simultaneously through what makes it special, that is, denial, and the reversal of this particularity, that is, the internationally recognised state. Palestinian identity is epitomised both through the denial, that is, what happens at present, and what is not yet realised. When this is established, Palestinian identity will be finally placed and localised somewhere in space and in international legality. The passport symbolises freedom of movement – 'not all the time being kicked out from everywhere' – that is, to be localised somewhere which is home and where Palestinians can be rooted without depending on the arbitrary goodwill of neighbouring states. To be a Palestinian was to 'feel like the British feel in Britain', that is, to have normalcy, as it was defined in international relations. It is what the Palestinians *used* to be and what they *will* become that is important. The present is merely a transitional period, a '*rite de passage*'.

From this perspective, the most important aspect of the agreements of 1993–95 was seen as the Israeli recognition of the PLO, representing formal recognition of the Palestinians as a people.

> The essence in the agreement and the mutual recognition between the PLO and Israel, it was that the Israelis [were] saying, they exist, they have rights, they have national rights, and this openly stood [in the agreement], [it was as though] someone said: 'We lied for the past seventy years, we can no longer lie. They are there.' (Interview with PNA minister and member of Fateh, 3 February 1995)

> As I understand the Oslo Agreement, it is the first document [in which] the Israeli government recognised the Palestinian people and its representative. . . . It's like [the] Balfour Declaration. It's the Oslo Declaration for the Palestinians [to have a] homeland. (Interview with Fateh representative, 23 October 1994)

'It's like the Balfour Declaration' for the Palestinians, that is, the Oslo Agreement was an historical document acknowledging Palestinian claims to land and a 'national home', as the Balfour Declaration did for the Jews. Highlighted in these remarks is the fact that the revolutionary PLO had now been elevated to the finest salons of international politics. A denied nationality was no longer denied. The Palestinians fearfully remember Golda Meir's statement in the late 1960s, that 'there were no Palestinians' (London *Sunday Times*, 15 June 1969), and Israel is still chilled by the Palestinian National Charter of 1964 and 1968, denying the existence of a Jewish nation.[2] With Israel's recognition, the USA followed, and the PLO received full international recognition. Recognition was an achievement in itself. Its significance was that the Palestinians now constituted a 'somebody' in the eyes of others, that is, an immaterial value had been partly fulfilled.

To 'struggle'

Perhaps the most substantial representation of Palestinian national identity is to 'struggle' – as formulated in and through both the revolution and the *intifada* – which serves as the action, the strategy through which to transcend the denial, the conditions of the present and reach the future, the state. 'Struggle' has persisted as the main means to overcome processes of victimisation and to transcend the current state of dispossession, denial and statelessness. Through the struggle, young men, *fedayyen* and *shabab*, have become active bearers of

Palestinian national identity: 'While I am struggling against the occupation I am a Palestinian' (interview with Fateh leader, 29 October 1994). It is in the *action*, in participation in resisting the occupation, that one becomes Palestinian. Palestinians perceive themselves as having an inherent right to their resistance:

> [To be a Palestinian] means that I am a fighter for human values, for [the] dignity of a nation and for what is right. Not what I believe, what I consider right, [but] what is really right according to international law, according to history, according to human values. So a Palestinian is [a] fighter for human rights and human values and [is the one] who will laugh at the end by achieving much of what we hope for right now. (Interview with DFLP sympathiser, 28 September 1994)

An emphasis on 'right' was even more explicit among the opposition than mainstream/official Fateh-dominated nationalism. Palestinian nationalism was thus an ideology of being 'right'. If Zionism was an ideology of the 'chosen people', Palestinianism was an ideology of the 'rightful people'. Connection with the land implied a perceived non-negotiable right, which also provided an imperative to fight. The 'struggle' would go on until what was 'right' was achieved.

The late 1990s phase of negotiations is also frequently described in terms of struggling: 'we continue to struggle, but in a peaceful way', 'the struggle of peace', 'the struggle of negotiations'. In Arabic, the peace process is sometimes referred to as 'the peace operation' (*amaliyyat al-salam*) (see Jayyusi, 1998: 210). It is not only a movement, the PLO or al-Fateh, which is to be transformed from a revolutionary/militarised structure to a civil/administrative apparatus, but the very denotation of being Palestinian is in a transitional period. This is bound to have consequences for people's feeling of meaning in life and sense of security and placement in time and space.

Struggle as the main representation of Palestinian-ness is also why Yasir Arafat still uses a revolutionary rhetorical style in many of his speeches. As an example, at a memorial ceremony in 1995, Arafat said: 'All of us are willing to be martyrs on our way to Jerusalem – the capital of Palestine . . . In the end, we will fly the Palestinian flag over the walls of Jerusalem' (*Jerusalem Post*, 15 January 1995). Such speeches put Israeli commentators on high alert and are immediately interpreted by Israel as a PLO and Palestinian determination *actually* to fight violently for Jerusalem, although they could be interpreted as part of an ideological and politico-cultural discourse on identity. They are part of a communicative style intended to place Palestinian national identity in time and space. There is still Jerusalem to fight for, *ergo* the significance of the struggling Palestinian is still valid. Furthermore, a struggle which is to take place through political/diplomatic means was dressed in a violent rhetoric.

Arafat's Independence Day speech of 15 November 1996 fed into this discourse on the continued struggle:

> You hold fast to the peace, the peace of the brave, and the peace process, and you sacrifice for its continuation and its stabilisation, and you place yourselves in the face of the world in your true and radiant picture, for you are the fighters, the fighters for peace. (Quoted in Jayyusi, 1998: 197)

'We decided to put an end [to] the past and we are trying to build a new Palestinian era by negotiations with the Israelis,' said one Fateh member. Struggle as the basis of Palestinian identity therefore found itself in a dilemma. On the one hand, there was no alternative notion with a similar potency to counter Palestinian vulnerability and insecurity (why 'struggle' had to prevail as the prime representation of Palestinianism). On the other hand, 'struggle' did not have the capacity to encapsulate the new era. Thus 'struggle' was in a process of being fulfilled. The period of interim self-rule marked not only an abrupt rupture between two kinds of situation, occupation and self-rule, but also a dramatic shift between two modes of identifying oneself as a Palestinian – the struggler and the state-builder. Still, the picture was too unclear and by 1993–98 the change had not yet been made; the Palestinian movement and the Palestinians found themselves between these two situations, causing disjunction and insecurity and a *crisis of identity*. This crisis was enlarged by the deadlock in the peace process during the first years of the Netanyahu era in Israel (1996–98), when little progress was being made but there was no possibility of falling back on either revolution or *intifada*, despite proud proclamations that everything was possible and that the *intifada* could be reactivated.

To 'suffer'

The struggle also requires suffering and sacrifice:

> I have suffered a lot and sacrificed a lot for Palestine. I have lost my brother, my cousin, four of my uncles, all because of Palestine. (Interview with Fateh activist, 26 August 1994)

> I am proud to be a Palestinian, even though it is very difficult to be a Palestinian in this stage. In this century, or in this time. Because being a Palestinian means to suffer, to be refused all over the world. (Interview with Fateh activist, 22 April 1995)

Loss of family members is *because* of Palestine. 'Suffering' as a structuring principle for identity may be found among other collective identities of minorities and diaspora populations. The image of the 'Palestinian' produced in political messages, the culture of martyrs, pictures in newspapers and magazines of the Palestinian prototype carrying a weapon, poetry, folk culture, songs and graffiti of someone who struggles, who fights, who resists – activities which are all bound to result in suffering – have had a profound impact. A Palestinian 'is' someone who resists, either with a kalashnikov or an RPG in the squalid camps of Lebanon, or with stones and Molotov cocktails in Gaza, and/or someone who suffers because of dispossession, longing, injustice and death. 'Struggle' and 'suffering' were *because* of being Palestinian, but it was also in the action of 'struggling' and 'suffering' the Palestinian identity was reconstructed in 'pride' and 'dignity':

> If I close my eyes and think of Palestine, I think of disasters, but I cannot be outside this circle. To be a Palestinian is to wait and have the steadfastness of waiting although you are seeing so many things that are wrong, and yet not say that this is the end. It is to be very sensitive and very militant at the same time. It is to have hope always. Because the people made an *intifada*. I have the hope in this people that they will have another *intifada*. (Interview with PFLP sympathiser, 29 October 1994)

This woman brought in a new dimension of Palestinian identity; it was to be *sensitive* and to be able to be touched by the Palestinian destiny. It was not to shy away from militant struggle and to be sensitive to what it might cause. Palestine was equated with 'disasters'. To be a Palestinian was to live disasters, but also to have 'steadfastness' and to be waiting, to be 'patient' and not give up; it was to have hope and to endure.

'Hope' as part of Palestinian identity is another strategy to counter processes of victimisation and feelings of powerlessness (Jørund Lønning, 1998: 163 f.). In circumstances of utmost misery, there is no alternative to hoping for better days. Such hopes are manifested in ideas about the bright future, a special kind of optimism. Jørund Lønning (1998) asserts that Palestinian support for the Oslo process is to be read within such a narrative on hopes for the future.

Identities in negotiation

Although many of the above meanings of Palestinian identity are common to the political factions, it is more appropriate to talk of Palestinian identities than identity and nationalisms than nationalism. There are ceaseless negotiations and internal bargaining processes on the meaning of identity. The various ideological streams represented in the factions have given rise to competing concepts of identity. In addition, regional, religious, class, 'inside' versus 'outside' and gender identities criss-cross with Palestinian identity to form a complicated pattern of threads and patches. However, all the factions still relate in one sense or another to Arabism.

Remnants of Arabism

Palestinian discourse is bitterly disappointed with the Arab states and lack of Arab unity. As in 1967, when the Palestinians embarked upon the road of revolution, resistance and armed struggle in response to Arab failure to come to their rescue, and like the *intifada* partly a response to the Arab League's neglect of the PLO at the summit of 1987, the 1993 decision officially to break the rhetorical ranks of Arab unity and sign a bilateral treaty with Israel can partly be seen as the result of again concluding that Arab regimes and the notion of 'Arab unity' would not act to the benefit of the Palestinians. 'Arab' constitutes a particular form of 'other'.

> The Arab countries after the Gulf War became not brother countries, they became enemies. The year of 1992 is the date of the defeat of Arab nationalism. The Palestinian question, which had been seen as an Arab question and a question for the world, now became a question for the Palestinians only, and not a question for the Arab brothers and even Muslim brothers. We became simply alone in the world. (Interview with Fateh activist, 18 September 1994)

Relations with the Arab world, and particularly with Jordan, remain an important factor in Palestinian political debate. Perceptions of these relationships change, however, according to contextual transformations and specific events and circumstances. Although it is doubtless the case that Palestinian national identity clearly distinguishes itself from Arab identity, this does not preclude a more pragmatic view within some Fateh circles that the most beneficial long-term solution is a confederation with Jordan.[3] In the autumn of 1995, after the signing of the Interim Agreement, new discussions on a confederation were held, although relations between the PNA and Jordan have been fluctuating, reaching a low with the peace agreement between Israel and Jordan (26 October 1994) and the acknowledgement of 'Jordan's role' in Jerusalem. Benyamin Netanyahu's period in office witnessed a thaw in Jordanian–PNA relations, although the release of Sheikh Ahmed Yasin seemed to downplay Arafat and the PNA.

The leftist factions, the PFLP and DFLP, still advocate an identity to a certain extent influenced by 'belongingness' to the broader Arab category. For the Marxist–Leninist fronts, the struggle for Palestine is first and foremost a *class* struggle, although this understanding is undergoing change. Although much of this discourse is today obsolete, the relationship between Palestinianism and Arabism remains a problem for the fronts.

> The 1990s are not the 1960s or 50s. We are in a very different era that is based on isolation of countries and peoples. So if, in the past, the common[4] thing was the first, and the particular[5] was the second, in the 1970s, 80s and 90s, it's the particular that takes the first priority. Do not expect us to think nation-wise, I mean pan-Arabism, while the Arabs are ignoring the Palestinians. They are the reason for our suffering. So our reaction to these regimes is unlimited. And when it comes to the real analysis, we Palestinians, we cannot live without the Arab countries. We cannot live without Jordan, we cannot live without Lebanon, without Syria,

> without Egypt. But when it comes to their way, how they behave, how they treat us, how they deal with us, it's almost impossible for us to admit being part of them. Even in spite of all these facts, we are Arabs, we are part of the Arab world. (Interview with DFLP sympathiser, 28 September 1994)

'It's almost impossible for us to admit being part of them,' and yet, in an organic view of nations, 'we are part of the Arab world'. The Palestinians were part of Arab-ness, but it was almost shameful to be an Arab, since the Arabs were perceived as those who had deserted the general, *al-'amm*. Self-image became complicated in this relationship, since the 'Arabs' were both 'others' and part of 'self'. To be a Palestinian was also to be an Arab, but yet to be differentiated from Arabs. The Arab states had inflicted an immense amount of suffering on the Palestinians, yet Palestinians and Arabs were organically linked to each other. The deep distrust and disappointment over Arab betrayals coexisted with a conviction that general and particular must be reunited.

PFLP/DFLP oppositional nationalism revealed a great deal of ambiguity in its views on Arabism and the Arab world, on the one hand rejecting being Arab and on the other feeling integral 'belongingness'. Some rejected it completely while others embraced it. Yet another category fell in between, despising the Arab regimes while recognising unbreakable links between the 'Arab nation' and the 'Palestinian people'. The relationship between 'Arab' and 'Palestinian' was even more complicated for the leftist opposition than for mainstream nationalism.

> Never ever were we like the Arab countries. It's the other way around. All our problems were left in . . . Arab hands for many years. So we have the heritage of being more Arab than anything else. We were first Arabs and then Palestinians. We tried to be Arabs and Palestinians on equal footing for two decades, the 60s and 70s. From the mid 1980s, and especially after Beirut, we started to be first Palestinians. First Palestinians, and then Arabs. And now it might be Palestinians first, Palestinians second, Arabs third. But in the Arab world, they are Kuwaitis first and second until ten. In 1982, *khallas*,[6] there was no way to be equally Arabs and Palestinians, we are first Palestinians. (Interview with DFLP sympathiser, 28 September 1994)

Palestinian leftism identified itself as both Arab and anti-Arab. Negative perceptions of 'Arabs' and the Arab world were *part* of the Palestinian self, and of the negative sides of selfhood and identity.

Identity betrayed

In leftist discourse there is in relation to the peace process a rejection of the notion of 'building' and instead a sense of betrayal and defeat which acts detrimentally to prospects for a common national identity. The DOP and its consequences are seen as disruptive, fragmentary and a betrayal of the cause and of identity.

> I don't know how we define Palestinian nationalism. When you are deceived, betrayed [by] your closest friends, allies, brothers, your own people, that gives no room for sticking to a certain definition of Palestinian nationalism. . . . I think we lost that. After what happened, this defeat, I wonder who can really give a definition. (Interview with PFLP sympathiser, 7 October 1994)

The retreat from Palestinianism is a rather bitter retreat, a defensive mechanism. 'Since Palestinianism has led only to "Oslo", what is the use of it?' is the rationale. Perceived betrayal gives rise to mounting internal disputes on identity and further emphasis on action.

> I should really say that a Palestinian [is somebody] who has Palestine in the heart, and not Palestine by birth. There are a lot of Palestinians by birth, who proved to be hostile against Palestine, either who were collaborators or people who fight for their own interests. And there are others who were not born in Palestine, [but] are Palestinians by heart, Palestinians by cause, proven to be more trusting and more committed than [those who are] Palestinians [by birth], so I cannot exclude them from being Palestinians, no. They should be Palestinians before the others. So my definition of Palestinians is a Palestinian who lives in this Palestinian ship in his heart and he feels part of it, he feels commitment for the cause. That's a Palestinian. (Interview with PFLP sympathiser, 7 October 1994)

It is not 'birth' which defines Palestinian identity, but the one who has 'Palestine in the heart', that is, a commitment, a dedication, an action. This situation fostered an even more action-oriented notion of identity than that embedded in the image of the struggling Palestinian. In this definition, it was not 'birth' which defined Palestinian identity, but *commitment to the cause*. Those who merely struggled for their own interests were not really Palestinians. This was a non-primordialist perception, stressing not only activism but devotion as the ultimate common denominator. Of course, this was also a highly politicised notion. Those who had 'betrayed Palestine' were less Palestinian. This was a subtle but clear indication towards those who were behind and supported the Oslo negotiations, whose Palestinian-ness was reduced and questioned. Internal 'betrayal' had led to a decline of Palestinian-ness; the 'family' had proved to include 'traitors'. Naturally, this had political connotations in the sense that PFLP leaders had an interest in claiming that leadership negotiations had led to a reduction of Palestinian-ness. Nevertheless, this indicates the extent to which Palestinian identities are non-coherent, vulnerable, disputed and in constant motion.

> Even our flag is empty now. Our flag which was something holy. Many, many kids died when they were carrying this flag and putting it metre by metre against the Israeli soldiers, and then they shot them, they were killed. They were not even

throwing stones, they were just putting the small flag. Someone was killed when he was obliged to remove the flag from the electricity lines. Now this flag is empty, because it is just moving in the Palestinian air in the Gaza Strip, but for nothing. We have nothing. (Interview with DFLP sympathiser, 18 May 1995)

The flag had been used by *intifada* fighters; it had been tossed on to the power lines with the help of stones, it had been used to cover the bodies of 'martyrs' – the flag had been stained with the 'blood of martyrs'. When forbidden, the flag symbolised self-reliance and defiance. It was a marker or a symbol of the denied Palestinian identity. When the flag as a symbol was recognised, however, it was not recognised in the way that the Palestinians had intended and imag- ined. Ironically, now that the flag was legitimate, allowed, co-opted into official nationalism and the power structure, it had lost much of its previous symbolic meaning. This is also observed by Salim Tamari:

> Forbidden during Israeli occupation it became a potent expression of defiance, and symbol of mass mobilisation, it was hoisted with great pride and fanfare on the eve of the Oslo Agreement, and again when Israeli troops made their withdrawal from Gaza and Jericho in August . . . [A] [f]ew months later the Palestinian flag lies forsaken and virtually ignored, with its green margins turning into dusty blue from the double exposure of the sun and benign neglect. Aside from the PNA no single political party today uses the flag as its own banner, and no attempts are made by the opposition parties to 'save' the flag from what they see as its defilement through territorial concessions made by Arafat. (Tamari, 1995: 11)

The Palestinian flag, once proudly connected with a struggling and suffering identity, no longer provided the symbolism of resistance, as it had been taken over by official nationalism and, as such, recognised internationally and by the Israelis. A symbol of non-power and aspiration could not easily be transformed into a legitimate symbol of power. Those symbols could not represent a half measure.

Islam, nationalism and identity: 'Islam is the main thing'

Islamism represents a competing concept of identity which is today more powerful than the Arabist-inspired concept. Although Hamas still stresses the importance of *umma*, its rhetoric is also filled with references to *wataniyya*, patriotism and to the territory of Palestine which is given sacred meaning, as outlined in Chapter 3.

The Palestinian people is defined as 'Muslim', but in many other ways, Islamist discourse shares the notions of mainstream Palestinian nationalism in the form of resistance, struggle and steadfastness. The main difference is that religion provides meaning and identity in the sense that Islam and religion provide the answer to the existential human query 'Why do I live?'

What's life? Why do I live? How can you prove that life is better than death? A good person dies, and a bad person dies, they're going to end up [in] soil. So life is meaningless without religion. So being Palestinian or non-Palestinian, that isn't [important]. There are other causes which make people close to me, just like relationships. As far as I am Palestinian, all Palestinians relate to me, but whoever carr[ies] the Islamic idea is closer to me than people who just relate to me. So there are some people that I have duties for like father, brother, wife, neighbour, Palestinian, a human being, Arab Palestinian, just like circles. The Palestinian circle is very important, we share many things that make us close to each other. We respect the nationalism. (Interview with Islamist sympathiser, 19 October 1994)

A reason for living is found in Islam. Islam provides guiding principles for action, norms and values. Like many other Islamic leaders, this man described his identity in terms of 'circles', and the most important circle was Islam. Islam was perceived as the total system which encompassed all of these other identities. In this mode of representation, identities were like Chinese boxes. The most important 'circle' was Islam, since it had the potentiality of including the rest. Theoretically, this mode of reasoning adds little to our understanding of identities, since there *are* no neat circles or boxes or levels through which to describe or analyse identities. Rather, identities are 'hyphenated' constructions, connecting with each other in a much more unsystematic and unstructured way than neatly bounded and easily definable categories. Identities could be defined in terms of fragments, patches and shreds woven together in some ends, while some ends are closed and others open towards the outside, existing not as levels of orders or systems but as juxtapositions. From the point of view of actors, however, attempts to describe identities in such terms, as circles or levels, become more understandable. From an actor's point of view, there are needs to create order in chaos, to position oneself. Although identities are frag-mented and de-centred, identities describe themselves in terms of wholeness and unification (Hall, 1992: 287). The hierarchisation of identities in this way is also part of politics.

I am a Muslim Arab Palestinian person, Muslim Arab Palestinian. Because what is [most] important to me is not this life. It is when I meet God. When I meet God, he will not ask me about my nationality, He will ask me if I am a Muslim or not, if I made good things or bad things. If you are not Muslim, OK, you are Christian, but if you did a bad thing or good thing, we have your code, your programme, your file. You made this and this and you are not a Palestinian or Syrian or French or Swedish or American. He will ask you about your belief. (Interview with Islamic Jihad sympathiser, 19 January 1995)

In a hierarchisation of identities, Islam is more important because what ultimately counts is not this life, but life after death, 'when I meet God'. God will not ask about nationality, but about faith and about deeds. Nationality remains a worldly affair, not relevant to the higher meanings of after-life.

I am proud to be a Palestinian, to be a Palestinian is [to be] a courageous people, and a people who is not ashamed. This is a good people who want their liberty and who do not accept to live like animals. But I am more proud to be a Muslim. I am a Muslim before anything. A Palestinian is someone who doesn't accept less than his rights, he didn't accept to have his territories taken and then leave, to be refugees or all these things. And this is what is good. But what is better is to be a Muslim. (Interview with Islamic Jihad sympathiser, 19 January 1995)

There is pride in Palestinian identity, because of Palestinian courage and Palestinian refusal to give up resistance and Palestinian pride. A Palestinian is someone who does not give in to wrongs done to them, 'this is a militant people', and here is the same discourse on the 'struggling Palestinians' as in other trends. To 'struggle' was part of a joint reading of a politicised Palestinian national identity. There was, however, debate over what the struggle should contain. 'The Palestinian identity means the homeland. The homeland in which I was born, and where my grandfather lived and where my sons will live' (interview with Islamic Jihad leader, 24 November 1994). To Islamists, the Palestinian aspect of identity also represented homeland (*watan*) and here was no rejection of *watan* and patriotic nationalism. *Wataniyya* could be included in an *umma* of believers, just as *watan* could be part of *qawm* to the Arabists. Islamism in a Palestinian context has, however, a clear territorial/ spatial component. The geographical entity is Palestine, which should be liberated not by Palestinians alone but through a common effort of a Muslim collectivity, given Palestine's pre-eminence in Islamic belief. There is a strong connection between nationalism/patriotism and Islam. '*Wataniyya* is not everything, but it is something for Islam. Islam is the sea, *wataniyya* the river' (interview with Islamist sympathiser, 7 May 1995). To be Palestinian was not only to be right, but to represent the universal 'good'. To be Palestinian was to exist at the crossroads between 'good' and 'evil', to 'exist' at an existential edge. 'To be a Palestinian is to live in the place which is the essence of universal conflict. Conflict between good and evil is at its maximum in Palestine. To stand in the line of good' (interview with Islamic Jihad sympathiser, 18 May 1995). The conflict involved universal issues; it was not only related to Palestinians and Israelis, but carried an holistic dimension. It was ultimately a conflict between good and evil, where to be Palestinian represented not only to be 'right' but also to be 'good'. Palestinians and Muslims were fighting for higher values than just the liberation of Palestine; they were representing the good of humankind.

The PNA: official nationalism: 'We don't have a magic stick'

One aspect of identity discourses is perceptions of internal relations. When accounting for a new political system, the political elite is either critical or defensive. The transformation causes stress on both the leadership and the population.

> I think we are going through one of the most difficult transformations [ever]. In April 1994, Palestinians threw stones at Israeli soldiers. On 13 May 1994, they saw joint Palestinian–Israeli patrols in the street. So we have to identify the difficulties that we face on the ground [concerning] the transformation within the Palestinian community, within Palestinian political life, we will never be the same. Secondly, we face the disastrous situation of what's left, what the Israelis left behind them. It's total devastation. We don't have an economy. [. . .] So we are starting from scratch. And we don't have a magic stick. And there is a huge mountain as high as Mount Everest entitled 'Things that must be done'. So we work twenty-four hours a day, seven days a week. So the piles of things done compared with the huge piles to be done will always look very small, very little in the eyes of the common Palestinian who has very high expectations. (Interview with PNA minister, 3 February 1995)

'We don't have a magic stick' was a frequently used metaphor to describe the difficulties the PNA was having in implementing projects and policies. Given the perception of being at point zero in history, it would take time to get the state-building process organised. A problem from the point of view of the Authority was the high popular expectations.

Among many outside the PNA, there was in the first year a 'wait and see' attitude. There was not complete satisfaction, but it was argued that the PNA should be given some respite; it should be given a chance to prove itself.

> [The performance of the PNA is] not as it should be. And it's not as bad as some people expected. So on the one hand, it's better than many people . . . expected, and on the other hand, it's still not on the level where you feel things are OK. I have a lot of criticism towards this authority, but knowing the very difficult conditions they are working under I find some excuses for what is happening, though there are things for which there are no excuses. (Interview with Fateh sympathiser, 26 October 1994)

Concerning relations between the PNA and PLO, there was confusion. What was the role of the PLO when most of its high-ranking officials had moved inside? The agreements had been signed by the PLO, which was thus ultimately responsible for the implementation of the agreements, and ultimately also for the PNA. Part of the PLO still remained outside, however. Furthermore, when the Executive Committee convened in Gaza in November 1994 (the first time ever on Palestinian soil), only nine out of eighteen delegates attended. In another Executive Committee meeting, held in Cairo in February 1995, the outcome was the same. In mid March 1995, the Executive Committee met again, this time in Tunis, a place more acceptable to the oppositional elements, and eleven out of eighteen delegates attended. Following the Interim Agreement

of September 1995, the Executive Committee met in Cairo, with seven delegates in attendance. The PLO was split and divided and its very existence was
questioned.

The PNA was created by the PLO, but only half of the members of the
Executive Committee agreed with its function and mandate. What was also confusing was the fact that the PLO was still defined as a 'liberation' organisation,
while the PNA was an 'administrative authority'. The function and *raison d'être*
of the two organisations were fundamentally different, and even contradictory.

Leftism and the PNA: 'It is so limited, so poor, so bad'

In leftist perceptions of the PNA – the representatives of power – deep resentment was revealed, particularly in 1994 and 1995. The PNA represented those
who had broken Palestinian ranks of unity and betrayed the cause.

> I don't think that they have a possibility or a chance to be qualified as [an authority].
> You have individuals that run authorities as they can, but it's not a matter of
> qualification. I think it is so limited, so poor, so bad, and the only thing operating
> in the country is the five bodies, instruments of security. And the rest of the
> Palestinian Authority is just trying to follow the instructions of the one-man regime
> and the five different security instruments. (Interview with DFLP sympathiser,
> 21 September 1994)

The Palestinian Authority was portrayed as completely unqualified. In opposition politics, the 'Palestinian Authority'[7] was based upon the preconditions of
fragmentation. Hence the Authority was void of national(ist) legitimacy. All
political strands were, however, affected by statist logic and the dominance of
state-building discourse. For the Marxist fronts, this was shown in a gradual
turning inwards in the redefinition of the struggle and in a newborn focus on
politics, governance and civil society:

> Now we have two kinds of struggle. There is the national struggle against the
> occupation, and the second is the democratic struggle, it means the struggle [against]
> the Palestinian Authority. The components of the democratic struggle are to
> struggle for the Palestinian independent civil society. [Regarding] the Authority
> itself, [we should] work with the Authority, according to the principle that the
> main relation with the Authority is related to contradiction, not cooperation. The
> problem is here how to try to avoid civil war. Our struggle against the occupation
> will be with all means [but] our struggle against the Authority will be in political,
> peaceful ways and through mobilising people without violence. But if we are fought
> against by the Authority, we will defend ourselves. (Interview with PFLP sym-
> pathiser, 27 September 1994)

With the Palestinian leadership cooperating with the 'other'/the enemy, then
to be a real Palestinian, or better Palestinian, must be to contradict also the

leadership, at least in the aspects in which the Authority was now connected to the leadership. This change is part and parcel of internal bargaining on identity. Adding to the national externally oriented struggle was now an internally oriented, anti-authoritarian struggle. 'Struggle' took on a new meaning. For Fateh, the new struggle was for democracy within the system, whereas for the left, struggle would now imply democratic and popular struggle against the system.

The Authority was seen as having been established because of, and in relation to, the occupation, and not as a structure opposed to occupation. Therefore, it was devoid of legitimacy.

> The Authority has no power to improve these things; to the contrary, it will sink even [further] down, and time will come, this is really [an] historical process, it's a revolution, time will come. Now, the Popular Front and others can accelerate that time, so people can stand up and can initiate [a] new *intifada*, [the] same way that they initiated the *intifada* against the occupation; this time they will initiate a new *intifada* against tyranny, against lack of democracy, against violation of human rights, against totalitarianism, against arbitrary detention, against monopoly, against many things. We are heading towards real dictatorship. (Interview with PFLP leader, 7 October 1994)

There was a strongly value-laden discourse on the Authority. Negative aspects of the process were believed to lead to mobilisation for a new uprising. The PFLP and other forces could accelerate the process through mobilisation, but in the PFLP way of analysing, using a kind of historical materialism and revolutionary discourse, it was inevitable. The use of the *intifada* gives the impression of a continuation of an endless Palestinian struggle against occupation and repression from whatever source. If repression were now to come from the Palestinian Authority, then the opposition would struggle against this Authority in the same way that the Palestinians resisted the British, the Jordanians and the Israelis.

> This Authority has the same way of lying as the Arab regimes. [. . .] The Palestinian people were convinced, this is something in the psychology of the Palestinian people that they are superior from the other Arab countries. . . . but it seems from the implementation that we are not superior, we are the same. (Interview with PFLP sympathiser, 27 September 1994)

The Authority was the 'same' as the Arab regimes; the ultimate disappointment for Palestinians, always claiming to be 'different' from the Arab states, and always claiming that whenever a Palestinian state was established, it would be the first democracy in the Arab world.

The opposition paid particular attention to the strong police and security apparatus. The PNA had a deal with Israel, implying an end to violence between the two parties. At the same time, the internal opposition still advocated armed struggle against Israel.[8] The dilemma of the opposition was how to deal with a new security apparatus, this time set up by their 'own people', while involved in what they perceived as a legitimate struggle against occupation.

> It's very hard for us to believe that still we have to suffer the same, or even more, and this time not by the Israeli occupation, but by other Palestinians who are supposed to be our brothers. We know that being killed or arrested by the enemy, by the occupation, is because we are doing something good to [our] own people and [our] own country, so it is considered as the normal and straightforward price for you to oppose the enemy and the occupation, but to suffer from those who are supposed to be you is not easy to believe. (Interview with DFLP sympathiser, 28 September 1994)

On the one hand, the opposition was Palestinian, like the Authority they were opposing. But this relationship of authority–opposition, combined with the fact that the Authority had not only been granted the legitimate use of violence but was also under external pressure to use it against the opposition, was exceedingly complicated. Thus they used to be 'the same', 'brothers' in the same cause, although with different approaches and strategies. Now they were posed against each other, and social boundaries were reordered. Intricate relations between 'us' and 'them' were also underlined; to be Palestinian was to be against the Israelis. To the Palestinian opposition, the newborn alliance between Israel and the Palestinian Authority represented a decline of Palestinian-ness and a surrender. Therefore, no longer was the cause the same, and therefore the PNA and the opposition suggested different collective entities and identities. They used to have the same enemy, but this was no longer as certain. No longer could it be argued that Palestinian rule was different and 'better' than Israeli or Arab rule.

Opposition against the Authority thrived on the concept of 'collaborators', and the opposition compared the Authority to Antoine Lahad, the commander of the South Lebanon Army, who was in cooperation with the IDF. Collaborators were trespassers and to accuse the Authority of collaborating was naturally a powerful symbol.

Despite all assurances of non-cooperation with the Authority, according to Walid Salem (interview, 13 June 1995) there was a decision by the PFLP's Political Bureau in June 1994 to allow employment in the Authority but not to participate in political decisions. According to PFLP-affiliated personnel, this decision was to a large extent based on a socioeconomic rationale that DFLP/PFLP members should also have access to new employment opportunities. PFLP members were, for example, allowed by the factional leadership to work in the civil police, but not in the intelligence or security forces (interview with PFLP sympathiser, 13 June 1995).

Although still very critical, the leftist factions were in 1997 more empathically oriented *vis-à-vis* the Authority than during the early years of self-rule.

This surely had something to do with the change in Israeli government. As the peace process went into a low gear in 1997 and 1998, the Palestinian opposition also found it possible to agree with the Authority on some points. 'Even though I am a person who is critical of the Authority['s] performance and behaviour, sometimes I find certain excuses for the Authority which are connected with the situation' (interview with PFLP leader, 10 October 1997).

The leftist factions were also bitter concerning the PLO:

> I used to fight for the PLO, to go to prison for the PLO, and to shout wherever I go for the PLO. Our people died because of the PLO and went to prison because of the PLO, [and] the PLO used to represent for us the hope, the future, the national rights, the liberation movement, that is the PLO. To liberate Palestine, that is to say, the right to return, the right to self-determination and the right to establish an independent Palestinian state. So for me, the PLO that I know, that I identify with, that I fight for, that I was ready to die for, does not exist any more. And anybody who says, well this is the PLO, in other words the autonomy, I want to shoot that autonomy. (Interview with DFLP sympathiser, 28 September 1994)

The PLO was no longer legitimate, as the current leadership had 'sold out' both territory and principles, both 'right' and 'struggle'. There was deep bitterness in the above remarks. The sacrifice of the people had reaped nothing but betrayal. The whole foundation of the PLO as the embodiment of Palestinian-ness had crumbled through the making of the PLO itself, and the PLO could no longer represent Palestinian identity. If there was no more struggle, then the legitimacy of the PLO could be questioned in 1994–95.

Islamism and the Authority: 'If they don't succeed, there are people to fill the gaps'

Ambiguity also prevailed concerning Hamas's perceptions of internal Palestinian politics. Some Islamist leaders were more conciliatory when it came to assessments of the Authority than were the leftists. According to this position, the Authority was a fact that could not be denied.

> I am a Muslim man, and the Palestinian government, they are like us, they are Palestinian and Muslim people, and we have the same history and the same religion and the same aim. There is no difference between any Palestinian people. We don't want to make problems to any Palestinian people, because we are the same people. (Interview with Islamist sympathiser, 7 May 1995)

The Authority was 'like us', and there was no reason to have differences, 'we are the same people'. When criticism was raised, however, it was much the same as that voiced by the PFLP/DFLP and critiques within the Fateh movement: 'Everything is in the hand of Arafat. Nothing can be done except by the hand of Arafat. Through this monopoly, you can't expect to create a new system. . . . There is social and moral deterioration. We have a lot of manifestations of corruption' (interview with Hamas leader, 11 January 1995). Although many asserted that it was not their intention to enter into opposition to the Authority, the concentration of power in the hands of Arafat was cited as the main problem. According to many Islamist-leaning figures, the Islamic movements did not aim to hinder the Authority, but merely to prove that it was not pursuing its duties as it should. The approach was rather one of letting the Authority prove itself. However, Islamist discourse, more openly than leftism, challenged the Authority's regime. One leading Islamist thinker said, 'If they don't succeed, then there are people to take over, and to fill the gaps' (interview, 19 October 1994). There was an explicit warning: if the Authority did not get its act together, there were people to fill its place; that is, Hamas was directly challenging the PNA over who would be the better leader.

> There is no performance at all. At all. The price of everything is high. Nobody is able to say yes or no, except Arafat. Ask Arafat . . . I think Arafat's attitude now became more hostile against the Palestinian Islamic side than before. (Interview with Hamas leader, 11 January 1995)

> They are responsible about all the corruption and the absence of democracy. So they are responsible for all the misery of the Palestinians. What they should do, they have to change their attitude, but according to my mind it is impossible for them, because they actually practised corruption, practised this absence of democracy among the PLO system for more than thirty-five years. So it's impossible for those people to change their minds and become more democratic. It's actually hopeless. (Interview with Hamas leader, 15 October 1997)

Many Islamist leaders rejected the performance of the Authority as completely incapable (e.g. interview with Hamas leader, 19 January 1995). It would, however, be possible to cooperate with the Authority in the fields of education and civil matters. In 1998, two years after the inauguration of the PLC, Hamas still remained outside the political structure (with the exception of those Hamas-affiliated who were elected to the Council) and opposed to the peace process. However, it also continued its path of multifaceted strategies, consisting of occasional violence against Israel, criticism of the Authority and some kind of accommodation with the Authority. Again, dogma and practice diverge.

The on-and-off dialogue between the Authority and Hamas indicates that the Authority did not wish to upset the Islamist position, but rather to appease it, co-opt it and bring it into the power structure so as to diminish its scope for opposition and criticism. A National Dialogue Committee was set up in order to smooth internal tensions. Statements made by Hamas leaders could be seen as an indication of accommodation to the situation and of cooperation with the Authority. Considering the history of Hamas, with a comparatively brief experience of militant activism and focus on the basic function of social and moral values (see especially Milton-Edwards, 1996), the movement back to a refocus on the Islamisation of Palestinian society should not be surprising – as pointed out by scholars such as Abu-Amr (1994).

Reformism and the Authority: 'There is much to be hoped for'

Reformists voiced severe criticism of the Authority on the basis of lack of democratic principles and organisational skills.

Democratisation was felt to be an urgent need. Criticism was raised against the large bureaucratic apparatus being established, both in terms of military personnel and civil officials. There was a fear of the military sector taking over the civil sector, but this criticism was not as rhetorical as leftist opposition.

Reformists criticised the Authority for promoting self-interest through the agreements, that is, enabling themselves to 'return', to hold positions and to get support from the international donor community (interview with PPP sympathiser, 5 October 1994). The administrative apparatus was seen as a new class of *comprador* which had distanced itself from the real hopes and aspirations of the people.

> I think that the Authority is weak and it lacks strategic vision and it doesn't serve the national objectives and aspirations of the Palestinian people. And people here didn't fight for twenty-seven years, especially the last five or six years during the *intifada*, in order to end up [in] a situation that is similar to or worse than the occupation. We fast in Ramadan, and there is a saying that you shouldn't fast and end up your fasting by eating onions. Onions [are] the cheapest thing you can find. And if you fast then you have to eat something worth the fasting, and here we have been fasting for twenty-seven years, and we shouldn't end up with this onion, the Palestinian Authority. (Interview with leading PPP personality, 5 October 1994)

The long Palestinian struggle deserved a better fate than to become a captive of the PNA, which did not represent the goal of Palestinianism.

From independents there was concern about the militarised structure, but not in quite the same way as among the opposition, which on a more immediate level perceived the security apparatus as a direct threat. Reformists' concerns were to a larger extent focused on the risk of creating a military society. The civil intelligentsia should be used more. This also communicated the concern of this social stratum, and its own interest in influence and position. This stratum had been part of the 'personalities' rising to political power with the Madrid negotiations, but was sidestepped by 'Oslo'.

> I think we haven't really used our best capabilities. The only resource we have is human. But also at the same time, I know that they are working with very severe handicaps. It doesn't justify it, I keep saying that they are accountable, but they don't have sufficient authority to be sufficiently accountable. We don't need slogans any more, we have to deal with the realities of life, respect people's intelligence.

And the military focus should completely change. Unfortunately this transformation in the mentality of the revolution and national liberation movement and
the military mind-set, and working in the dark and secrecy and manipulation
and so on, has not really taken place smoothly. We need now statesmen and
women, not revolutionary people. (Interview with independent political personality,
24 February 1995)

In the above quotation, there is outright rejection of the revolution outside.
Instead, there should be investment in civic structures. There is competition between the 'class' of previously exiled revolutionaries and an internal
intelligentsia.

Internal conflicts: official nationalism: 'Hamas are our brothers'

Factionalism was now institutionalised on the level of formal authority/
'government' versus the opposition. One dilemma of the Authority was that
the opposition did not recognise its legitimacy, that is, it rejected being a 'loyal
opposition'. In practice, however, there were indications of coexistence in some
fields. Another related problem was the continued and, in terms of the number
of civilian Israelis killed, even escalated attacks against Israel. The Authority
was caught in an intricate dilemma, aspiring to peace with both Israel and
its internal opposition. Israel called on the PNA to assist in boosting Israel's
security, in practice implying a crackdown on Islamists while doing so was
dangerous in terms of internal politics. The image of the Palestinian police and
quasi-military apparatus cracking down on fellow Palestinians, or 'brothers',
was sensitive and troubled, as highlighted on 18 November 1994, when thirteen
Palestinians were shot dead by Palestinian police after Friday prayers at the
Palestine mosque.[9] The incident was named 'Sad Friday', or 'Black Friday',
adding yet another day of grievance to the Palestinian calendar of remembrance and suffering; and this time it was internally inflicted. The incident
gives rise to a number of questions concerning the factions' relations and
perceptions of each other.

From the point of view of the PNA, the dominant but challenged elite,
there was a great deal of irritation towards the opposition, which was not willing to play according to what were the structured regulations. This was to be
seen as pluralism within a unified whole.

That's the Palestinian situation, always. We, the Palestinians, like to complicate
our lives. This is the Palestinian life. This is Palestinian politics. I don't like to be so
selfish, but I can say that the Fateh movement is the most realistic, pragmatic and
serious about the Palestinian cause and the Palestinian people. It is so easy to go to
the opposition, to sleep well, to issue statements, to have some people around you,
and to walk in the street as a hero: 'I am against,' 'I'm against,' 'I'm against.' The

people will say OK. But this is not the way, this is not in the interests of the people. (Interview with PNA minister and member of Fateh, 21 February 1995)

It is easy to be against, but more difficult to be realistic and to take responsibility for authority and governance. Thus Fateh was the responsible part and the part which acted according to the true interests of the people. Therefore, Fateh was the 'better' representative of Palestinian-ness.

Concern about the future role of Hamas was revealed, but at the same time there were attempts to conceal splits. Internal conflicts were instead described as 'political pluralism'. 'We are brothers, we are part of the same nation, they are Palestinians' (interview with PNA official and Fateh member, 10 November 1994). This statement is part of a discourse on the Palestinian nation as an extended family, with relations of brotherhood. On the one hand, the Palestinians constituted one people, one nation, one 'family', in which Hamas and Fateh, Hamas and the PNA were brothers. On the other hand, there were signs of boundary-making between 'us' and 'them'. '*They* are Palestinians,' that is, they were *also* Palestinians, like *us*, like the Fateh people or those who supported the agreement. A new 'them' was created. Thus the PNA and mainstream nationalism were in a position to define who were Palestinians. Islamists were not the *same*, they were brothers but not us, not we, not the *core* of Palestinian identity. Ghazi Jabali, head of the Palestinian Authority civil police in Gaza, dismissed the Palestinian-ness of Hamas and Islamic Jihad: 'Hamas and Islamic Jihad are not Palestinians. They belong to Iran and Jordan. I am sure about that' (*Jerusalem Post*, 22 November 1994). Palestinian-ness was thus defined according to commitment to the Palestinian cause as it was defined by the leadership. Such statements communicated that there was no room for deviant definitions of Palestinianism. *Palestinianism in its dominant, official interpretation was what defined a Palestinian*. Hence nationalism defined the nation in a very real sense. The opposition also used the agreements as a starting point for redefinitions of nationalism. To resent the agreements made you a better national in this view.

Incidents of internal disputes or violence such as 'Black Friday' are usually discussed in terms of external conspiracies. Many blamed 'someone else', external factors, for what happened on that occasion in November 1994. Disharmony, disunity and disorder were all states of affairs which stemmed from the threatening 'outside' of the boundary.

There were also warnings from the PNA that there could be only one authority in the Palestinian areas: 'We have all of us to recognise that there is only one authority. We can have many political groups, but no one in the world can build a state or build his country while there are many authorities' (interview with PNA minister and Fateh member, 18 October 1997). Stability is sought in this turbulent era, and from an Authority point of view, centralisation is crucial in order to ensure solidity. Hamas competition is seen as fragmenting and as a challenge on the level of who is most able to represent the Palestinians.

Islamist leaders tended to see the agreements as conflict-generating, although they also played down the differences and conflicts. The main enemy was still Israel. The Islamic movements had an interest in concealing Palestinian–Palestinian conflict and presenting a picture of a plural Palestinian society. Internal struggle and the risks of internal violence appeared to be a trauma for all factions. There was also a verbal consensus that such risks must be minimised:

> This issue of relations between Hamas and the Authority is dependent upon the Authority itself, not the Islamic movements. The Islamic movement policy is not to fall in clashes with the Authority and not to change their line, the confrontation line with the Israeli authority. If the Authority understands this attitude, no clashes will occur, but if it keeps going in response [to] the pressure, it will force the other parties to protect themselves. (Interview with Islamic Jihad leader, 24 November 1994)

This position was more in line with the leftist opposition when arguing that whether conflicts would occur depended on the Authority. To the Islamists, the main line of confrontation was Israel, and this they would not depart from. If the Authority continued to adhere to Israeli pressure in cracking down on the Islamic movements, then the opposition would 'protect' itself.

Rather than interpreting the conflict as being between Hamas and the Authority, Islamists argued in the same way as many of the leftist oppositional leaders: that the conflict was between the Authority and the people; that is, the Authority was not perceived as an Authority of the people. As the authoritarianism of the PNA became increasingly obvious, both leftist and Islamist opposition focused on the mismanagement and violence of PNA rule, the legitimacy of which became increasingly questioned.[10]

The Islamist movements were thus testing the ground with the Authority in order to find out how far they could go in casting themselves as the main political force in Palestinian society, continuing to base their actions and nationalism upon 'resistance' while at the same time not ruling out cooperation. The Islamist movements, particularly Hamas, showed skill in the management of brinkmanship, while at the same time having to relate to the facts of the peace process. Self-rule represented a pressing situation for the Islamic movements. How could Hamas manoeuvre as a 'resistance' movement, a 'liberation' movement, when circumstances were pushing for a completely new agenda, that is, state-building, the creation of institutions, the building of a polity, and when people's identities were confused between the sense of having given up and the urge at least to try the new setting through a new kind of struggle?

'Inside'–'outside': 'They have to change their mentality'

Another issue of internal dichotomisation and potential tension, although in a different setting altogether, is the question of 'inside' and 'outside', a dichotomy to a large extent structuring Palestinian discourse and ideas of selfhood. This pair of relations also influences politics in a number of ways. 'Inside'–'outside' is important both on the level of human relations and in terms of politics between and within movements/factions.

Among PNA ministers, there was a tendency to play down the prospect of complications between the 'inside' and 'outside'. At the same time, however, many subscribed to the commonly held view that those who came from outside had a different mentality from those who had lived under and with the occupation since 1967. Those who lived outside had lived their experience in the Arab world, under the Arab regimes which were, *par définition*, undemocratic. Palestinians in the West Bank and Gaza, on the other hand, had been exposed to Israel and internal Israeli democracy, leading them to be more democratic, and more critical. This created a gap between the two experiences.

> During twenty-seven years, we have developed in an alternative way, being exposed to Israeli democracy which has changed and influenced our behaviour. It's true that this occupation was very tough, very hard, very bad, but we saw how the Israelis behaved among themselves, they behaved in a different way, they have democracy for the Israelis and we want to have the same. Our brothers who came from outside don't understand. (Interview with Fateh representative, 26 October 1994)

Again, the concept of 'brothers' was used. 'They' who came from outside were 'our' brothers and 'we' were those who stayed 'inside'. Hierarchisation of Palestinian-ness was therefore part of the process of identity in a number of ways.

> I think that the people who are coming from outside cannot understand the facts like us, like the people here. And there are some of them considering themselves that they are the only ones who were struggling and that they have the right to govern. And they ignore the people here. I think they are wrong. Because the people here suffered during twenty-seven years in the prisons, in the jails, in the streets, in the economic situation, in everything, in education, and they were steadfast against the enemy. They stood against the Israelis, and they were making the *intifada*, and through the *intifada* the people who were outside could return back. And the people who are coming from outside, they have to change their mentality. They have to understand the psychology of the people who were suffering under the occupation and the people who revolted against everything. It's not easy to govern this people, like the Arab systems or regimes. This people believes in democracy, and exercised that in the jails. We were electing our leaders in the jails. (Interview with Fateh leader, 23 October 1994)

The revolutionary structure was built up in exile, whereas the 'inside' experience was more civic, implying that the transformation mainly relied upon the returnees. There was a dispute between the 'insiders' and the 'outsiders' about who were the better strugglers, and therefore, by implication, who were the better Palestinians. Who struggled more, who suffered more? Moreover, 'insiders' often argued that it was through the *intifada* and the inside struggle that outsiders were able to return.

> They cannot say anything in Jordan, and in Syria it's much worse. In Egypt you disappear, in Iraq there is no way to know where you are buried if you oppose the regime. So this mentality is different. We have abandoned the fears of being oppressed. We are oppressed, we are still oppressed, but we have broken the bars if you like, at least, theoretically, mentally. But we do not fear our oppressor as they do. This will need some time, because they will get infected very soon [by] the positive realities. And the system is an oppressive one, so it is very easy for them to adapt, because it is similar to Jordan, Syria, etc., to the other Arab regimes. (Interview with DFLP sympathiser, 28 September 1994)

The 'inside' leadership of all PLO factions emphasised the more democratic fabric of West Bank/Gaza society. Like Fateh respondents, PFLP/DFLP interviewees spoke about the fact that despite the oppressive system of the occupation, the West Bank and Gaza populations had rid themselves of fear.

> It's true that we still talk about ourselves that we belong to the same people, but we can't talk about people with the same backgrounds. No, we were separated for the last forty-five years. Even you notice that in the attitudes, in their way of dress, or even the talk. People who are coming from Egypt, their accent is Egyptian. They lost the Palestinian accent. So what more can you fear, if you lose your accent, through which you will be recognised immediately? Anyone that was defined as Palestinian was defined by his accent. So if you lose your accent, you lose certain important identification, national identification, and this is really happening. (Interview with PFLP leader, 7 October 1994)

In this interview there was even a slight hesitation in describing the Palestinians as the same people and nation. Divisions in backgrounds and experiences had fostered a dangerous phenomenon. Acquiring other colloquial accents was seen as a reduction of one's Palestinian-ness. Returning Palestinians had lost some of their national characteristics through which they could be identified, a process which was used politically to underline perceptions of the weakness of the peace process.

'Inside'–'outside' represents a tension on two levels: (1) regarding identity, that is, who is the better Palestinian, who has struggled and suffered more; and (2) on position and influence. 'Insiders' feel that returnees came and took positions without deserving them; returnees feel it was the other way round. For the returnees, societal transformation in the West Bank and Gaza can be as

142

disturbing an experience as for the 'insiders' watching the 'outsiders' coming back.

Exiled movements and dispersed populations face specific problems in nationalist politics. This is a general problem, not specific to the Palestinian movement. The exiled relationship with the territory is one of longing, whereas the 'inside' has a relationship of being 'steadfast' and continued connection with the land. To be 'outside' was to be absent, while 'insiders' were present on the land. These are completely different notions as regards the land, and the differences are not easily overcome when the movement is reunited. How much does the struggle of exile count among 'insiders' and vice versa? Has there been a process of accommodating different experiences during the years of division? To an exiled leadership, there is some sort of paradoxical privilege in exile. While in exile, the leadership is less questioned than when in control of territory and constituency, bringing along its varied and different experiences which are to be merged with the 'inside'. When moving from an exiled position to one of returning, the returnees also move from the situation of 'strangers' to 'homecomers' (Hannerz, 1992: 133). For both, taken-for-granted ideas and perspectives of social structures can no longer be taken for granted.

NOTES

1 See also Khader (1997) for a recent description of the border experience.
2 As part of the peace process, the PNC met in April 1996 to decide upon the inevitable change of the Palestinian Charter. The vast majority of the members voted in favour of amending the Charter in accordance with Israeli demands.
3 As agreed in the Jordanian–Palestinian Accord, Amman, 11 February 1985.
4 In Arabic *'amm*, meaning general, universal, is used in referring to *qawmiyya*, the general principle.
5 In Arabic *khass*, particular, specific, refers to *wataniyya* as the specific as opposed to the general principle.
6 In Arabic: 'enough'.
7 It is worth noting that in the terminology of the opposition, it is not the Palestinian National Authority, but the Palestinian Authority.
8 PFLP/DFLP militant activism was, despite such proud announcements, low key.
9 In August 1995, new confrontations occurred in Gaza, leaving thirty Palestinians injured.
10 In the population, trust for Cabinet ministers declined from 63 per cent in December 1996 (CPRS Poll No. 31, 22–30 December 1997) to 53 per cent in June 1998 (CPRS Poll No. 34, 25–27 June 1998).

Perceptions of the 'other'

To reiterate what we have already determined, a 'self' requires an 'other'. No identity emerges or exists in a vacuum, in the absence of significant 'others'.

> This entails the radically disturbing recognition that it is only through the relation to the Other, the relation to what it is not, to precisely what it lacks, to what has been called its *constitutive outside* that the 'positive' meaning of any term – and thus its 'identity' – can be constructed (Derrida, 1981; Laclau, 1990; Butler, 1993). Throughout their careers, identities can function as points of identification and attachment only *because* of their capacity to exclude, to leave out, to render 'outside', abjected. Every identity has at its 'margin' an excess, something more. The unity, the internal homogeneity, which the term identity treats as foundational is not a natural, but a constructed form of closure, every identity naming as its necessary, even if silenced and unspoken, other that which it 'lacks'. (Hall, 1996: 5)

If we stick to Barth's notion of ethnic and national identity as dependent on boundaries, it is important to add to this that culture in the form of collectively shared meaning also has an effect upon the boundary and vice versa. A pattern of interaction characterised by conflict obviously creates an emphasis on difference and 'otherness'. Stereotypes or fixed perceptions of the 'other' provide norms and patterns of behaviour and action. In line with Simmel (1971), 'self' and 'other', friend and foe, are the basic forms of sociation. They help to bring order in chaos; 'inside' is purity, order, truth, beauty, good and right. 'Outside' the boundary is pollution, chaos, falsity, ugliness, bad and wrong (Bauman, 1990). 'The repugnant and frightening "out there" of the enemies is, as Derrida would say, a supplement: both the addition to, and displacement of, the cosy and comforting "in here" of the friends' (Bauman, 1990: 143). If and when conflict declines, the social location of the boundary does not necessarily move, but its nature shifts. In relation to the peace process, Israelis were becoming more benign 'others'. When the stereotype changes in character, it poses problems, since it is no longer clear how to act and behave *vis-à-vis* the 'other'. Turbulence replaces the previous sense of order and harmony.

Inferiority

Palestinians were often suspicious of Israeli intentions and believed that what Israel wanted, after all, was no more than limited self-rule for parts of the West Bank and Gaza; that Israel was finally implementing the part on Palestinian autonomy of the Camp David Accords; and that it was reorganising the occupation using Palestinians in manipulating and dividing the Palestinian leadership. In this primarily oppositional discourse, the DOP was the outcome of Israeli calculations and conspiracies. Many tended to see the Israelis as having a detailed grand plan or scheme which they were going to implement to its finest detail. Among supporters of the peace process, however, the relationship was thought to be more complex. One could not fully trust the Israelis, yet the 'objective circumstances' would open the way to mutual understanding. There was also suspicion and distrust among political representatives with relations with the Israelis through participation in negotiations. Formal recognition on an official level had thus yet to break and change enemy images and mutual distrust.

> The Israelis are still seeking this kind of peace equation where they can continue settlements, continue [to be occupiers] and at the same time have peace. And that's the irony in the Israeli thinking. In peace-making, you must picture a win–win situation. That's the essence in any agreement. The Israelis are still thinking a lose–win situation, the Israelis are still thinking in the mentality of occupiers, not in the mentality of those who signed an agreement. So unless the Israelis divorce themselves from this way of thinking, I don't think that we will ever reach a peace treaty. (Interview with PNA minister, 3 February 1995)

The basic problem in the negotiations was perceived as Israeli arrogance. There was an ambiguity in terms of Israeli goals, creating insecurity on the Palestinian side. Such insecurity further fed into feelings of subordination, since Israel's unwillingness to define its intentions clearly might indicate a hidden agenda. A predefined inferiority informed interpretations of Israeli intentions in the sense that, since Israel was strong and the Palestinians weak, Israeli motives and intentions must be contrary to Palestinian aspirations. There was thus a mixture of pessimism in the short run and optimism in the long run, called 'pessoptimism' by Palestinian author Habibi (1989) or, expressed differently, distrust in the Israelis, but trust in history.

> So you have to have patience, first of all, to work with them, and you have to be a politician to go through with them, and to know what you want and to continue to ask for it. And that's how we can work with the Israelis. The Israelis are not easy. You cannot get more out of them. Because I know them. (Interview with independent, former PNC member, 14 November 1994)

Israel was seen as still clinging to the land through a continuation of the occupation. Since this was not internationally acceptable, Israel was, according to many, in the process of camouflaging it. This suspicion again increased with the election of the Netanyahu government.

In the interviews, the Israelis were portrayed as being smart and cunning, and as able to run the course of events in the direction they preferred, which was, needless to say, perceived to be to the disadvantage of the Palestinians. The Israelis represented the superior with whom the Palestinians were endlessly comparing themselves. If Israelis were smart, then the Palestinians were not equally smart. Palestinians were incessantly observing the Israelis and in that process constructing Palestinian identity. A woman activist said: 'We have to be as foxy as them,' that is, the Israelis were perceived as wily and, in order to gain a better influence over the negotiations, the Palestinians should learn from the Israelis and become sly themselves. These perceptions also stem from the history of the Palestinian–Israeli conflict as it is experienced and felt by the Palestinians and the structural asymmetry between them. There was, on the one hand, a sense of almost total subordination to Israeli rational calculations, and the Palestinians had hardly any choice but to follow Israeli rule. On the other hand, the Palestinians were to make the Israelis understand that it would be better for them to stay out of the West Bank and Gaza.

> The Israelis are very smart, very intelligent. They could manage to have somebody like Yasir Arafat sign, as if the whole Palestinian problem is solved, as if the Palestinian–Israeli conflict is solved, and as if the Arab–Israeli conflict has been solved. And as a matter of fact, the agreement does not oblige Israel to do much. (Interview with DFLP sympathiser, 21 September 1994)

Thus by the opposition parties as well, Israelis were perceived as shrewd enough to make Arafat sign something which was detrimental to the Palestinian people. Israelis were manipulating and calculating to an even greater extent than within official discourse. However, this same sense of Israelis as superior led the factions to different conclusions as to how to act *vis-à-vis* Israelis.

The notion of a balance of power strongly favouring Israel was not as frequent among the opposition as among supporters. Palestinian struggle could compensate for Palestinian weakness in other regards.

> If you want to compare the PLO and the Palestinians with Israel, that is a superpower in this area and in the world, with Israel who has 154 nuclear bombs, with Israel who [has] highly advanced technology, of course we are weak, but nations, peoples are never weak compared to anything else, because we Palestinians during our *intifada*, we could neutralise not only the atomic bombs of Israel, but also we neutralised the Israeli economy; we neutralised all sorts of arms and equipment. (Interview with DFLP sympathiser, 21 September 1994)

The opposition here differed from supporters in not perceiving the equation between Israelis and Palestinians as degrading to the Palestinians. There was no need to 'give in' as the mainstream dominant discourse had done. Palestinian rightfulness made them morally superior. Israelis were certainly perceived as smart and as militarily stronger, but there was a Palestinian asset in the struggle for 'what was right'. Israeli superiority was in fact based on false premises, since it was 'better' to be 'right' than to be 'smart'. The *intifada* was imagined as the ultimate evidence of this reversed strength.

Also among supporters of the peace process, there were divergences regarding the intentions of Israel. One trend believed that the Israelis had a real interest in withdrawing from all the occupied territories, whereas another trend was of the opinion that Israel wanted to keep as much as possible of the West Bank and would withdraw only as a result of inescapable facts, that is, the irreversible creation of a Palestinian state. There were also Israeli weaknesses, however.

> The Israelis have during fifty years been living with the war, with victims, with bombs. So it is not only the Palestinians who have the chance to be liberated from the occupation. Oslo also implies an historical chance for the Israelis to liberate themselves from the occupation. So we are like other peoples, we don't say, like the Israelis do, that we are the God-chosen people, we are not like that, we are like any other people in the world. They are living with the complex of security. We have to liberate them from this. (Interview with Fateh leader, 23 October 1994)

The occupation was therefore a burden to the Israelis, and something from which Israel needed to be liberated. The notion of 'liberation' also applied to Israel, which could be 'liberated' from both the yoke of the occupation and from its 'security complex'. In recognising Israel's preoccupation with security, this quotation also departs from Palestinian perceptions of the Israelis as superior. The 'security complex' is seen as an Israeli weakness.

Israeli security as a Palestinian interest

There was also, however (in 1994–96), a great deal of sensitivity towards Israeli pressure on the Palestinian Authority and the Palestinian police to act against the Islamic movements in order both to prevent attacks from taking place and to punish attacks that had already taken place. This was increasingly so during the spring of 1995. The turning point was the Beit Lid attack and, as Nabil Sha'ath pointed out, this represented a new Palestinian political discourse: 'a political discourse in the Palestinian ranks, that is for the first time fundamentally based on the fact that protecting Israeli security is inherent in protecting Palestinian national interests' (Sha'ath in Lindholm Schulz and Schulz, 1995: 14). PNA ministers thus not only recognised Israeli security considerations, but made Israel's security a *Palestinian* concern. This represented a dramatic change in Palestinian official politics. The arch-enemy, the most significant and antagonised/antagonising 'other', had now to be protected from fellow Palestinians, who in turn claimed simply to be exercising a basic right. *To protect Israeli security became a fundamental ingredient in Palestinian state-building.* The revolutionary and confusing consequences of this cannot be overestimated. The implications of such a shift in discourse amount to no less than a demand for a change in the content of identity. A nation-building project and nationalism that had been firmly based on the 'struggle' was to be transformed into a state-building project based on the protection of the 'other'. The message from the Oslo process was clear and sharp: no state without the protection of Israeli security. At the same time, the very national(ist) foundation of a Palestinian state was represented through its struggle. This was highly problematic in terms of popular legitimacy, and the PNA therefore attempted to create legitimacy through arguing that its actions were in fact according to Palestinian needs and interests:

> We recognise that they have a problem about security. I am against any Palestinian procedures or acts that will come according to the Israeli demands. If the Israelis ask us to arrest, we should not arrest. If the Israelis ask me to create a security state court, I will not do it but if I need it, I should do it. It is a matter that I need it. Therefore, if what we are doing is a Palestinian policy, then it's OK. It is much more easy to destroy the agreement, and to say bye, bye, and go to fight, or go to *intifada* again, but what's the result? Therefore, we should be realistic, but also maintain our power and responsibilities. Not according to the Israeli request or orders, but according to our interests. (Interview with PNA minister, 21 February 1995)

After the Islamic Jihad attack in Beit Lid which killed twenty-two people, Arafat said at a rally in Gaza that 'No one has any right to use the Palestinian liberated land to carry out acts against the Authority and the state. Why is it that every time we want to reach an agreement a problem occurs? Those who won't stop firing, what exactly do they want? They want to kill the Palestinian dream' (*Jerusalem Post*, 25 January 1995). Here he underlined the argument that the Authority tried to delegitimise the opposition through arguing that its activities hurt Palestinians as much as Israelis.

Another perception altogether was the leftist argument that the Israelis could now claim there was no more occupation and had been relieved of the inconvenience of causing suffering to the Palestinians. Instead, the Palestinian police were doing the 'dirty' job of the Israeli soldiers. Israelis felt moral deprivation when inflicting pain upon others, but were shrewd enough to see to it that things were going their way, in fact succeeding in turning the PLO into collaborators. The Israelis felt bad about what they were doing, but only because *they were the ones causing suffering*. It was not Palestinian suffering which affected them, but the fact that *Israelis* were the cause of it.

> The Israelis are very happy now because they don't have to run after [children in] Jabaliya or Nuseirat and they don't have to get stoned by these kids, they will not

be exposed to the bullets of al-Qassem or Jihad or [the] Democratic Front or other bullets. So they are very happy, because they see that Gaza is still under their occupation, but in another way. And this is what the occupation wants. (Interview with DFLP sympathiser, 18 May 1995)

Israel had liberated itself from a moral burden while at the same time assuring itself of greater security and maintaining the occupation, since it had convinced the Palestinian leadership to dismiss the 'struggle', which had been the sole Palestinian means through which to compensate for Israeli supremacy.

Learning from the 'neighbour'

For future relations on a human level, in mainstream discourse, Israelis and Palestinians must live together, perhaps separately but at least as neighbours.

That's a fact that in this holy land, there are two different peoples and one cannot destroy one another or the other people. We must live together. It's very difficult, but that's a fact. (Interview with Fateh activist, 4 December 1994)

I have no problems with the Israelis, [we have a] relation of trust and no-trust, but they will be our neighbours for ever. (Interview with Fateh activist, 29 October 1994)

The concept of 'neighbours' implies that Israelis and Palestinians were to live not together, among each other, but next to each other, related but separated. It would be very difficult, but 'it's a fact'. Changing perceptions from 'enemies' to 'neighbours' is naturally a complicated and painful transformation. As long as one has 'enemies', the boundaries between 'self' and 'other' are clear and unambiguous. However insecure the situation of conflict, the boundaries between 'self' and 'other' create a sense of security and order. To be 'neighbours' also implies boundaries. They don't live together, but neighbours can be good friends; one can visit one's neighbours and vice versa. As conflict declines and changes, boundaries become less rigid and less decided, which in transitional periods creates uncertainty. The character of the boundary alters from being strict, guarded and disputed to becoming looser, more relaxed and less disputed. To be neighbours implies a different definition of the boundary and also has implications for the definition of 'self'. That is to say, both the cultural content of 'self' and 'other' and the nature of the boundary change. 'In fact, for both Palestinians and Israeli Jews, the agreement hurt longstanding cognitive maps – of who the "enemy" is, of the "intentions" of the "other", and of the imperatives of collective memories and amnesia – without any proper preparation' (Kimmerling, 1997: 241). One of the main effects of the peace process was the breaking down of enemy images. Enemy images and constructions of 'self' and 'other' had until then provided an unquestioned, secure sphere in which to place oneself and to find categories for acting. When all of a sudden cooperaration was the favoured action, this created confusion at a popular level on both sides.

To those who supported the peace process, relations with the Israelis were perceived as *potentially* good. Many pointed out that during the occupation, Palestinians and Israelis had got to know each other, they had met as occupier and occupied, as soldier and stone-thrower, as soldier and gunman, as prison guard and inmate, as employer and employed; always in an asymmetrical relationship in terms of power and control – one ruling and the other being ruled – but still, the meeting and facing each other had created a space where actors had met and become acquainted. Many Palestinians learned Hebrew, often as part of being employed in Israel or as part of 'prison education' (Kimmerling, 1997: 233).

However asymmetrical (power being a fundamental part of it), the relationship could not be denied, and although also marked by distrust, bitterness and hatred, positive elements of envisioning a better future, *together but separated*, were also portrayed. Palestinians and Israelis were seen as destined to live side by side, to share the land for which they had fought so bitterly. Official discourse (on both sides) had confirmed that the other side would not go away, but was there as a real fact. One Fateh activist who spent twelve years in prison for attempting to kill a collaborator decided that he would dedicate his time in prison 'to learning the Israeli mind':

> I learned that they are very open-minded. They have democracy among themselves. I believe that they have an open mind, and they know what they want, but they like themselves. They think high of themselves. I think the Israeli state is democratic. It's not democratic between Israelis and Palestinians, you can't have democracy and occupation, but I mean democratic between the Israelis themselves, and we must learn that from them. (Interview with Fateh activist, 4 December 1994)

Respondents often stressed that Israeli society *in itself* was democratic and that the Palestinians must learn from that in their own building of state and society. This is also reflected in opinion polls on attitudes towards democracy. In a December 1996 poll, 53.1 per cent of the respondents rated Israeli democracy as 'very good' and 25.0 per cent rated it as 'good' (CPRS Opinion Poll No. 25, 26–28 December 1996). In another study, 71 per cent of the sample thought that the Israeli parliamentary system should serve as a model for Palestinian society (Hanf and Sabella, 1996: 85). In a more recent study (November 1997) 16.4 per cent of the Palestinian population in the West Bank and Gaza preferred Israel as a model for the political system to be established in a future Palestinian state. This was the highest percentage received by any one state, with 22.5 per cent of those questioned believing that there does not exist a model society for the Palestinians to be inspired by.[1] At the same time, there was strong resentment against what was perceived as Israeli self-congratulation.

In Palestinian discourse about the 'other', there is also a comparison be-tween Palestinians and Jews: '[The] Palestinians are the Jews of this century. We are like the Jews, the Jewish people' (interview with Fateh activist, 29 Octo-ber 1994). There are similarities between 'self' and 'other'. Both are peoples who have 'suffered'. Official discourse links Palestinian suffering with Jewish suffering. They are not 'brothers' but 'cousins' or 'relatives'. Both have been victims and betrayed by the world. Bassam Abu Sharif once said:

> Sometimes when I read or listen to Israeli officials' reactions, I laugh, because they are exactly like us, the way they react, the way they stick to things. The 'return' is a key word in Jewish history. We were telling the Israelis that the right of return is not only theirs, but ours. (In Wallach and Wallach, 1997: 35)

In fact, both Israeli (see Kimmerling, 1997) and Palestinian identities are pro-duced around the dual concepts of 'suffer' and 'struggle', or 'warrior'.

The 'other' in Islamism

Islamist discourse is rather ambiguous when it comes to perceptions of Israelis and Jews. On the one hand, Hamas displays an 'almost blind hatred' and racism against Jews, partly inspired by European antisemitism (Milton-Edwards, 1996: 185). Israel, Jews and Zionism are viewed as one entity. On the other hand, Hamas discusses Israel in a religious perspective and regards Jews as a *dhimmi* people. The conflict between Palestinians and Israelis was not solely between two peoples, but between believers and non-believers. Ultimately, it was a conflict between 'right' and 'wrong', 'good' and 'evil'.

> The Arab people believes that Israel existing in the Arab world is a dangerous situation. Up till this moment, the Arab people don't even accept the idea for Israel to be in the Arab world. Because it shows that it is an enemy state to the Arab people. [If the Israelis withdrew from the West Bank] it would be a positive point for the Arab people to consider. They never showed us any positive sign. They do things we will never forget. Now I am talking about the history of the Jews. 1492 they were in Spain, they [received] very bad treatment in Spain, so they came to us, and they had a very good situation being among us. When they started to think about kicking out the Arab residents from Palestine, this is when the problem started. So they can live here, we accept them to live here. We don't think even to kick them out from here, but if they think negatively about us, we don't have an imagination of what we think about them in the future. (Interview with Islamist sympathiser, 19 October 1994)

Although Israel has no right to exist in the 'Arab world', if there was an Israeli withdrawal from the West Bank, it would be a 'positive point to con-sider', indicating a certain willingness to consider West Bank and Gaza as the Palestinian state, rather than a liberated Islamic Palestine 'from the river to the sea'. In this remark there was in fact openness, although the interviewee also discussed, in what could be labelled typical Islamist discourse, Jews as always protected by the totality of Islamic rule while persecuted in Europe. History had shown, according to Islamists, that this was the best choice for Muslims, Christians and Jews. And, he continued, it was a fact that the Muslims were in a majority in the Middle East; hence the Muslims should rule.

> From where did the Jews come? Are they the main race of this land? Of course not. They came as immigrants from abroad and made our own people emigrate, and substitute them in the place of our own people. If an Islamic state is built in the Palestinian land, we give them a choice, any one of them who wants to live in Palestine, he will be welcome to live like us, and if anybody wants to leave, we will not prevent him to leave. (Interview with Islamic Jihad leader, 24 November 1994)

Jews were seen as 'aliens', strangers who did not belong in the land. They had migrated there, and infringed a social and physical boundary. Immigration represented travel 'in', while Palestinian flight symbolised a forced migration 'out'. These 'artificial' waves of migration had altered a demographic situation and created chaos. The natural order of people had been disrupted and order must now be restored. In an Islamic state, Israelis would be turned again into the religious category of Jews and would be given a choice whether to stay subordinated to Islamic rule.

Islamic Jihad more explicitly separates Jews and Zionism, although also convinced (like Hamas) that the Jews constitute the main enemy of Islam. It views Israel as a Western colonialist implant devoid of any legitimacy whatsoever (cf. Milton-Edwards, 1996: 207).

> We can't resolve the question of Israel by pushing the Jewish people in the sea, like some Arab leaders said, like Abdel Nasser. But if there will be a solution, a radical solution, the Israel state must be . . . I don't want to use some vocabulary that the West uses, destroy, no. We hope that Israel as a regime disappears, as an organ, an executive organ. We want the Jewish people to be here. This is the goal of the Islam, but we don't want that these people come to be leader and we are [subordinate]. This is enough, we want that Israel disappears as an organ, and the Jewish people stay still here with us. Like they lived with us during fourteen centuries. (Interview with Islamic Jihad sympathiser, 19 January 1995)

Israel represented a false Judaism and was a Western creation which could not be accepted. Israel should thus 'disappear', cease to exist as a state, but the 'Jewish people should stay here with us': if the Jews accepted their rightful position, that is, subordinated to Islam, as in a glorious past, then coexistence between the two populations would be possible. Jews constituted a minority in the Middle East and Muslims a majority, and that was how society should be organised. Numbers were seen as politically decisive, not in terms of democratic practices but in the number of believers.

Also in Islamist discourse, Israelis were seen as placing themselves in a superior position:

> Israel wants very much. Israel wants all the Arabic and Islamic countries, to catch the economy in all Arabic and Islamic countries, and Israel wants to fight the Muslim people in their countries, not with weapons, but with mind, and culture and economy, and their religion. (Interview with Islamist sympathiser, 7 May 1995)

Israel was perceived as a cultural infiltrator in the process of 'fighting' Muslims with the 'mind', that is, a kind of threat and penetration more subtle than the use of military might. The war between believers was a war between cultures, and Israel was perceived as having a mission to try to mislead the Muslim population of Palestine and spread cultural heresy, stemming from the West.

> Israel wants that all the world is suitable to her. Israel wants that all the things march like Israel wants. Israel is a racist state in her own society. They want all the things. This is a complex in the Israeli person. Since the beginning of this century, after the killing of the Jewish people in Europe, the complex of security, the complex of wanting to be more than the other, the complex that they are hated by the others, and they want to prove to others that they are much better than them. This is a complex in the psychology of the Israeli people. (Interview with Islamic Jihad sympathiser, 19 January 1995)

There was also – as in the other trends – a rejection of what was perceived as Israeli self-perceptions of being superior, and Israel was described as greedy. Although Islamist leaders also revealed a strong dislike of ideas of Jewish self-perception as 'above', the Islamist movements did not reveal the same sense of inferiority. Islamic movements had found a way to deal with this sense among Palestinians: in terms of numbers, Jews were really inferior to the Muslims. In using religious categories and classificatory systems, it was possible to reverse and compensate for Palestinian inferiority.

Transcending the boundary?

Reformists had a rather sophisticated view of the 'other', in the sense that in a 'realistic' way they did not trust Israeli intentions but thought that Israel still wanted all of the West Bank. At the same time, they revealed no clear negative stereotypes, but were ready to enter an interactive process of altering relationships between Israelis and Palestinians. Relations of power and asymmetries had to be altered and a greater amount of equality had to be created. This was not because reformists suffered so much from the inferiority complex – they rather saw themselves as equal to Israelis in all regards except in terms of power – but because the Israelis were unilaterally placing themselves at the top of a hierarchy which did not exist.

Reformists argued in terms of a right to have an identity and a right to belong to a people, which was not, however, to be asserted at the expense of Israeli identity. One bold way of boundary-transcending was provided by a leftist feminist definition.

> It is not easy for me, what is going on in the Israeli side. After this incident in Tel Aviv,[2] it was difficult for me to sleep. And if I express this feeling to my people, they will say: 'Crazy.' I have been touched by Israeli people. Sometimes I feel that they are victims, and they are under a great deal of pressure. When I started to make dialogue with them, there was all the time a good response. Even when they were arresting my companion in a demonstration. Sometimes they say: 'You are right. Go away. Please go away. Don't push me to do something. I hate it.' Even at the checkpoints. I never had permission and I went with the car without permission to Gaza.[3] And at Eretz checkpoint, I made dialogue with them. And I told the soldier: 'Why are you still here? I heard that we have a peace process and I expected to see you in Ashkelon maybe.' He said: 'You didn't read the newspaper? I'm here for ever.' And I said: 'Why? It's very strange. It's not good for you to be here. It's good to be with your girlfriend or your wife or your kids, to enjoy your life. Really.' And he said: 'You are right, maybe you are right.' But I don't believe in the identification of the Palestinians as our political leaders believe in. Because they try to separate you from your emotions, from your own feelings, and it's not a good way, it is a mechanical way. It will not work. (Interview with woman activist, 5 November 1994)

For this woman, an inherent conflict existed between the struggle for rights and equality on the one hand, and an understanding of the 'other', supposed to be enemies, on the other. Her empathy towards the 'other' created disruption between her and the surrounding Palestinian society and within herself. Politics served to *fragment* identity. On the one hand, she was Palestinian, with all the common notions related to Palestinian-ness and the joint political struggle. At the same time, she had transcended the boundary between 'us' and 'them' and felt in community with Jewish women. This transcendence stemmed from feminism and a genderised perspective, and her basic political insight of the PLO and Palestinianism as male structures. Feminism led her to meeting Jewish women in joint discussions and actions. Asymmetry is surely part of such processes in the sense that it is the sons of Israeli Jewish women who constitute the army and the occupation forces. It is the sons of Israeli Jewish women who inflict suffering upon Palestinian women and require their sacrifice. Through the meeting and transcendence of boundaries, however, new identities emerged, criss-crossing with established ones. The woman was critical of the leadership trying to separate feelings of mutual understanding and those of exclusion and political struggle. The political identity of the leadership did not take into account deeper emotions of empathy and sympathy, but was 'mechanical' in its emphasis on the particularity of Palestinian political identity.

Here I think it is relevant to bring in Bauman's discussion of different forms of 'togetherness' and the difference between a postulated togetherness of the 'brotherhoods and sisterhoods of nations, races, classes, genders and other shadowy and abstruse dream-communities' (Bauman, 1995: 47) and the togetherness of 'being for':

> The being-for, I propose, means an *emotional* engagement with the Other *before* it is committed . . . to a specific course of action regarding the Other. . . . First, emotion marks the exit from the state of *indifference* lived among thing-like Others. Second, emotion pulls the Other from the world of finitude and stereotyped certainty, and casts her/him into the universe of under-determination, questioning and openness. Third, emotion extricates the Other from the world of convention, routine and normatively engendered monotony, and transmits her/him into a world in which no universal rules apply, while those which do apply are overtly and blatantly non-universal, specific, born and shaped in the self-containment of the face-to-face, protected from the outside influence by the wall of sentiment . . . emotional engagement makes the Other into a problem and the task of and for the self . . . ; now it is up to the self, and the self alone, to do something . . . about the Other. The Other turns into the self's *responsibility*, and this is where morality begins as the possibility of choice between good and evil. (Bauman, 1995: 62)

The 'postulated togetherness' formulated by official nationalism imposed sanctions against interaction with, and feelings of empathy for, the 'other'. The woman quoted above was torn between this postulated, obligatory togetherness of the nation and her emotional engagement with the 'other'. Israelis were part of her responsibility and she owed a moral commitment in her 'being for'. She could 'be for', owing to her meetings with Israelis. No longer could simplified stereotypes be applied to either Palestinians/'self' or Israelis/'other'. Instead, it was up to her consciously to overcome the boundary and to allow openness. To accept that there are no easy ways of excluding–including when human interaction is involved is to allow for uncertainty and to invite chaos.

NOTES

1 This poll was conducted as part of a research project concerning Palestinian state-building and democracy, financed by the Swedish International Development Authority. The research was conducted jointly by BirZeit University Department of Sociology and the Peace and Development Research Institute, Göteborg University. The results have not yet been published.
2 The interview took place shortly after the suicide bus bomb in Tel Aviv on 18 October 1994, which killed twenty people.
3 For Palestinians from the West Bank or Gaza, it is necessary to get permission from the Israeli authorities to go from the West Bank to Gaza, Jerusalem or Israel, and to go from Gaza to the West Bank, Jerusalem or Israel.

Conclusions:
nationalism in flux

This book has dealt with nationalisms and their reconstructive capacity in relation to external impact as well as internal creation through a case study of Palestinian nationalisms. Particular emphasis has been placed on the context of external conflict in a period of transition and how decline of conflict affects internally defined concepts of identity and nationalism.

The study has underlined the ambiguity of nationalism and national identity. Even within one and the same political faction and within the official leadership, concepts of identity and nationalism are unevenly distributed. Identity processes are open-ended, in a sense chaotic, and not always clear to the actors themselves. There are some important basic themes of Palestinian identity and political goals and strategies common to the various factions, such as 'struggle', 'right' and 'suffer', for gaining 'statehood' and international 'equality', but there are also individual and group variations. Neither 'self' nor 'other' is represented as a monolithic construct, but as variegated, fluid, composite and complex. The sometimes ambiguous narratives should also be seen against the contextual background of the (uncertain and limping) decline of the Palestinian–Israeli conflict, changing the political agenda as far as goals and strategies are concerned. The study has also illuminated the intricate relationship between 'other' and 'self' in identity processes and nationalism. The relationship is one of dynamic dialectics, and changes within the content of one of them immediately act upon the other.

Historical formation of Palestinian nationalism

Palestinian nationalism is not as straightforward as sometimes described (by its apologists as well as its antagonists), but has changed dramatically in the course of history. There is nothing natural or given about it, just as there is nothing natural or given about any nationalism. Neither is it, however, simply an ideology of reaction and negation. Surely, external factors served as a catalyst for sparking the nationalist movement, but the ideology and its content are also internally formulated. It is in the meeting and crossing between external push factors, large-scale processes and internal creative dynamics that the interesting processes occur, that nationalism is in fact being produced, and where studies of nationalism ought to be carried out. Nationalism as an ideology is thus highly flexible, and is reshaped depending on situations and conjunctures. Palestinian nationalism has not developed in an evolutionary process, but has seen disruptive changes and has been redefined at several points in history. Although the main cause of the emergence of a specific Palestinian nationalism at that particular juncture in history (i.e. 1917 onwards) was the encounter with Zionism (and later Israel) and the ensuing process of land alienation, other factors cannot be downplayed. These include European colonialism, the spread of nationalism as an ideology in the Middle East, the rise of Arab nationalism in relation to World War I and the falling asunder of the Ottoman empire, the actions (or lack of action) of Arab states, and internal factors, such as the role of elites. In addition, Palestinian-ness is ultimately connected with modernity, the spread of nationalist ideologies since the late 1800s, and the modern idea of the nation-state as the optimal and ultimate organising principle in the international system. The modern ideology of nationalism, or perhaps the paradigm of nationalism structuring the inter-state system, is hence an *ideology about culture as an organising principle*. Nationalism is also related to conflict and wars. World War I gave rise to both Arab nationalism and embryonic Palestinianism and enhanced Zionism. In the early phase of the emerging Palestinian movement, that is, between 1917 and 1939, a proto-nationalism on the elite level was formed. World War II led to the establishment of the state of Israel, which in turn led to the Arab/Palestinian–Israeli conflicts which in the late 1990s appear to be leading to a Palestinian state. The catastrophe and the 1967 war led to the two main meanings of being Palestinian (i.e. to suffer and to struggle) in a political sense.

In the mid 1930s, the traditional elite was challenged by a new, non-dominant elite, the bourgeoisie, professionals and intellectuals, that is, the social stratum generally connected with the formulation of nationalism, and the lower social strata, affected by the dispossession of land and urbanisation processes. Radicalisation and militant politicisation occurred, paving the way for the Great Revolt of 1936–39, and a popular discourse on national identity challenged the elite.

British repression of the Great Revolt left the Palestine Arabs devoid of effective leadership. One of the internal factors that disrupted a continuation of nationalist politics was factional rivalry. From 1945 onwards, the Arab states pursued their own interests, manipulating the Palestine question. Following the *nakba*, the national(ist) leadership was even further fragmented and in disarray, and politics were to a large extent determined by the Arab states. Arabism was the dominant ideology.

From 1959 onwards there was a period of germinating Palestinian mobilisation from below. al-Fateh had a radically different ideology from the pan-Arabists, advocating the strategy that the liberation of Palestine should precede Arab unity. al-Fateh's ideas began to gain widespread support after the 1967 war. The late 1960s and 1970s were a time of mass mobilisation, and al-Fateh's Palestinianism became both dominating and popular nationalism. The nationalist struggle and discourse were based on the exile experience, on camp life and the *fedayeen* as the ideal 'Palestinian'. al-Fateh took the leading role in fostering Palestinian identity and nationalism in the revolutionary era. Military training of *fedayeen* and the fostering of the guerrilla fighter as a national/cultural hero further served to integrate and homogenise the Palestinian camp population. There was a conscious use of 'struggle' as well as 'suffer' to enhance Palestinianism.

In the West Bank and Gaza, the very *absence* of formal authority and statehood in fact served as a unifying factor in the immediate aftermath of the occupation. Palestinians were defined out of what they did not have; their loss knitted them together. Oppositional nationalism was formulated by intellectuals in the Marxist–Leninist organisations. Arabism has always been a troubled part of Palestinian identity. The late 1960s and early 1970s were remarkable times for Palestinian nationalisms. Many authors have asserted that al-Fateh and the revolutionary era succeeded in creating a mass base for Palestinian-ness. It has seldom been pointed out, however, that it was also now that to be a Palestinian came to mean to be a resistance fighter, a struggler, at least in the abstract discourse of politicised identity, as this study has emphasised.[1] The meaning of Palestinian identity is thus not only modern (cf. Gellner, 1983; Hobsbawm, 1990; Anderson, 1991), but *new and recent*. The newness of this concept does not mean, however, that it is of any less importance than if it had been based on historical continuity.

In the West Bank and Gaza, popular mobilisation reached a climax through the *intifada*. One of the most significant achievements of the *intifada* – if seen from an 'inside' perspective – was the *redefinition of Palestinian national identity and nationalism*. Palestinian nationalism was now largely determined from *inside* the West Bank and Gaza, and it was the Palestinians from the occupied territories who communicated to the international community. Previous studies (e.g. McDowall, 1989; Peretz, 1990; Schiff and Ya'ari, 1990; Hunter, 1993) have asserted that the important contribution of the *intifada* was its reorientation of goals in the Palestinian movement and its promotion of a new class (Robinson, 1997a). It has rarely been stressed that it also altered the concept of Palestinian-ness. The *intifada* was a spontaneous uprising set in motion by lower social strata, by the refugee dwellers, by the unemployed and young workers. There was a combination of informal folk concepts and formal nationalism, which blended into the highly revolutionary, romanticised language of the struggle and the *intifada*. 'Struggle' and 'resistance' were given new meaning through both the idiom and the practice of the *intifada*. As the revolution in the 'outside' had served as a unifying principle, *intifada* was now the ideology which provided a movement of unification in the 'inside'. The *intifada* represented both change and continuity of 'struggle' as the main image of the Palestinians.

An oppositional definition of national identity implying a redrawing of social boundaries was provided by an Islamically defined nationalism based on the concept of liberation of all of 'Palestine'. The right, *al-haq*, was in Islamist discourse also a matter of rights attributed by God and not merely to international legality. Hamas and Islamic Jihad represent a new form of nationalism capitalising on the notions of resistance and liberation of the homeland, in combination with a sacrilisation of territory and a moralistic pitch. Thus political Islam is not a challenge against nationalism as such, but against the secularised, Western version of it.

What we can conclude from an historical overview of Palestinian nationalism is also that national(ist) mobilisation went hand in hand with land alienation in different forms, urbanisation, industrialisation, migration and the creation of workforces. During the British era, urbanisation and industrialisation increased and the urban poor and unemployed contributed to the Great Revolt. Land alienation increased after the *nakba* and the first refugee flow. From the 1960s, Palestinians were increasingly made into a reserve workforce in the Arab states as well as Israel. In Lebanon, in the Gulf and under Israeli rule in the occupied territories, Palestinian labour forces were devoid of rights as citizens, and could be used on a more or less *ad hoc* basis, that is, when there was a need in the labour market. The *intifada* was also to a large extent sparked by an urbanised *Lumpenproletariat*, Gaza city with its surrounding refugee camps being a large slum city, sending its workers commuting through the Eretz checkpoint.

Particular nationalisms (1) are created in relation to 'others' and perceived threats against security and identity, but also in relation to more benign 'others'; and (2) depend on a leadership which is capable of and willing to formulate an ideological content convincing enough for a large enough population. That is to say, politicised identities are formed out of peril and anxiety but also need creativity.

> It would appear that this propensity of peoples to reassess fundamental attitudes and beliefs at times of major historical shifts is a general pattern, and not one exclusive to this time and place. Clearly, more must be involved than simply a situation of crisis, great stress, and a threat to existing values and attitudes: there also must be a vision or a goal, or at least a viable alternative for people to be drawn

to, since stress and crisis by themselves could simply lead to the shattering of a community. (Khalidi, 1997: 161)

In order to understand nationalism, one must therefore understand the complexities of the combination of external and internal events in changing the direction of nationalist political discourse. Also, the Palestinian case has highlighted the pluralism of each nationalism in terms of content and substance. This pluralism is by no means unique to the Palestinian case, but is inherent in the malleability of nationalism.

From revolution to state-building

Palestinian nationalism has historically been a nationalism formulated around the concepts of liberation and self-determination. With the contextual change of the Palestinian–Israeli conflict, the previously common national idea was now being questioned. Palestinianism found itself undergoing a dramatic change, in the process of becoming more 'inward-looking'; that is, effective state-building nationalism must look into internal structures and patterns of politics and governance. A liberation nationalism rather draws its initial advantage on its external orientation, focusing political energy on an antagonistic relationship with an 'other' in the form of the 'enemy'. With state-building, internal negotiations and discursive struggles over the content of nationalism increase.

In general terms, official 'state' nationalism in its early phase has always unleashed reactions from the intelligentsia and other social strata. In this case, struggles are enacted between an official 'state' nationalism striving to achieve the largest possible internal unity while at the same time keeping to its obligations to Israel and oppositional nationalisms. The peculiar circumstances of Palestinian nationalism in the mid 1990s meant tremendous hardship in this mixture of external and internal considerations. The success of official nationalism will depend upon how all-embracing the PNA succeeds in being, and how efficient it will be in promoting symbols of identity recognisable and legitimate to all social strata. It is also dependent on the establishment of a socioeconomic basis for the now radically altered national project. The national cause is not fulfilled but changing, implying traumatic reconsiderations for Palestinian nationalisms.

The agreements between Israel and the PLO dramatically altered the contextual background of Palestinian nationalism. A Palestinian National Authority gained formal authority – responsibilities over a population and legitimacy over military violence – but not (yet) territorial sovereignty. Through the agreements, the external enemy decreased in importance with consequences for the ideological content of Palestinianism. The alliance between Israel and the PLO/PNA made the old concepts of 'liberation' and 'struggle' increasingly redundant, and for the Fateh-based Authority new concepts of building, constructing and creating legitimacy for a controversial policy and for clinging to power by a certain elite entered its formulation of discourse. The PNA and Israel were new partners in the peace process. The PLO had not succeeded in achieving the old goals of 'liberation of Palestine' or the more recent goal of 'establishing an independent Palestinian state'. The leadership continuously argued that the state was in the making, that a process of state-building had begun. Yet contextual change is not capable of causing immediate and rapid change in identity discourse, but to 'struggle' is still part of the structure informing nationalism and identity, including among supporters of the agreements. Identity moves more slowly than surrounding circumstances. The Palestinian leadership was internally still using popular notions of 'struggle' while not acting in that sense, which was confusing.

The problem of transition from liberation and anti-structure/anti-thesis to construction appears systemic; it is inherent in the nationalism of liberation. Its main problem is precisely the overemphasis on external factors and enemies and a neglect of internal cleavages, internal policy and distribution of resources. The Fateh movement has portrayed itself as the uniting force. Its mission to keep the Palestinians united has meant a lack of a coherent strategy for state- and society-building. The acute need of a reorientation of politics in state-building may under certain conditions prove fragmenting. States emerging out of anti-colonial struggles are therefore vulnerable.

Double movement of 'stateness' and fragmentation

To accept self-government had, on the one hand, historical foundations, in the sense that the objectives of the PLO had changed over time and the political leadership could now argue that self-rule was a logical step in the right direction, following the 1974 decision to shift its goal from liberation of Palestine to accepting intermediate stops and the 1988 Declaration of Independence. On the other hand, it was a highly controversial matter, since self-government and 'partial solutions' were always rejected, as in the *intifada* calls. Despite deep divergences and fragmentation of Palestinian nationalism – in fact implying that it is more appropriate to talk about nationalism*s* – there was, however, a more or less common understanding that a two-state solution was the only, or the most realistic, solution to the Palestinian–Israeli conflict, at least for the time being and in the short run. Despite ideological rhetoric, both the PFLP/DFLP and at least part of Hamas have more or less, and in *practical* terms, accepted the West Bank and Gaza as the locus for a Palestinian state, at least as an intermediate stage.

Official nationalism interpreted the agreements as the first step in an irreversible process towards an independent Palestinian state. The structure of *time* is important in this context. On the one hand, the agreements were described as a continuation of a natural, evolutionary process of the Palestinian political movement. On the other hand, time was now at point zero, the Palestinians had to start from scratch and the many years of struggle were a transport to this turning point in history. Self-rule marked the beginning of a new era where a total reversal of strategies and politics had to be made. 'Realism' and 'responsibility' were important notions used to describe the era of state-building and the role of those manifesting self-rule. Palestine was 'a country to be made', and the agreements represented the 'first step' towards the making of the state. The agreements were not ideal but the only 'realistic option'. The period of transition represented neither the struggle/process nor the statehood/outcome, but a stage in 'between', hence new means of measuring time were needed. Palestinian nationalism found itself 'between and betwixt'; it was neither in a process of struggling nor in an era of statehood, but displayed a little bit of both. There was a redefinition of the 'struggle' in different ways.

Oppositional nationalism defined self-rule as leading to continued occupation combined with limited self-rule by a non-legitimate Palestinian authority. The PNA was not legitimate since it had deserted the path of liberation and struggle.

To the PFLP and DFLP, 'right' stemmed from the land and from international law. To give up 'right' was to give up struggle and thence Palestinianness. Hamas and Islamic Jihad based their politics on 'struggle' and 'resistance'; the goal was to 'liberate all of Palestine' and establish an Islamic state. The competition between the PNA/Fateh and Hamas was, on the ideological level, to a large extent a struggle between the politics of 'realism' and the politics of 'resistance' and who were the 'better' Palestinians. Hamas also made use of the concept of 'right' which was divine and which was thus a powerful symbol. Palestinian 'right' in the land was not derived solely from the Palestinians being a people of the land, but from the land being a land of God, providing the geography with a non-negotiable value and giving it a prominent place in the world of national spaces. However, Hamas was also going through a phase of change where it was torn between ideology and the overwhelming situation of political change.

The change from revolutionary nationalism to state-building in general terms implies a fundamental change and a reorientation of unprecedented proportions. A revolutionary liberation nationalism is abstract and mystified in its underground existence, concentrating its energies on the foe. Objection and resistance are promoted *vis-à-vis* the outside, and disicipline and conformity are required on the inside. State-building is official, based on formal and legitimate authority or governance and probing internal relations. The 'other' may remain, but its importance and meaning change.

Reconstruction of self and the meaning of identity

Palestinian identity in its general sense, that is, in the denominators common to all factions, is both *process* and *outcome*. By this is suggested that it represents both the struggling and suffering of Palestinian selfhood, that is, what Palestinians perceive themselves to be *doing* in the process and the aspired *outcome* of that action/struggle, that is, statehood and equality, described in terms of 'rights', derived either through 'land', 'international law' or 'God'. In this sense, the meaning of Palestinian identity is still to 'struggle' and 'suffer', but the content of these concepts was in a process of change from military/popular struggle to the struggle of state-building in official nationalism. To many *intifada* activists in the Fateh ranks and to PLC members, struggle is now widened so as to embrace also the internal struggle for democracy. To the leftist opposition, change in the struggle lay in an orientation towards political and democratic struggle against the new authoritarian structure. The loss of military and/or popular struggle implied a partial loss of identity. Identity was no longer coherent. Struggle had represented a way of life, at least for guerrilla fighters and *intifada* activists. What to do when the fight was over, and neither socioeconomic nor identity expectations had been fulfilled? What it entails is identity as process and action; *it is what people do which helps them to define national identities.*

The second part of Palestinian identity was related to the *outcome*, the *future* which was defined as statehood, which was now on its way to becoming realised (or at least closer to realisation than ever before). This part had never been given any concrete meaning. It was always abstract, mystified and ideal, despite the concrete statism of the PLO in exile. There was in this sense an imbalance between the two parts of process/'struggle' and outcome/'statehood' in the sense that struggle could be given concrete and practical meaning in everyday actions and strategies, while outcome was always far away; it was always in a distant, diffuse future. The biggest challenge for the Palestinian leadership was now to fill this part of Palestinian identity with 'meaningful meaning'.

The most important internal tensions were perceptions of who were the 'better' Palestinians, who had the right to define national identity. The new dispute was, then, about who was the better struggler. Was it Fateh, the movement which first introduced the political path of 'resistance' and 'struggle', and the historical legitimacy of which in this sense remained spotless? Or was it Hamas, which had recently entered the road of struggle, but on the other hand was not ready to give it up for poor compromises? Was it the activists in the 'interior', who triumphed in their 'glorious' *intifada*, enabling a new vision of pride and dignity and who suffered in Israeli prisons and through martyrdom? Or was it the 'outside' – the community still in exile – who led the struggle for decades in miserable circumstances and who suffered the 'exile', the longing and the dispersal? Was it the PNA, the ex-exile who always represented the privileged strata with privileged lives in Arab or European capitals or in relative wealth in the 'inside', who had taken on the lead in the 'new struggle' of building and construction? Or was it the opposition, who refused half measures and insisted on the rightfulness of a legitimate struggle of resistance? In this very struggle, new social boundaries were drawn and created, but in a different order than the boundaries between Palestinians and Israelis. Both official and oppositional nationalisms made internal hierarchisations of Palestinian identity. Out of their own contextualised definitions of Palestinian-ness, the trends defined who were the 'better' or 'more' Palestinian and who were 'less' Palestinian. Deviations from the norm gave rise to new internal hierarchisations of Palestinian-ness. There was a clear-cut division between 'outside' and 'inside'. There were now two kinds of struggle with different goals, thus further emphasising the rift between the two societies. 'Return' was no longer necessarily a common agenda. To the 'inside', it was more important to build internal structures. With the agreements, it had also become clear that the issue of 'return' was highly problematic. What to 'return' to? It was not the agreements *per se* that caused this change, but they clearly manifested existing divisions and gave them new meaning.

Palestinian identity was thus ambiguous. Two basic dimensions stand out as particularly important; that is, the simultaneous presence of

1   *Vulnerability.* Palestinians perceived themselves to be highly subordinated in relation to Israel, as well as to the international system. They perceived themselves to a large extent to be victims, those who have always to sacrifice and suffer, and

2   *Pride.* Despite their vulnerability, Palestinians described themselves as those who still resist and fight, those who do not give up. In the notion of struggle, there is a great deal of pride and self-acclaimed strength. The notion of struggle is the one component capable of challenging the Israelis and compensating for the inferiority complex.

These concepts appear paradoxical, and so they are in a way, trapping Palestinian politics in a mystification and romanticisation of a victimised self. In another way, however, these basic notions function in an interacting process, reinforcing a common base for politics and action. Anguish and torment are what have been inflicted by way of 'others', ever stronger and more powerful forces. The acts and strategies to decrease and counter the weakness created the new Palestinian – the struggler. What mobilised Palestinian political identity was the perceived and inherent 'right' stemming from being 'sons of the soil', from international law and religion/God. The 'right' gave rise to Palestinians as acting agents, and in the process of acting as Palestinians, Palestinian-ness was constructed and created. Palestinians were what they did, that is, they 'struggled' and 'suffered', but simultaneously that identity could not be firmly established unless a Palestinian state was established and the Palestinians gained what they did not have, that is, a position in the international system and a recognised identity. Palestinians were both what they *did* and what they *did not have*, what they struggled for. In relation to others, they were weak and vulnerable, they were victims. There was a simultaneous existence of all these concepts and meanings which existed as juxtapositions. This underlines the fundamental plurality of each nationalism. The specific content of Palestinian identity in the form of struggle and suffering could not exist without the Israelis as the 'other' and without the Palestinian–Israeli conflict. At the same time, however, the meaning given to these contents is internally defined. Furthermore, this is not to say that there would be no Palestinians were there no Israelis. A Palestinian identity could, of course, have been established without Zionism, but the content of Palestinian-ness would most probably have been different. In addition, to stress constructivism is not to say that identities are devoid of meaning. Meanings can have very recent origin and need not be historically based. The meaning of the Palestinian as the fighter has profound meaning, as it provides Palestinians with a self-image which can counter Israeli strength and provide a feeling of pride and dignity.

The dichotomisation of Palestinian identity into suffering victim versus struggling hero, *feday*, martyr, finds its direct counterpart in Israeli Jewish identity.

> Israeli political culture is characterised by a mixture of permanent anxiety and a power-oriented culture. On one hand, the Jewish–Israeli polity is driven by a code of self-perceived weakness, permanent wretchedness, and existential threat. A sense of permanent siege and potential annihilation in a hostile Gentile world of antisemites . . . is perceived as the state of nature, or the cosmic order. [. . .] The 'new Israeli' – in counter-distinction to the 'Jew-of-exile', shaped and disdained by Zionist ideology and mythology – is first and foremost a warrior. Jewish–Israelis adore *macht* (action); they are confident that force, now that they have it, will solve most societal and political problems, making the power-orientation the touchstone of their political culture. [. . .] The weakness and power-oriented components of this culture complement each other, yet they are also a source of internal strain. (Kimmerling, 1997: 229)

Therefore, despite or because of the deep-rooted conflict, and the hard to erase negative stereotypes on both sides, Palestinian and Israeli identities are mirror images in a very concrete way. Both identities thrive on a victimised and traumatised self, pushing them to militancy to overcome their own weaknesses and anxieties and to counter the threats that are posed against them.

Generally speaking, when a strongly influential external variable or context is changed, it has a dramatic impact upon concepts of self and identity. An uncertain future in a sense reinforces old concepts of identity, since they are what remain as secure structures. There is thus a pull in both directions: to stick to what is known and secure and to change what is becoming ever more an anomaly. Not only to give old concepts of identity new meaning but to change them requires boldness. In this case, there is a potential for the concept of 'neighbour' to establish itself, to provide shared meaning for people.

Therefore, we cannot actually separate content and boundary the way Barth did. Content in the form of meaningful 'stuff' is formed by the boundary and its character as well as influencing the boundary. This is not to say that we should study so-called 'objective criteria' or language, religion, history as straightforwardly informing content and meaning. There are rather contents, or meaningful information, of different characters. Such meaningful content can only be known through empirical studies. In the interviews, Palestinian identity is very clearly placed in the struggle, and not only in the land as is usually assumed. National identities are therefore much more complex than merely being connected with territory, language, traditions, and so on. When the boundary changes, it has an impact upon the content, although not in a straightforward, unproblematic sense. In another way, however, this study has reinforced the argument of Barth, that it is not the 'cultural stuff' which defines ethnicity/national identity. Neither is it, however, entirely a form of social organisation but cultural meaning has a profound impact. This study illustrates how people's self-identities are clearly defined as *actions, as processes, as something which they do.* 'People's categories are for acting' (Barth, 1969: 29). That is to say, although Palestinians imagine themselves as rightful inheritors of the soil they inhabit through a primordialist nationalist discourse, they are also defining themselves in a highly non-primordial way, that is, they *are* what they *do.* Since culture is about doing, what needs to be done in ethnicity studies is further to emphasise cultural content and 'stuff' in the form of active processes.

Deconstruction of the enemy image

Perceptions of Israeli intentions were negative in all three trends, but least so among the supporters of the peace process. Suspicions and doubts about Israel's real desires were revealed, as well as frustration over obstacles and delays in the on-going negotiations. A change was occurring in official nationalism, being in effect allied with Israel's government in the peace process as well as in protecting Israeli security, representing a drastic change of the enemy image. Those who were previously fought were now to be protected. For the first time in the history of Palestinian nationalism, Israeli security was interpreted as a Palestinian national interest, although respondents in the interviews made a point of arguing that harsher security measures were for Palestinian needs. How does such change influence the image of the 'other'? The enemy image

166

has historically been marked by a feeling of inferiority. Now, in the altered relations, Israelis were in need of Palestinian protection; in fact the Palestinians could not be as weak as the Palestinian–Israeli conflict has implied and as the Palestinians have felt themselves to be.

The perception of Israel as almost a super-agent, as having an exacting and calculated strategy on how to keep control of the West Bank while allowing Palestinian rule to govern civil affairs, was a widely held idea. Conspiracy theories were still common, implying that Israel was seen as responsible for all evils in Palestinian society, especially among the opposition. Israelis were seen as very smart, as clever and cunning and exceedingly strong. There was in this regard a very clear inferiority complex among the Palestinians. There were basically two ways of coping with it: (1) learning from the Israelis, that is, accepting that for Israelis and Palestinians to become equal, they had to enter a process of learning. This strategy stemmed from a certain sense of admiration for the Israelis, that is, what was defined as Israeli was affirmed in positive terms. Palestinians had to learn from the Israelis, both from their internal democracy and from their slyness, and to in a sense join them; and (2) negation and rejection of everything that was perceived as Israeli, in the form of politics, values and culture.

This led the various factions to different conclusions. To the mainstream, official nationalism, the conclusion was that they had to move from resistance to *Realpolitik*. Representatives of official nationalism in the interviews showed signs of admiring the Israelis but were frustrated over this admiration. Their strategy was to become more similar to the Israelis, both in external negotiations and in internal society-building. Through becoming similar, Palestinians could become equal. Also, in allying themselves with Israel, they gained recognition and Israeli need for their assistance, which in a way boosted self-perception. On behalf of official nationalism and its political representatives, a new identity production could be discerned, in the form of a political identity common to Israeli and Palestinian peace negotiators. In the process of negotiations, Israelis and Palestinians met and shared a new form of togetherness. Official nationalism referred to the concept of 'neighbour', implying that a separation had to occur between the two populations but, at the same time, they were to share their fought-for territory and to live next to each other. Thus the boundary remained but was becoming softer in its edges. The political process of separation in fact led to the stressing of similarities in identity. There was a *potential* for a new identity. 'Learning from the Israelis' and 'joining them' must be followed by 'equality'. Among Fateh and PNA representatives, as well as in the reformist camp, stereotypes were in fact much less negative and more open to change than is usually supposed.

Representatives of oppositional leftism advocated in the long term a tearing down of boundaries, the creation of a new national identity out of the two collectivities in the territory of Palestine, that is, 'one democratic state for all'. The insight that this – at least in this historical perspective – could not be fulfilled has led the Marxist fronts in the short run to embrace the 'separation' strategy. That is, for the foreseeable future, the two-state solution is the preferred goal. Ideally, however, they advocate the creation of a new society. 'Struggle' should remain as a means to challenge Israel's superiority.

Islamists in the interviews represented the most radical position, turning Palestinian *qualitative* inferiority (i.e. in terms of military might, technology, political power, strategic allies and economic dominance) to Muslim *quantitative* superiority. In terms of sheer numbers, Muslims outweighed Jews. This equation was also based on the non-territoriality of Islamism. In regional or global terms, Jews could never compete with Muslims. Using this numerical calculation, Muslims should rule. However, territoriality was also important in relation to Palestine. Territory was connected with divine right, that is, Palestine was God-given and hence Muslims should rule as God's representatives.

What has also been revealed through this study, and the interviews and material upon which it is based, is the truly open-ended character and ambiguity of national identity. Identities are multi-faceted not only (or mainly) in the sense that one individual can simultaneously identify as a father, a son, a member of a particular family, a member of a faction, a West Banker, a Palestinian, an Arab and a Muslim – which means that there are shared identities and loyalties with different peoples at different times – but rather that there are *several forms* and contents of Palestinian-ness. To be a Palestinian does not mean a sole thing or a simple thing, but the meaning embedded in being Palestinian is multiple, even to one and the same individual. It remains to be seen how the Palestinian leadership will deal with such concepts of identity and whether there is a potential in the notion of 'building' together with the 'neighbour'.

NOTE

1 The prime exception is Sayigh (1997a).

BIBLIOGRAPHY

Primary sources

Interviews

Details of interviews with interviewees who wish to remain anonymous are given in the text.

ACADEMICS

Abu-Amr, Ziad, 22 July 1994, Ramallah, and 18 January 1995, BirZeit; Associate Professor of Political Science at BirZeit University.
Barghouti, Iyad, 16 July 1994, Nablus; PhD, Political Scientist, an-Najah University.
Abdel Hadi, Mahdi, 31 May 1995; Head of Palestinian Association for the Study of International Affairs, PASSIA, Jerusalem.
Heidar, Aziz, 27 October 1994, BirZeit; Professor at Department of Sociology, BirZeit University.
Izzat, Nader, 20 May 1995, Nablus; Researcher at the CPRS, Nablus.
Jarbawi, Ali, 10 October 1994, BirZeit, and 27 June 1995, BirZeit; PhD, Political Scientist, BirZeit University.
Jawwad, Islah, 12 October 1994, BirZeit; PhD, Political Scientist, works at Cultural Studies at BirZeit University and at Women's Studies Programme, BirZeit.
Abdel Jawwad, Saleh, 31 January 1995, Ramallah; Director, BirZeit Research and Documentation Centre.
Kuttab, Eileen, 7 and 11 November 1994, BirZeit; PhD, Department of Sociology, BirZeit University, and involved in Women's Studies Programme, BirZeit, and in Bisan Research Centre, Ramallah.
Shqaqi, Khalil, various occasions in 1994, 1995 and 1997, Nablus; Head of CPRS, Nablus.
Tamari, Salim, 4 August 1995, BirZeit, and lecture at BirZeit University, 27 June 1995; Professor at Department of Sociology, BirZeit University.
Taraki, Liza, 25 October 1994, BirZeit; PhD, Department of Sociology, BirZeit University, and involved in Women's Studies Programme, BirZeit.

POLITICAL FIGURES AND REPRESENTATIVES

Abu Ala, or *Qreia, Ahmed*, 1995, a-Ram, Fateh; Minister of Trade and Economy, PNA; Director-General of PECDAR; after elections in 1996, Speaker of the PLC.
Aldiik, Ahmed, 1994, Ramallah, Fateh; after elections in 1996, Member of the PLC.
Allouh, Diab, 1995, Gaza, Fateh.
Ashrawi, Hanan, 1995, Jerusalem, independent; after elections in 1996, Member of the PLC and subsequently Minister of Higher Education until August 1998.
Assad, Nafez, 1995, Gaza, Islamic Jihad.
Bahhar, Ahmed, Sheikh, 1995, Gaza, Hamas leader.
Barghouti, Bashir, 1994, Jerusalem, General Secretary of the PPP; editor of the weekly *al-Ta'lia*; from 1996, Minister of Industry, resigned in 1997 due to health reasons.
Barghouti, Marwan, 1994, 1997, Ramallah, Fateh; General Secretary of Fateh Higher Committee in the West Bank; after elections in 1996, Member of the PLC.

169

Bitawi, Imad, Sheikh, 1995, Nablus; judge in Islamic court in Nablus.

Erakat, Sa'eb, 1995, Jericho, Fateh; Minister of Municipal and Local Affairs, PNA, from 1994; after elections in 1996, Member of the PLC.

Fada, Majeda, 1995, Nablus; women's activist with Islamist opinions.

Freij, Elias, 1994, Bethlehem, 21 June 1995, Bethlehem, independent; Mayor of Bethlehem since 1972; Minister of Tourism and Antiquities, PNA, from 1994; died in autumn of 1997.

Abdel Hadi, Izzat, 1994, Ramallah, independent; Bisan Research Centre.

Haj, Abdel Latif Muhammad, 1995, Gaza; DFLP sympathiser.

Hamameh, Jamil, 1994, Jerusalem/a-Ram; Executive Director of Islamic Committee of Sciences.

Abu Hillel, Ali, 1994, Jerusalem; DFLP sympathiser.

Husayni, Feysal, 1994, Jerusalem, Fateh; Minister without Portfolio, PNA, from 1994.

Jadallah, Muhammad, 1994, 1997, Beit Safafa; DFLP, physician/surgeon; Head of the Union of Health Care Committees; Member of Medical Association, Jerusalem.

Jarrar, Bassam, Sheikh, 1994, al-Bireh; Islamic teacher in a United Nations Relief and Works Agency school in al-Bireh; Imam of Ramallah Mosque; member of Higher Islamic Council, Jerusalem.

Jihad, 1994, Fateh, Nablus.

Juul, Mona, 1995, Embassy of Norway, Tel Aviv.

Jwabrah, Atiyehe, various occasions, 1994, 1995, Fateh.

Kamal, Zahira, 1994, Jerusalem, Fida; Chairwoman, Palestine Federation of Women's Action.

Kanaan, Sameh, 1994, Nablus; Fateh in Nablus.

Abu Khalil, Muhammad 1994, Nablus; Fateh activist in Nablus.

al-Khateeb, Ghassan, 1994, 1997, Jerusalem; PPP, Director of the JMCC.

Abu Khosa, Abdel Hadi, 1995, Gaza; PPP in Gaza.

Koura, Nahla, 1994, Ramallah, Fateh; active in Association of Women's Committees for Social Work in Palestine.

Kreishe, Amal, 1994, Ramallah; PPP.

al-Krunz, Sa'edi, 1997, Member of the PLC, Fateh-affiliated.

Larsen, Terje Rød, 1995, Gaza; UN Special Coordinator.

Malki, Riad, 1994, 1997, Jerusalem; Spokesperson for PFLP; Professor of Engineering, BirZeit University.

Abu Middein, Freih, 1995, Gaza, independent; Minister of Justice, PNA, from 1994; after elections in 1996, Member of PLC.

Muhanna, Rabah, 1995, Gaza; PFLP sympathiser.

Nasser, Fathi, 1994, Nablus, Fateh.

Nasser, Maha, 1994, Ramallah; PFLP sympathiser; teacher of science and physics in private high schools.

Natsche, Rafiq, 1997, Member of the PLC, Fateh-affiliated.

Ramadan, Mahmoud, 1995, Nablus, Fateh; works at an-Najah University, Nablus.

Saftawi, Ala, 1995, Gaza; Islamic Jihad sympathiser.

Saleh, 1994, Nablus, Fateh.

Salem, Walid, 1994, Jerusalem; PFLP sympathiser.

Abdel Shafi, Heidar, 1994, Gaza, independent; physician; President of Red Crescent Society; after elections in 1996, Member of PLC; resigned in autumn of 1997 due to discontent with internal political processes.

Shami, Abdullah, Sheikh, 1994, Gaza, Islamic Jihad.

Shtayyeh, Muhammad, 1994, a-Ram, Fateh, PECDAR.

Shu'aibi, Azmi, 1994, 1997, Ramallah, Fida; Minister of Youth and Sports, PNA, 1994–96; after elections in 1996, Member of PLC.

Bibliography

Tarifi, Jamil, 1994, Ramallah, Fateh; Head of the Liaison Committee with Israel; after elections in 1996, Member of PLC and Minister of Civil Affairs.

Tawfiq Daragmeh, Muwaffaq, 1995, Nablus; Fateh in Nablus.

Toubbasi, Alfred, 1994, Ramallah, independent.

Umm Jihad, or al-Wazir, Intisar, 1994, Gaza, Fateh; Minister of Social Affairs, PNA from 1994 and after elections in 1996, Member of PLC.

Ya'iesh, Imad, 1995, Nablus, Fateh; Nablus representative in Fateh Higher Committee.

Zahhar, Mahmoud, 1995, 1997, Gaza; spokesperson for Hamas.

Abu Zayde, Sufiyan, 1994, Gaza, Fateh.

Abu Zayyad, Ziad, 1994, 1997, Jerusalem; Fateh sympathiser, journalist, negotiator; after elections in 1996, Member of PLC.

Documents

PALESTINIAN

Address to the UN General Assembly, 13 November 1974, by Yasir Arafat, quoted in Walter Laqueur and Barry Rubin (eds), 1984, pp. 504–18.

Charter of the Islamic Resistance Movement (Hamas) of Palestine, translated by Muhammad Maqdsi for the Islamic Association for Palestine, Dallas, Texas, 1990, *Journal of Palestine Studies*, Vol. XXII (88), No. 4, Summer 1993, pp. 122–34.

Draft Basic Law for the National Authority in the Transitional Period, Tunis, April 1994, *Journal of Palestine Studies*, Vol. XXIII (92), No. 4, Summer 1994, pp. 137–45.

Draft Basic Law for the National Authority in the Transitional Period, December 1995, published by JMCC, Jerusalem, as Occasional Document Series, February 1996, No. 5.

Expanded Outline: Palestinian Internal Self-Government Authority: Preliminary Measures, and Elections Modalities, 3 March 1992, *Journal of Palestine Studies*, Vol. XXI (83), No. 3, Spring 1992, pp. 135–41.

Hani al-Hasan, Critique of Palestinian Peace Strategy, Tunis, mid March 1992, excerpts in *Journal of Palestine Studies*, Vol. XXI (84), No. 4, Summer 1992, pp. 142–9.

Mahmoud Abbas' (Abu Mazen), 'Apology' to Arab Gulf States concerning PLO Gulf War Stance, Riyadh, 11 January 1993, *Journal of Palestine Studies*, Vol. XXII (87), No. 3, Spring 1993, pp. 144–5.

The Palestine Declaration of Independence, 15 November 1988, in Yehuda Lukacs (ed.), 1992, pp. 411–15.

The Palestine Independence Document Prepared by Feysal Husayni of the Jerusalem Arab Studies Society, in Don Peretz, 1990, Appendix 4, pp. 204–7.

Palestinian Leadership, Statement on Current Developments, Tunis, 23 July 1992, in *Journal of Palestine Studies*, Vol. XXII (85), No. 1, Autumn 1992, pp. 139–41.

PLC Report on the Findings of the General Control Office, August 1997, translated and provided by JMCC.

PLC Self-Evaluation Report, October 1996, *Journal of Palestine Studies*, Vol. XXVI, No. 2, Winter 1997, pp. 160–1.

Palestinian Figures, Memorandum to Yasir Arafat, November 1993, *Journal of Palestine Studies*, Vol. XXIII (90), No. 2, Winter 1994, pp. 136–8.

Palestinian National Authority, Ministry of Planning, 1996–97 Human Development File.

The Palestinian National Charter: Resolutions of the Palestine National Council, 1968, in Walter Laqueur and Barry Rubin (eds), 1984, pp. 366–72.

The Palestinians' Fourteen Demands, 14 January 1988, *Journal of Palestine Studies*, Vol. XVII (67), No. 3, pp. 63–5.

171

Bibliography

Platform of the Popular Front for the Liberation of Palestine, in Walter Laqueur and Barry Rubin (eds), 1984, pp. 379–83.

PLO Central Council, Statement of the Peace Process, Tunis, 10 May 1992 excerpts, *Journal of Palestine Studies*, Vol. XXI (84), No. 4, Summer 1992, pp. 149–53.

PLO Central Council, Statement on the Peace Process and the Regional Situation, Tunis, 17 October 1992, *Journal of Palestine Studies*, Vol. XXII (86), No. 2, Winter 1993, pp. 144–7.

PLO Chairman Yasir Arafat to Israeli Prime Minister Yitzhak Rabin, PLO and Israeli Letters of Mutual Recognition, Tunis and Jerusalem, 9 September 1993, *Journal of Palestine Studies*, Vol. XXIII, No. 1, Autumn 1993, pp. 114–15.

PLO Executive Committee, Statement on Israeli–Palestinian Declaration of Principles, Tunis, 12 September 1993, *Journal of Palestine Studies*, Vol. XXIII (90), No. 2, Winter 1994, pp. 131–3.

PNC Meeting, 20th, Political Statement, Algiers, 28 September 1991, *Journal of Palestine Studies*, Vol. XXI (82), No. 2, Winter 1992, pp. 151–5.

PNC, Political Communiqué, Algiers, 15 November 1988, in Yehuda Lukacs (ed.), 1992, pp. 415–20.

PNC, Political Programme, 8 June 1974, in Yehuda Lukacs (ed.), 1992, pp. 308–11.

Revolutionary Council of Fateh, 'Political Statement', Tunis, 15 November 1993, *Journal of Palestine Studies*, Vol. XXIII (90), No. 2, Winter 1994, pp. 133–6.

The Seven Points, passed by the Central Committee of al-Fatah, January 1969, in Walter Lacqueur and Barry Rubin (eds), 1984, pp. 372–9.

Speech by Yasir Arafat to the UN General Assembly, 13 November 1974, in Yehuda Lukacs (ed.), 1992, pp. 317–33.

Statements by General Secretary of the PDFLP, Nayif Hawatmeh, Defending the Establishment of a Palestinian National Authority in Territories Liberated from Israeli Occupation, 24 February 1974, in Yehuda Lukacs (ed.), 1992, p. 307 f.

LEAFLETS

Commandement National Unifié (UNLU), 01A (Palestine National Forces), 8 January 1988; 02B, 10 January 1988; 03A, 16 January 1988; 03B, 18 January 1988; 04A, 21 January 1988; 06B, 5 February 1988, reprinted in Arabic and translated into French in Legrain, 1991a.

JHD01 (Islamic Jihad), 10 December 1987, reprinted in Arabic and translated into French in Legrain, 1991a.

HMS01 (Hamas), 14 December 1987; HMS02 (Hamas), January 1988; HMS03A and C, 22 January 1988, reprinted in Arabic and translated into French in Legrain, 1991a.

Hamas2, in Mishal and Asharoni, 1994: 204.

Hamas37, 3 March 1989, in *Filastin al-Muslimun*, Issue No. 3, March 1989 (in Arabic).

Hamas49, 27 October 1989, from archives of Arab Studies Society (in Arabic).

Hamas54, 11 March 1990, from archives of Arab Studies Society (in Arabic).

Hamas65, 10 November 1990, from archives of Arab Studies Society (in Arabic).

Hamas78 (no date), in *Filastin al-Muslimin*, Issue No. 10, October 1991 (in Arabic).

Hamas83 (no date), in *Filastin al-Muslimun*, Issue No. 3, March 1992 (in Arabic).

Hamas94 (no date), in *Filastin al-Muslimun*, Issue No. 3, March 1993 (in Arabic).

Hamas94a, 4 January 1993; 95, 3 February 1993; 97, 5 April 1993 (provided by staff of *al-Fajr*, in English).

Hamas100, 7 July 1993, from archives of Arab Studies Society (in Arabic).

Hamas105 (no date), in *Filastin al-Muslimun*, Issue No. 1, January 1994 (in Arabic).

Hamas114, 6 August 1994, in *Filastin al-Muslimun*, Issue No. 9, September 1994 (in Arabic).

Hamas Special Leaflet, 10 November 1988, in Mishal and Aharoni, 1994: 270.

Hamas No. 1, January 1988, in Mishal and Aharoni, 1994: 201.

Islamic Jihad, 3 November 1992, from the archives of JMCC, Jerusalem (in Arabic).

'Izz al-Din al-Qassem, 19 November 1994 (in Arabic).

UNLU1, 8 January Nos 1–47, 8 January 1988–15 October 1989 in *No Voice is Louder than the Voice of the Uprising*, Ibal Publishing (in English).

UNLU3, 18 January 1988, in Mishal and Aharoni, 1994: 60–3.

UNLU11, 19 March 1988, in Mishal and Aharoni, 1994: 72–5.

UNLU12, 2 April 1988, in Mishal and Aharoni, 1994: 76–81.

UNLU16, 13 May 1988, in Mishal and Aharoni, 1994: 93–7.

UNLU21, 6 July 1988, in Mishal and Aharoni, 1994: 108–12.

UNLU25, 6 September 1988, in Mishal and Aharoni, 1994: 123–9.

UNLU32, 9 January 1989, from archives at BirZeit Research and Documentation Centre (in Arabic).

UNLU35, 26 February 1989, in *Filastin al-Thawra*, 5 March 1989, Issue 739 (in Arabic).

UNLU41, 13 June 1989, in Mishal and Aharoni, 1994: 143–8.

UNLU45, 5 September 1989, from archives of *al-Tal'ia* in Jerusalem (in Arabic).

UNLU55, 26 March 1990, from archives of Arab Studies Society, Jerusalem (in Arabic).

UNLU61, no date, printed in *Filastin al-Thawra*, 9 September 1990, Issue 811 (in Arabic).

UNLU71, 1 June 1991, from the archives of JMCC, Jerusalem (in Arabic).

UNLU81, 12 April 1992, from the archives of JMCC, Jerusalem (in Arabic).

UNLU83, 30 May 1992, excerpts, in *Journal of Palestine Studies*, Vol. XXII (85), No. 1, Autumn 1992, pp. 138–9.

UNLU91, January 1993; 93, 1 February 1993; 93, 1 March 1993; 94, 1 April 1993; 95, 29 May 1993 (in English, provided by staff of *al-Fajr*), from the archives of the JMCC.

UNLU96, 3 July 1993, from the archives of Arab Studies Society (in Arabic).

UNLU100, 3 November 1993, from the archives of Arab Studies Society (in Arabic).

UNLU (special call), 25 February 1994 (in Arabic), from archives of Jerusalem Media and Communication Center.

ARAB

Address by King Hussein on Jordan's Disengagement from the West Bank, 31 July 1988, in Yehuda Lukacs (ed.), 1991, pp. 520–25.

Statement by Jordanian Prime Minister Zaid al-Rifai on the Implementation of Jordan's Disengagement from the West Bank, 20 August 1988, in Yehuda Lukacs (ed.), 1991, pp. 525–6.

INTERNATIONAL

Amnesty International, 1996, 'Palestinian Authority: Prolonged Political Detention, Torture and Unfair Trials', London, December.

Middle East Watch, 1992a, 'Human Rights Watch World Report 1992: "The Israeli-Occupied West Bank and Gaza Strip"', *Journal of Palestine Studies*, Vol. XXI (84), No. 4, pp. 113–29.

Middle East Watch, 1992b, 'The Israeli-Occupied West Bank and Gaza Strip', *Journal of Palestine Studies*, Vol. XXI (84), No. 4, Summer 1992, pp. 113–29.

UN Security Council Resolution 242, 22 November 1967, in Yehuda Lukacs (ed.), 1991, pp. 1–2.

UN Security Resolution 338, 23 October 1973, in Yehuda Lukacs (ed.), 1991, p. 13.

UN Security Resolution 799, 18 December 1992, *Journal of Palestine Studies*, Vol. XXII (87), No. 3, Spring 1993, p. 137.

Bibliography

AGREEMENTS

Agreement on the Gaza Strip and the Jericho Area, 4 May 1994, Cairo, Ministry of Foreign Affairs, Jerusalem, Government of Israel.

Declaration of Principles, Washington, DC, 13 September 1993, *Journal of Palestine Studies*, Vol. XXIII (89), No. 1, Autumn 1993, pp. 115–21.

Israel and the PLO, Agreement on Preparatory Transfer of Powers and Responsibilities', Eretz Checkpoint, Gaza, 29 August 1994, *Journal of Palestine Studies*, Vol. XXIV (94), No. 2, Winter 1995, pp. 109–26.

Israeli–Palestinian Interim Agreement on the West Bank and the Gaza Strip, Washington, DC, 28 September 1995, Israel Information Service Gopher, Israeli Ministry of Foreign Affairs, Jerusalem.

The Jordanian–Palestinian Accord, Amman, 11 February 1985, in Yehuda Lukacs (ed.), 1991, pp. 488–92.

Protocol on Economic Relations, Paris, 29 April 1994, in Agreement on the Gaza Strip and the Jericho Area.

Protocol on Further Transfer of Powers and Responsibilities, 27 August 1995, Israel Information Service Gopher, Israeli Ministry of Foreign Affairs, Jerusalem.

Treaty of Peace between the State of Israel and the Hashemite Kingdom of Jordan, 26 October 1994, copy provided by Israeli Ministry of Foreign Affairs, Jerusalem.

The Washington Declaration, Israel–Jordan and the United States, 25 July 1994, copy provided by Israeli Ministry of Foreign Affairs, Jerusalem.

WORKS OF REFERENCE

Chronology of Journal of Palestine Studies, Vol. XVII (67), No. 3, Spring 1988, to Vol. XXVI (102), No. 2, Winter 1997.

CPRS, *Opinion Polls*, January 1994 to June 1998, Nablus.

Palestinian Bureau of Statistics, 1994, Current Status Report Series (No. 1), *Demography of the Palestinian Population in the West Bank and Gaza Strip*, Ramallah, December.

Palestinians in Profile: A Guide to Leading Palestinians in the Occupied Territories, 1993, Jerusalem: Panorama; the Centre for the Dissemination of Alternative Information.

PCBS, 1997–98, www.pcbs.org.

Newspapers and periodicals

al-Filastin al-Muslima, connected with Hamas, published in London.

al-Filastin al-Thawra, PLO organ, published in Nicosia, Cyprus.

al-Istiqlal, Gaza, weekly paper connected with Islamic Jihad, publication started in Autumn 1994.

al-Quds, East Jerusalem, daily newspaper.

Jerusalem Media Communication Centre Weekly Report, published by JMCC, East Jerusalem; changed name in August 1993 to *Palestine Report*.

Jerusalem Post, Jerusalem, daily newspaper.

Jerusalem Post International, Jerusalem, weekly paper, summary of *Jerusalem Post*.

Jerusalem Report, biweekly magazine.

The Jerusalem Times, weekly paper, East Jerusalem, replaced *al-Fajr*, in English.

Middle East, monthly magazine, London.

Middle East International, biweekly, published in London and Washington.

Middle East Report, Middle East Research and Information Project, quarterly, Washington.

News from Within, published by Alternative Information Center, monthly, Jerusalem.
Palestine Report, published by JMCC, weekly, East Jerusalem.

Secondary sources

Abbas, Mahmoud (Abu Mazen), 1993, 'Apology' to Arab Gulf States Concerning PLO Gulf War Stance, Riyadh, 11 January 1993, *Journal of Palestine Studies*, Vol. XXII (87), No. 3, Spring, 144–5.
—— , 1995, *Through Secret Channels: The Road to Oslo. Senior PLO Leader Revealing Story of the Negotiations with Israel*, Garnet Publishing.
Abu-Amr, Ziad, 1990, 'The Politics of the *Intifada*', in Michael Hudson (ed.), pp. 3–23.
—— , 1992, *Emerging Trends in Palestinian Strategic Political Thinking and Practice*. Jerusalem, PASSIA.
—— , 1993, 'Hamas: A Historical and Political Background', *Journal of Palestine Studies*, Vol. XXII (88), No. 4, Summer, pp. 5–19.
—— , 1994, *Islamic Fundamentalism in the West Bank and Gaza: Muslim Brotherhood and Islamic Jihad*, Bloomington and Indianapolis, Indiana University Press.
—— , 1997, 'The Palestinian Legislative Council: A Critical Assessment', *Journal of Palestine Studies*, Vol. XXVI, No. 4, Summer, pp. 90–7.
Aggestam, Karin and Christer Jönsson, 1997, '(Un)Ending Conflict: Challenges in Post-War Bargaining', *Millennium: Journal of International Studies*, Vol. 26, No. 3, pp. 771–93.
Ahmed, Hisham H., 1994, *Hamas: From Religious Salvation to Political Transformation – The Rise of Hamas in Palestinian Society*, Jerusalem, PASSIA.
al-Qasem, Anis, 1994, 'The Proposed Charter of the National Authority in the Transitional Phase', in JMCC (ed.), pp. 45–55.
Anderson, Benedict, 1991, *Imagined Communities*, London, Verso.
Antonius, George, 1938 (reprinted 1969), *The Arab Awakening: The Story of the Arab National Movement*, Beirut, Libraire du Liban.
Ardant, Gabriel, 1975, 'Financial Policy and Economic Infrastructure of Modern States and Nations', in Charles Tilly (ed.), 1975a, pp. 164–243.
Armstrong, John A., 1982, *Nations before Nationalism*, Chapel Hill, University of North Carolina Press.
Aronson, Geoffrey, 1997, 'Settlement Monitor', *Journal of Palestine Studies*, Vol. XXVII, No. 1, Autumn, pp. 126–35.
Aruri, Nasser (ed.), 1984, *Occupation: Israel over Palestine*, London, Zed Books Ltd.
Aruri, H. Nasser and John J. Carroll, 1994, 'A New Palestinian Charter', *Journal of Palestine Studies*, Vol. 92 (XXIII), No. 4, Summer, pp. 5–16.
Aybui, Nazih N., 1991 *Political Islam: Religion and Politics in the Arab World*, London and New York, Routledge.
al-Azmeh, Aziz, 1988, 'Arab Nationalism and Islamism', *Review of Middle East Studies*, No. 4, pp. 33–51.
Axell, Karin (ed.), 1993, *States in Armed Conflict 1992*, Report No. 36, Department of Peace and Conflict Research, Uppsala University.
Bahiri, Simcha, 1987, *Industrialization in the West Bank and Gaza*, Jerusalem, The West Bank Data Base Project.
Bargouti, Husain Jameel, 1990, 'Jeep versus Bare Feet: The Villages in the *Intifada*', in Jamal R. Nassar and Roger Heacock (eds), 1990a, pp. 107–23.
Barth, Fredrik, 1969, *Ethnic Groups and Boundaries: The Social Organization of Culture Difference*, Bergen and Oslo, Universitetsforlaget; London, George Allen and Unwin.

Bibliography

Barth, Fredrik, 1994, 'Enduring and Emerging Issues in the Analysis of Ethnicity', in Hans Vermuelen and Cora Govers (eds), 1994a, pp. 11–32.

Bauman, Zygmunt, 1989, *Auschwitz och det moderna samhället*, Göteborg, Daidalos (original: *Modernity and the Holocaust*, first published 1989 by Polity Press).

——, 1990, 'Modernity and Ambivalence', in Mike Featherstone (ed.), pp. 143–70.

——, 1995, *Life in Fragments: Essays in Postmodern Morality*, Oxford, Blackwell Publishers.

Baumgarten, Helga, 1990, ' "Discontented People" and "Outside Agitators": The PLO in the Palestinian Uprising', in Jamal R. Nassar and Roger Heacock (eds), 1990a, pp. 207–26.

Beblawi, Hazem and Giacomo Luciani (eds), 1987, *The Rentier State*, London, Croom Helm.

Ben-Dor, Gabriel, 1988, 'Ethnopolitics and the Middle Eastern State', in Milton Esman and Itamar Rabinovich (eds), pp. 3–24.

Benvenisti, Eyal, 1990, *Legal Dualism: The Absorption of the Occupied Territories into Israel*, The West Bank Data Base Project, Boulder, San Francisco, Oxford, Westview Press.

Benvenisti, Meron, 1986, *Report: Demographic, Economic, Legal, Social and Political Developments in the West Bank*, Jerusalem, West Bank Data Project.

Benvenisti, Meron and Shlomo Khayat, 1988, *The West Bank and Gaza Atlas*, Jerusalem, The Jerusalem Post Press.

Bishara, Azmi, 1995, 'Bantustanisation or Bi-nationalism?', *Race and Class*, October–December.

——, 1998, 'Reflections on the Realities of the Oslo Process', in George Giacamen and Dag Jørund Lønning (eds), pp. 212–26.

Bourdieu, Pierre, 1977, *Outline of a Theory of Practice*, tr. Richard Nice, Cambridge, Cambridge University Press.

Brand, Laurie, 1988a, *Palestinians in the Arab World: Institution Building and the Search for State*, New York, Columbia University Press.

——, 1988b, 'Nasir's Egypt and the Reemergence of the Palestinian National Movement', *Journal of Palestine Studies*, Vol. XVII, No. 2, Winter, pp. 29–45.

——, 1990, 'The Shape of Things to Come: Policy and Politics in the Palestinian State', in Michael Hudson (ed.), pp. 227–57.

Breuilly, J., 1985, *Nationalism and the State*, Manchester, Manchester University Press.

Brynen, Rex (ed.), 1991, *Echoes of the Intifada: Regional Repercussions of the Palestinian–Israeli Conflict*, Boulder, Westview and Oxford, Westview Press, Westview Special Studies on the Middle East.

——, 1992, 'Post-Rentier Democratization in the Arab World: The Case of Jordan', *Canadian Journal of Political Science*, Vol. 25, No. 1.

Butenschøn, Nils, 1998, 'The Oslo Agreement: From the White House to Jabal Abu Ghneim', in George Giacamen and Dag Jørund Lønning (eds), pp. 16–44.

Butler, Judith, 1993, *Bodies that Matter*, London, Routledge.

Buzan, Barry, 1991, *People, States and Fear: An Agenda for International Security Studies in the Post-Cold War Era*, Second Edition, Hemel Hempstead, Harvester Wheatsheaf.

Chaliand, Gerard, 1972, *The Palestinian Resistance*, Harmondsworth, Penguin Books.

Chase, Anthony B. Tirado, 1997, *The Palestinian Authority Draft Constitution: Possibilities and Realities in the Search for Alternative Models of State Formation*, Jerusalem, IPCRI Law and Development Programme, Civil Society Publications.

Chelkowski, Peter J. and Robert J. Pranger (eds), *Ideology and Power in the Middle East*, Durham, NC, and London, Duke University Press.

Cobban, H., 1984, *The Palestinian Liberation Organization: People, Power and Politics*, Cambridge, Cambridge University Press.

Cohen, Abner (ed.), 1974, *Urban Ethnicity*, London, Tavistock.

Cohen, Amnon, 1982, *Political Parties in the West Bank under the Jordanian Regime, 1949–1967*, Ithaca and London, Cornell University Press.

Bibliography

Connor, Walker, 1972, 'Nation-building or Nation Destroying', *World Politics*, Vol. XXIV, No. 3, April, pp. 319–55.

Corbin, Jane, 1994, *Gaza First: The Secret Norway Channel to Peace between Israel and the PLO*, London, Bloomsbury.

Curtis, Michael (ed.), 1986, *The Middle East Reader*, New Brunswick and Oxford, Transaction Books.

Dahbour, Omar and Micheline R. Ishay (eds), 1995, *The Nationalism Reader*, Atlantic Highlands, NJ, Humanities Press.

Derrida, J., 1981, *Positions*, Chicago, University of Chicago Press.

Diamond, Larry, Juan J. Linz and Seymour Martin Lipset, 1990, *Politics in Developing Countries: Comparing Experiences with Democracy*, Boulder and London, Lynne Rienner Publishers.

Divine, Donna Robinson, 1980, 'The Dialectics of Palestinian Politics', in Joel S. Migdal (ed.) 1980b, pp. 212–32.

Emerson, Steven, 1992, 'The Palestinian Meltdown', *The New Republic*, 23 November.

Eriksen, Thomas Hylland, 1992a, *Us and Them in Modern Societies: Ethnicity and Nationalism in Mauritius, Trinidad and Beyond*, Oslo, Scandinavian University Press.

—— , 1992b, 'Ethnicity and Nationalism: Definitions and Critical Reflections', *Bulletin of Peace Proposals*, Vol. 23, No. 2, June, pp. 219–24.

—— , 1993, *Ethnicity and Nationalism: Anthropological Perspectives*, London and Boulder, Pluto Press.

Esman, Milton and Itamar Rabinovich (eds), 1988, *Ethnicity, Pluralism and the State in the Middle East*, Ithaca and London, Cornell University Press.

Fanon, Franz, 1968, *The Wretched of the Earth*, New York, Grove Press.

Farsoun, Samih K. and Jean M. Landis, 1990, 'The Sociology of an Uprising', in Jamal R. Nassar and Roger Heacock (eds), 1990a.

Featherstone, Mike, 1990, *Global Culture: Nationalism, Globalization and Modernity*, London, Sage.

Fichte, Johann Gottlieb, 1808 [1995], 'Address to the German Nation', in Omar Dahbour and Micheline K. Ishay (eds), pp. 62–70.

Finer, Samuel, 1975, 'State- and Nation-building in Europe: The Role of the Military', in Charles Tilly (ed.), 1975a, pp. 84–164.

Flapan, Simha, 1987, *The Birth of Israel: Myths and Realities*, London, Croom Helm.

Frangi, Abdallah, 1982, *The PLO and Palestine*, London, Zed Books.

Frisch, Hillel, 1997a, 'From Palestine Liberation Organization to Palestinian Authority: The Territorialization of "Neopatriarchy", in Sela and Ma'oz (eds), 1997a, pp. 55–72.

—— , 1997b, 'Modern Absolutist or Neopatriarchal State Building? Customary Law, Extended Families, and the Palestinian Authority', *International Journal of Middle East Studies*, Vol. 29, pp. 341–58.

Gabriel, Judith, 1988, 'The Economic Side of the *Intifada*', *Journal of Palestine Studies*, Vol. XVIII (69), No. 1, pp. 198–213.

Gellner, Ernest, 1983, *Nations and Nationalism*, Oxford, Basil Blackwell.

Ghamina, Ziad Abu, 1989, *The Islamic Movement and the Issue of Palestine*, Amman, in Arabic, quoted in Haddad, 1992, p. 268.

Ghanem, As'ad, 1996, 'Founding Elections in a Transitional Period: The First Palestinian General Elections', *Middle East Journal*, Vol. 50, No. 4, Autumn, pp. 513–28.

Giacamen, George and Dag Jørund Lønning (eds), 1998, *After Oslo: New Realities, Old Problems*, London and Chicago, Pluto Press.

Giddens, Anthony, 1979, *Central Problems in Social Theory: Action, Structure and Contradiction in Social Analysis*, London, Macmillan Press.

—— , 1981, *A Contemporary Critique of Historical Materialism*. Vol. 1: *Power, Property and the State*, Berkeley and Los Angeles, University of California Press.

Golan, Galia, 1980, *The Soviet Union and the Palestine Liberation Organization: An Uneasy Alliance*, New York, Praeger Publishers.

——, 1997, 'Moscow and the PLO: The Ups and Downs of a Complex Relationship', in Avraham Sela and Moshe Ma'oz (eds), 1997a, pp. 121–41.

Granott, A., 1952, *The Land System in Palestine*, London, Eyre and Spottiswoode.

Gresh, A., 1983, *The PLO – The Struggle Within: Towards an Independent Palestinian State*, reprinted in 1988, London, Zed Books.

Habermas, Jürgen, 1988, *On the Logic of the Social Sciences*, Cambridge, Polity Press.

Habibi, Emile, 1989, *The Secret Life of Saeed: The Ill-Fated Pessoptimist: A Palestinian Who Became a Citizen of Israel*, Columbia, La., Readers International.

Haddad, Yvonne, 1992, 'Islamists and the "Problem of Israel": The 1967 Awakening', *Middle East Journal*, Vol. 4, No. 2, Spring, pp. 268–85.

Hall, Stuart, 1992, 'The Question of Cultural Identity', in Stuart Hall, David Held and Tony McGrew (eds), pp. 274–314.

——, 1996, 'Introduction: Who Needs Identity?', in Stuart Hall and Paul du Gay (eds), *Questions of Cultural Identity*, London, Sage Publications Ltd.

Hall, Stuart, David Held and Tony McGrew (eds), 1992, *Modernity and its Futures*, Cambridge, Polity Press in association with the Open University.

Hanf, Theodor and Bernard Sabella, 1996, *A Date with Democracy: Palestinians on Society and Politics. An Empirical Survey*, Freiburg, Arnold Bergstraesser Institut.

Hannerz, Ulf, 1992, *Cultural Complexity: Studies in the Social Organization of Meaning*, New York, Columbia University Press.

Al-Haq, 1988, *Punishing a Nation: Human Rights Violations During the Palestinian Uprising, December 1987–December 1988*, Ramallah, al-Haq, Law in the Service of Man.

Al-Haqiqa al-Gha'iba, [The Absent Truth], n.d., a booklet published by the Muslim Brotherhood Society in the Occupied Territories. Author, publisher, date and place of publication not provided, quoted in Ziad Abu-Amr, 1994, *Islamic Fundamentalism in the West Bank and Gaza: Muslim Brotherhood and Islamic Jihad*, Bloomington and Indianapolis, Indiana University Press, p. 141 n. 13.

Harris-Rolef, Susan, 1997, 'Israel's Policy Towards the PLO: From Rejection to Recognition', in Sela and Ma'oz (eds), 1997a.

Hart, Alan, 1984, *Arafat: A Political Biography*, Bloomington and Indianapolis, Indiana University Press.

Hastings, Adrian, 1997, *The Construction of Nationhood: Ethnicity, Religion and Nationalism*, Cambridge, Cambridge University Press.

Heiberg, Marianne, 1993, 'Opinions and Attitudes', in Marianne Heiberg and Geir Øvensen, pp. 249–82.

Heiberg, Marianne and Geir Øvensen (eds), 1993, *Palestinian Society in Gaza, West Bank and Arab Jerusalem: A Survey of Living Conditions*, Fagbevegelsens senter for forskning, utredning og dokumentasjon, FAFO report 151, Oslo, Falch Hurtigtrykk.

Heidar, Aziz, 1988, 'The Different Levels of Palestinian Identity', in M. Esman and I. Rabinovich (eds), pp. 95–120.

Heller, Mark, 1980, 'Politics and Social Change in the West Bank Since 1967', in Joel S. Migdal (ed.), 1980b, pp. 185–211.

——, 1997, 'Towards a Palestinian State', *Survival*, Vol. 39, No. 2, Summer, pp. 5–22.

Heller, Mark A. and Sari Nusseibeh, 1991, *No Trumpets, No Drums: A Two-State Settlement of the Israeli–Palestinian Conflict*, New York, Hill and Wang.

Hettne, Björn, 1992, *Etniska konflikter och internationella relationer*, Lund, Studentlitteratur.

Hilal, Jamil, 1992, 'West Bank and Gaza Strip Social Formations under Jordanian and Egyptian Rule (1948–1967)', *Review of Middle East Studies*, 5.

—— , 1998, 'The Effect of the Oslo Agreement on the Palestinian Political System', in George Giacamen and Dag Jørund Lønning (eds), pp. 162–88.

Hiltermann, Joost, 1990a, 'Mass Mobilization and the Uprising: The Labour Movement', in Michael Hudson (ed.), pp. 44–62.

—— , 1990b, 'Work and Action: The Role of the Working Class in the Uprising', in Jamal R. Nassar and Roger Heacock (eds), 1990a, pp. 143–57.

—— , 1991, *Behind the Intifada: Labor and Women's Movements in the Occupied Territories*, Princeton, Princeton University Press.

Hobsbawm, Eric, 1990, *Nations and Nationalism Since 1780: Programme, Myth, Reality*, Cambridge, Cambridge University Press.

Hobsbawm, Eric and Terence Ranger (eds), 1983, *The Invention of Tradition*, Cambridge, Cambridge University Press.

Holt, Maria, 1992, *Half the People: Women, History and the Palestinian Intifada*, Jerusalem, Palestinian Academic Society for the Study of International Affairs.

Horowitz, D.L., 1985, *Ethnic Groups in Conflict*, Berkeley, University of California Press.

Hourani, Albert, 1962, *Arabic Thought in the Liberal Age 1798–1939*, reissued with new preface 1983 and reprinted 1991, Cambridge, Cambridge University Press.

—— , 1991, *A History of the Arab Peoples*, New York, Warner Books.

Hroch, Miroslav, 1985, *Social Preconditions of National Revival in Europe*, Cambridge, Cambridge University Press.

Hudson, Michael, 1977, *Arab Politics: The Search for Legitimacy*, New Haven, Yale University Press.

—— (ed.), 1990, *The Palestinians: New Directions*, Washington, Georgetown University, The Center for Contemporary Arab Studies.

—— , 1991, 'After the Gulf War: Prospects for Democratization in the Arab World', *Middle East Journal*, Vol. 4, No. 3, Summer, pp. 407–26.

Hunter, Robert F., 1993(first edition 1991), *The Palestinian Uprising: A War by Other Means*, Berkeley and Los Angeles, University of California Press.

Interview with Eric Rouleau, *Journal of Palestine Studies*, Vol. XXII, No. 4, Summer 1993, pp. 45–61.

Jad, Islah, 1990, 'From Salons to the Popular Committees', in Jamal R. Nassar and Roger Heacock (eds), 1990a, pp. 124–42.

Jarbawi, Ali, 1990, 'Palestinian Elites in the Occupied Territories: Stability and Change through the *Intifada*', in Jamal R. Nassar and Roger Heacock (eds), 1990a, pp. 287–305.

Jarbawi, Ali and Roger Heacock, 1993, 'The Deportations and the Palestinian–Israeli Negotiations', *Journal of Palestine Studies*, Vol. XXII, No. 3, pp. 32–45.

Jawwad, Islah Abdul, 1990, 'The Evolution of the Political Role of the Palestinian Women's Movement in the Uprising', in Michael Hudson (ed.), pp. 63–76.

Jawwad Atta and Saleh Abdel, 1991, *Al-Bayanat al-Israe'iliyya al-Muzawwara. Dirasa Khassa Hawla-l-Harb al-Nafsiyya Didd al-Intifada (The Israeli Fake Leaflets. Study of the Psychological War Against the Intifada)*, Amman, Markaz al-Quds li-l-Dirasat al-Inm'iyya. An unpublished, briefer version exists in English under the title *Fake Leaflets*.

Jayyusi, Lena, 1998, 'The "Voice of Palestine" and the Peace Process: Paradoxes in Media Discourse After Oslo', in George Giacamen and Dag Jørund Lønning (eds), pp. 189–211.

Jerusalem Media and Communication Centre, 1993, *Israeli Military Orders in the Occupied Palestinian West Bank 1967–1992*, compiled by Jamil Rabah and Natasha Fairweather, Jerusalem, JMCC.

—— , 1994, *Challenges Facing Palestinian Society in the Interim Period*, Jerusalem, JMCC.

Al-Jihad fi Filastin: Farida Shar'iyya wa-darura Bashariyya (*The Jihad in Palestine: A Religious Obligation and Human Necessity*), author, publisher, date and place of publication not given. Quoted in Ziad Abu-Amr, 1994, p. 113.

JMCC, 1992, *Israeli Obstacles to Economic Development in the Occupied Palestinian Territories*, Jerusalem, JMCC.

Johnson, Nels, 1982, *Islam and the Politics of Meaning in Palestinian Nationalism*, London, Routledge and Kegan Paul.

Joint Report on the 1996 Palestinian Elections, by al-Haq, Article 19, International Commission of Jurists, May 1997, Ramallah.

de Jong, Jan, 1998, 'The Geography of Politics: Israel's Settlement Drive After Oslo', in George Giacamen and Dag Jørund Lønning (eds), pp. 77–120.

Jørund Lønning, Dag, 1998, 'Vision and Reality Diverging: Palestinian Survival Strategies in the Post-Oslo Era', in George Giacamen and Dag Jørund Lønning (eds), pp. 162–88.

Kahan, David, 1987, *Agriculture and Water Resources in the West Bank and Gaza (1967–1987)*, Jerusalem, the West Bank Data Base Project.

Kapferer, Bruce, 1988, *Legends of People, Myths of State: Violence, Intolerance and Political Culture in Sri Lanka and Australia*, Washington DC and London, Smithsonian Institution Press.

Kaufman, Edy, Abed B. Shukri and Robert L. Rothstein (eds), 1993, *Democracy, Peace and the Israeli–Palestinian Conflict*, Boulder, Lynne Rienner Publisher.

Kellas, James, 1991, *The Politics of Nationalism and Ethnicity*, London, Macmillan.

Khader, Hassan, 1997, 'Confessions of a Palestinian Returnee', *Journal of Palestine Studies*, Vol. XXVII, No. 1, Autumn, pp. 85–95.

Khalaf, Issa, 1991, *Politics in Palestine: Arab Factionalism and Social Disintegration 1939–1948*, New York, State University of New York Press.

Khalidi, Rashid, 1997, *Palestinian Identity: The Construction of Modern National Consciousness*, New York, Columbia University Press.

Khalidi, Walid (ed.), 1971, *From Haven to Conquest: Readings in Zionism and the Palestine Problem until 1948*, Beirut, The Institute for Palestine Studies.

—— , 1992, *Palestine Reborn*, London and New York, I. B. Tauris.

al-Khalil, Samir, 1989, *Republic of Fear: Saddam's Iraq*, Berkeley, University of California Press.

Khoury, Philip and Joseph Kostiner (eds), 1990, *Tribes and State-formation in the Middle East*, London and New York, I. B. Tauris.

Kimmerling, Baruch, 1992, 'Sociology, Ideology, and Nation-Building: The Palestinians and their Meaning in Israeli Sociology', *American Sociological Review*. Vol. 57, No. 4, August, pp. 446–60.

—— , 1997, The Power-Oriented Settlement: PLO–Israel – The Road to the Oslo Agreement and Back?', in Avraham Sela and Moshe Ma'oz (eds), 1997a, pp. 223–52.

Kimmerling, Baruch and Joel S. Migdal, 1993, *Palestinians: The Making of a People*, New York, The Free Press.

Krishna, Sankaran, 1996, 'Cartographic Anxiety: Mapping the Body Politics in India', in Michael J. Shapiro and Hayward R. Alker (eds), *Challenging Boundaries: Global Flows, Territorial Identities*, Minneapolis and London, University of Minnesota Press.

Kuttab, Daoud, 1992, 'Current Developments and the Peace Process', *Journal of Palestine Studies*, Vol. XXII, No. 1, Autumn, pp. 100–7.

—— , 1993, 'Report from the Occupied Territories', *Journal of Palestine Studies*, Vol. XXIII, No. 1, Autumn, pp. 80–9.

Laclau, E., 1990, *New Reflections on the Revolution of Our Time*, London, Verso.

Landau, J. M., 1993, *The Arab Minority in Israel 1967–1991, Political Aspects*, Oxford, Clarendon Press.

Bibliography

Laqueur, Walter and Barry Rubin (eds), 1984, *The Israel–Arab Reader: A Documentary History of the Middle East*, New York, Penguin Books.

Legrain, Jean-François, 1990, 'The Islamic Movements and the *Intifada*', in Jamal R. Nassar and Roger Heacock (eds), 1990a, pp. 175–89.

——, 1991a, *Voix du soulèvement Palestinien 1987–1988*, in cooperation with Pierre Chenard, critical edition of the leaflets of UNLU and Hamas. French translation with Pierre Chenard. CEDEJ: Centre d'Études et de Documentation Economique, Juridique et Sociale, Le Cane.

——, 1991b, 'A Defining Moment: Palestinian Islamic Fundamentalism', in James Piscatori (ed.), 1991a, pp. 70–87.

——, 1994, 'Palestinian Islamisms: Patriotism as a Condition of their Expansion', in Martin E. Marty and R. Scott Appleby (eds), pp. 413–27.

Lesch, Ann Mosley, 1973, 'The Palestine Arab Nationalist Movement Under the Mandate', in William Quandt, Fuad Jabber and Ann Mosley Lesch, pp. 5–42.

——, 1979, *Arab Politics in Palestine 1917–1939: The Frustration of a Nationalist Movement*, Ithaca and London, Cornell University Press.

——, 1984a, 'Gaza: Life under Occupation', in Ann Mosley Lesch and Mark Tessler, 1989a, pp. 238–54.

——, 1991, 'Palestinians in Kuwait', *Journal of Palestine Studies*, Vol. XX, No. 4, Summer, pp. 42–54.

——, 1992, *Transition to Palestinian Self-Government*, Bloomington and Indianapolis, Indiana University Press.

Lesch, Ann Mosley and Mark Tessler, 1989a, *Israel, Egypt and the Palestinians: From Camp David to Intifada*, Bloomington and Indianapolis, Indiana University Press.

——, 1989b, 'The West Bank and Gaza: Political and Ideological Responses to Occupation', in Ann Mosley Lesch and Mark Tessler (eds), 1989a.

Libdeh, Hasan Abu, Geir Øvensen and Helge Brunborg, 1993, 'Population Characteristics and Trends', in Marianne Heiberg and Geir Øvensen (eds), 1993, pp. 35–80.

Lindholm Schulz, Helena and Michael Schulz (eds), 1995, *Visions for a New Middle East: Prospects for Regional Co-operation and Institution Building in the Context of the Peace Process – Israel, the Palestinian Entity and Jordan*, proceedings from a one-day conference in Jerusalem, 11 April 1995, organised by UNU/WIDER, Göteborg, Padrigu Papers.

Litvak, Meir, 1997, 'Inside versus Outside: The Challenge of the Local Leadership, 1967–1994', in Avraham Sela and Moshe Ma'oz (eds), 1997a, pp. 171–96.

Lockman, Zachary and Joel Beinin, 1989, *Intifada: The Palestinian Uprising Against Israeli Occupation*, Boston, South End Press.

Luciani, Giacomo (ed.), 1990, *The Arab State*, London, Routledge.

Lukacs, Yehuda (ed.), 1992, *The Israeli–Palestinian Conflict: A Documentary Record 1967–1990*, Cambridge and New York, Cambridge University Press.

Lustick, Ian, 1980, *Arabs in the Jewish State: Israel's Control of a National Minority*, Austin and London, University of Texas Press.

Ma'oz, Moshe, 1984, *Palestinian Leadership on the West Bank: The Changing Role of the Mayors under Jordan and Israel*, London, Frank Cass.

——, 1993, *Democratization Among the West Bank Palestinians and its Relevance to Palestinian–Israeli Relations*, Jerusalem, The Harry S. Truman Research Institute for the Advancement of Peace and The Hebrew University of Jerusalem, reprinted from Edy Kaufman, Shukri B. Abed and Robert L. Rothstein (eds).

Maqdsi, Muhammad, 1993, Translation of the Charter of Hamas, *Journal of Palestine Studies*, Vol. XXII, No. 4, Summer.

Marty, Martin E. and R. Scott Appleby (eds), 1994, *Accounting for Fundamentalisms: The Dynamic Character of Movements*, Chicago and London, The University of Chicago Press.

Mattar, Philip, 1988, *The Mufti of Jerusalem: Al-Hajj Amin al-Husayni and the Palestinian National Movement*, New York, Columbia University Press.

Mayer, T., 1990, 'Pro-Iranian Fundamentalism in Gaza', in Emmanuel Sivan and Menachem Friedman (eds), pp. 143–56.

McDowall, David, 1989, *Palestine and Israel – The Uprising and Beyond*, London, I. B. Tauris.

—— , 1994, *Palestinians: The Road to Nationhood*, London, Minority Rights Publications.

Migdal, Joel, S., 1980a, 'The Effects of Regime Policies on Social Cohesion and Fragmentation', in Joel S. Migdal (ed.), 1980b, pp. 3–98.

Migdal, Joel S. (ed.), 1980b, *Palestinian Society and Politics*, Princeton, Princeton University Press.

Miller, Ylana N., 1980, 'Administrative Policy in Rural Palestine: The Impact of British Norms on Arab Community Life, 1920–1948', in Joel S. Migdal (ed.), 1980b, pp. 124–45.

Milton-Edwards, Beverley, 1996, *Islamic Politics in Palestine*, London and New York, Tauris Academic Studies.

Mishal, Saul, 1978, *West Bank/East Bank: The Palestinians in Jordan, 1949–1967*, New Haven and London, Yale University Press.

—— , 1997, '*Intifada* Discourse: The Hamas and UNL Leaflets', in Avraham Sela and Moshe Ma'oz (eds), 1997a, pp. 197–212.

Mishal, Saul and Reuben Aharoni, 1994, *Speaking Stones: Communiqués from the Intifada Underground*, Syracuse, NY, Syracuse University Press.

Mitchell, Richard P., 1969, *The Society of the Muslim Brothers*, London, Oxford University Press.

Morris, Benny, 1987, *The Birth of the Palestinian Refugee Problem 1947–1949*, Cambridge, Cambridge University Press.

—— , 1990, *1948 and After: Israel and the Palestinians*, Oxford, Clarendon Press.

Muslih, Muhammad, 1988, *The Origins of Palestinian Nationalism*, New York, Columbia University Press.

—— , 1993, 'Palestinian Civil Society', *Middle East Journal*, Vol. 47, No. 2, Spring, pp. 258–74.

—— , 1995, 'Palestinian Civil Society', in Augustus Richard Norton (ed.), Vol. 1, pp. 243–68.

Nairn, Tom, 1977, *The Break-up of Britain*, London, New Left Books.

Nassar, Jamal, 1991, *The Palestine Liberation Organization: From Armed Struggle to the Declaration of Independence*, New York, Westport and London, Praeger.

Nassar, Jamal R. and Roger Heacock (eds), 1990a, *Intifada: Palestine at the Crossroads*, New York, Westport and London, Praeger.

—— , 1990b, 'The Revolutionary Transformation of the Palestinians Under Occupation', in Jamal R. Nassar and Roger Heacock (eds), 1990a, pp. 191–206.

Noble, Paul, 1991, 'The PLO in Regional Politics', in Rex Brynen (ed.), pp. 131–64.

Norton, Augustus Richard (ed.), 1995, *Civil Society in the Middle East*, Vols 1 and 2, Leiden, New York and Cologne, E. J. Brill.

Øvensen, Geir, 1994, *Responding to Change: Trends in Palestinian Household Economy*, FAFO Report 166, Oslo.

Owen, Roger, 1982, *Studies in the Economic History of Palestine in the Nineteenth and Twentieth Centuries*, London, Macmillan Press.

—— , 1992, *State, Power and Politics in the Making of the Modern Middle East*, London and New York, Routledge.

Palestinian Legistative Council, 1997, 'Self-Evaluation Report, Ramallah, 31 October 1996', *Journal of Palestine Studies*, Vol. XXVI, No. 2, Winter, pp. 160–1.

Parry, Geraint and Michael Moran (eds), 1994, *Democracy and Democratization*, London and New York, Routledge.

Patrick, Neil, 1994, *Democracy under Limited Autonomy: The Declaration of Principles and Political Prospects in the West Bank and Gaza Strip*, Jerusalem, Panorama: Centre for the Dissemination of Alternative Information.

Peretz, Don, 1986, *The West Bank: History, Politics, Society and Economy*, Boulder and London, Westview Press.

—— , 1990, *Intifada, the Palestinian Uprising*, Boulder, Westview Press.

Peteet, Julie, 1991, *Gender in Crisis: Women and the Palestinian Resistance Movement*, New York, Columbia University Press.

Piscatori, James, 1986, *Islam in a World of Nation-States*, Cambridge and New York, Cambridge University Press.

—— (ed)., 1991a, *Islamic Fundamentalism and the Gulf Crisis*, Chicago, The Fundamentalism Project at the American Academy of Arts and Sciences.

—— , 1991b, 'Religion and *Realpolitik*: Islamic Responses to the Gulf War', in James Piscatori (ed.) 1991a, pp. 1–27.

PLO Chairman Yasir Arafat to Israeli Prime Minister Yitzhak Rabin, PLO and Israeli Letters of Mutual Recognition, Tunis and Jerusalem, 9 September 1993, *Journal of Palestine Studies*, Vol. XXIII, No. 1, Autumn.

Polk, William R. and Richard L. Chambers (eds), 1968, *Beginnings of Modernization in the Middle East*, Chicago, Chicago University Press.

Porath, Yehoshua, 1974, *The Emergence of the Palestinian–Arab National Movement 1918–1929*, London, Frank Cass.

—— , 1977, *The Palestinian Arab National Movement: From Riots to Rebellion, 1929–1939*, London, Frank Cass.

—— , 1986, *The Palestine-Arab Nationalist Movement*, in Michael Curtis (ed.), pp. 265–70.

Portugali, Yuvali, 1993, *Implicate Relations: Society and Space in the Israeli–Palestinian Conflict*, Dordrecht, Kluwer Academic Publishers.

Potter, David, David Goldblatt, Margaret Kiloch and Paul Lewis (eds), 1997, *Democratization*, Cambridge, Polity Press.

al-Qasem, Anis, 1994, 'The Proposed Charter of the National Authority in the Transitional Phase' in JMCC, 1994, pp. 45–55.

Quandt, William, 1973, 'Political and Military Dimensions of Contemporary Palestinian Nationalism', in William Quandt, Fuad Jabber and Ann Mosley Lesch, pp. 43–153.

Quandt, William, Fuad Jabber and Ann Mosley Lesch, 1973, *The Politics of Palestinian Nationalism*, Berkeley, Los Angeles and London, University of California Press.

Renan, Ernest, 1995, 'What is a Nation?', in Omar Dahbour and Micheline R. Ishay (eds), pp. 143–55.

Richards, Alan and John Waterbury, 1990, *A Political Economy of the Middle East: State, Class and Economic Development*, Boulder, San Francisco and Oxford, Westview Press.

Rigby, André, 1997, *The Legacy of the Past: The Problem of Collaborators and the Palestinian Case*, Jerusalem, PASSIA.

Robinson, Glenn, 1997a, *Building a Palestinian State: The Incomplete Revolution*, Bloomington and Indianapolis, Indiana University Press.

—— , 1997b, 'The Growing Authoritarianism of the Arafat Regime', *Survival*, Vol. 39, No. 2, Summer, pp. 42–56.

Rolef, Susan Hattis, 1997, 'Israel's Policy Toward the PLO: From Rejection to Recognition', in Avraham Sela and Moshe Ma'oz (eds), 1997a, pp. 253–72.

Roosens, Eugeen, 1994, 'The Primordial Nature of Origins in Migrant Ethnicity', in Hans Vermuelen and Cora Govers (eds), 1994a, pp. 81–104.

Bibliography

Rothschild, Joseph, 1981, *Ethnopolitics: A Conceptual Framework*, New York, Columbia University Press.

Rouhana, Nadim, 1990, 'The *Intifada* and the Palestinians of Israel: Resurrecting the Green Line', *Journal of Palestine Studies*, Vol. XIX, No. 3, Spring, pp. 57–89.

Roy, Sara, 1991, 'The Political Economy of Despair: Changing Political and Economic Realities in the Gaza Strip', *Journal of Palestine Studies*, Vol. XX, No. 3, Spring, pp. 58–69.

—— , 1993, 'Gaza: New Dynamics of Civic Disintegration', *Journal of Palestine Studies*, Vol. XXII (88), No. 4, Summer, pp. 20–31.

—— , 1994, 'Development or Dependency? The Gaza Strip Economy Under Limited Self-Rule', *The Beirut Review*, No. 8, Fall, pp. 59–80.

—— , 1995a, *The Gaza Strip: The Political Economy of De-development*, Washington, DC, Institute for Palestine Studies.

—— , 1995b, 'Civil Society in the Gaza Strip: Obstacles to Social Reconstruction', in Augustus Richard Norton (ed.), Vol. 2, pp. 221–58.

Rustow, D., 1970, 'Transitions to Democracy', *Comparative Politics*, Vol. 2, pp. 327–63.

Saftawi, Ala, 1994, Eulogy, *al-Istiqlal*, Vol. 5, No. 18, November.

Sahliyeh, Emile, 1988, *In Search of Leadership: West Bank Politics since 1967*, Washington, DC, Brookings Institution.

Said, Edward, 1978, *Orientalism: Western Concepts of the Orient*, reprinted in 1991, London and New York, Penguin Books.

—— , 1980, *The Question of Palestine*, London and Henley, Routledge and Kegan Paul.

—— , 1993, *Culture and Imperialism*, London, Vintage.

—— , 1994, *The Politics of Dispossession: The Struggle for Palestinian Self-Determination*, London, Chatto and Windus.

—— , 1995, *Peace and its Discontents: Gaza–Jericho 1993–1995*, London, Vintage.

Sayigh, Rosemary, 1979, *Palestinians: From Peasants to Revolutionaries*, London, Zed Books.

—— , 1994, *Too Many Enemies: The Palestinian Experience in Lebanon*, London and Atlantic Highlands, NJ, Zed Books.

Sayigh, Yezid, 1989, 'The *Intifada* Continues: Legacy, Dynamics and Challenges', *Third World Quarterly*, Vol. 11, No. 3, July, pp. 20–47.

—— , 1997a, *Armed Struggle and the Search for State: The Palestinian National Movement, 1949–1993*, Oxford, Clarendon Press.

—— , 1997b, 'The Armed Struggle and Palestinian Nationalism', in Avraham Sela and Moshe Ma'oz (eds), 1997a, pp. 23–36.

Sayigh, Yusif, 1986, 'The Palestinian Economy Under Occupation', *Journal of Palestine Studies*, Vol. XV, No. 4, pp. 46–67.

Schiff, Ze'ev and Ehuri Ya'ari, 1990, *Intifada: The Palestinian Uprising – Israel's Third Front*, New York, Simon and Schuster.

Schulz, Michael, 1996, 'Between Conflict and Accommodation: Transformations of Collective Identities in a Multi-Melting Pot Process', dissertation, forthcoming 1996, Department of Peace and Development Research, Göteborg University (Padrigu).

Segal, Jerome, 1993, 'Strategic Choices Facing the Palestinians in the Negotiations', *Journal of Palestine Studies*, Vol. XXII, No. 2, Winter, pp. 17–29.

Sela, Avraham and Moshe Ma'oz (eds), 1997a, *The PLO and Israel: From Armed Conflict to Political Settlement, 1964–1994*, New York, St Martin's Press.

—— , 1997b 'The PLO in Regional Arab Politics: Taming a Non-State Actor', in Avraham Sela and Moshe Ma'oz (eds), 1997a, pp. 97–121.

Seton-Watson, Hugh, 1977, *Nations and States*, London, Methuen.

Shadid, Muhammad, 1988, 'The Muslim Brotherhood Movement in the West Bank and Gaza', *Third World Quarterly*, Vol. 10, No. 2, April, pp. 658–82.

184

Shadid, Muhammad and Rick Seltzer, 1988, 'Political Attitudes of Palestinians in the West Bank and Gaza Strip' *Middle East Journal*, Vol. 42, No. 1, Winter, pp. 16–32.

Shain, Yossi and J. J. Linz (eds), 1995, *Between States: Interim Governments and Democratic Transitions*, Cambridge, Cambridge University Press.

Shalev, Aryeh, 1991, *The Intifada: Causes and Effects*, Boulder, Westview Press.

Shamir, Shimon, 1980, 'West Bank Refugees – Between Camp and Society', in Joel S. Migdal (ed.), 1980b, pp. 146–68.

Shapiro, Michael J., 1992, *Reading the Postmodern Polity: Political Theory as Textual Practice*, Minneapolis and Oxford, University of Minnesota Press.

Sharabi, Hisham, 1990, *Theory, Politics and the Arab World: Critical Responses*, New York and London, Routledge.

Shemesh, Moshe, 1988, *The Palestinian Entity 1959–1974: Arab Politics and the PLO*, London, Frank Cass.

Shkaki, Khalil, 1996a, 'The Peace Process, National Reconstruction, and the Transition to Democracy in Palestine', *Journal of Palestine Studies*, Vol. XXV, No. 2, Winter, pp. 5–20.

—— , 1996b, *Transition to Democracy in Palestine: The Peace Process, National Reconstruction and Elections*, Nablus Centre for Palestine Research and Studies.

Sicker, Martin, 1989, *Between Hashemites and Zionists: The Struggle for Palestine 1908–1988*, New York and London, Holmes and Meier.

Simmel, Georg, 1971, *On Individuality and Social Forms: Selected Writings*, edited with an introduction by Donald N. Lerine, Chicago, University of Chicago Press.

Sivan, Emmanuel, 1985, *Radical Islam: Medieval Theology and Modern Politics*, New Haven and London, Yale University Press.

Sivan, Emmanuel and M. Friedmann, 1990, *Religious Radicalism and Politics in the Middle East*, New York, State University of New York Press.

Smith, Anthony, 1971, *Theories of Nationalism*, London, Duckworth.

—— , 1979, *Nationalism in the Twentieth Century*, Oxford, Martin Robertson.

—— , 1983, *Theories of Nationalism*, second edition, London.

—— , 1986, *The Ethnic Origins of Nations*, New Haven and London, Yale University Press.

—— , 1991, *National Identity*, London, Penguin Books.

—— , 1994, 'The Problem of National Identity: Ancient, Medieval and Modern?', *Ethnic and Racial Studies*, Vol. 17, No. 3, July, pp. 375–99.

Smooha, Sammy, 1978, *Israel, Pluralism and Conflict*, London, Routledge and Kegan Paul.

—— , 1989, *Arabs and Jews in Israel*, Vol. 1: *Conflicting and Shared Attitudes in a Divided Society*, Boulder, Westview Press, Westview Special Studies on the Middle East.

—— , 1992, *Arabs and Jews in Israel*, Vol. 2: *Change and Continuity in Mutual Intolerance*, Boulder, Westview Press, Westview Special Studies on the Middle East.

Starr, Joyce R. and Daniel C. Stoll (eds), 1988, *The Politics of Scarcity: Water in the Middle East*, Boulder and London, Westview Press.

Stavenhagen, Rodolfo, 1990, *The Ethnic Question: Conflicts, Development and Human Rights*, Tokyo, United Nations University Press.

Steinberg, Matti, 1989, 'The Worldview of Hawatmeh's Democratic Front', *Jerusalem Quarterly*, No. 50, Spring, pp. 23–40.

Steinberg, Paul and Ann-Marie Oliver, 1994, *The Graffiti of the Intifada: A Brief Survey*, Jerusalem, PASSIA.

Tamari, Salim, 1984, 'Israel's Search for a Native Pillar: The Village Leagues', in Nasser Aruri (ed.), pp. 377–90.

—— , 1990, 'Revolt of the Petite Bourgeoisie: Urban Merchants and the Palestinian Uprising', in Michael Hudson (ed.), pp. 24–43.

——, 1991, 'The Palestinian Movement in Transition: Historical Reversals and the Uprising', *Journal of Palestine Studies*, Vol. XX, No. 2, Winter, pp. 57–70.

——, 1993, 'The Transformation of Palestinian Society: Fragmentation and Occupation', in Marianne Heiberg and Geir Øvensen (eds), pp. 21–33.

——, 1995, 'Fading Flags and the Crisis of Legitimacy', *Middle East Report*, July/August, pp. 10–12.

——, 1997, 'Social Science Research in Palestine: A Review of Trends and Issues', in *Palestine, Palestiniens: National Territory, Community Spaces*, ed. Riccardo Bocco, Blandine Destremau and Jean Hannoyer, Beirut Centre of Studies and Research into the Contemporary Middle East, pp. 17–37.

Taraki, Liza, 1990, 'The Development of Political Consciousness among Palestinians in the Occupied Territories, 1967–1987', in Jamal R. Nassar and Roger Heacock (eds), 1990a, pp. 53–71.

Tibi, Bassam, 1971, *Arab Nationalism: A Critical Inquiry*, second edition, New York, St Martin's Press, 1991.

——, 1988, *The Crisis of Modern Islam: A Preindustrial Culture in the Scientific-Technological Age*, Salt Lake City, University of Utah Press.

——, 1991, *Islam and the Cultural Accommodation of Social Change*, Boulder, San Francisco and Oxford, Westview Press.

——, 1992, *Conflict and War in the Middle East, 1967–91*, London, Macmillan Press.

——, 1997, *Arab Nationalism: Between Islam and the Nation-State*, third edition, London, Macmillan.

Tilly, Charles (ed.), 1975a, *The Formation of National States in Western Europe*, Princeton, Princeton University Press.

——, 1975b, 'Reflections on the History of European State-Making', in Charles Tilly (ed.), 1975a, pp. 3–84.

Tsimhoni, Daphne, 1987, 'Demographic Trends of the Christian Population in Jerusalem and the West Bank 1948–1978', *Middle East Journal*, Vol. 37, No. 1, Winter, pp. 54–64.

Turner, Victor, 1969, *The Ritual Process: Structure and Anti-Structure*, Chicago, Aldine.

Usher, Graham, 1997, 'The Return of the Tribes', *al-Ahram Weekly*, 30 October–5 November.

——, 1998, 'The Politics of Internal Security: The Palestinian Authority's New Security Services', in George Giacamen and Dag Jørund Lønning (eds), pp. 146–61.

Verdery, Katherine, 1994, 'Ethnicity, Nationalism and State-Making: Ethnic Groups and Boundaries, Past and Future', in Hans Vermuelen and Cora Govers (eds), 1994a, pp. 33–58.

Vermuelen, Hans and Cora Govers (eds), 1994a, *The Anthropology of Ethnicity: Beyond Ethnic Groups and Boundaries*, Amsterdam, Het Spinhuis.

——, 1994b, 'Introduction', in Hans Vermuelen and Cora Govers (eds), 1994a, pp. 1–10.

Von Herder, Johann Gottfried, 1784–97 [1995], 'Reflections on the Philosophy of the History of Mankind', in Omar Dahbour and Micheline K. Ishay (eds), pp. 48–57.

Wallach, Janet and John Wallach, 1997, *Arafat: In the Eyes of the Beholder*, revised and updated, Secaucus, NJ, Carol Publishing.

Weber, Max, 1947, *The Theory of Social and Economic Organization*, New York, The Free Press.

Wise, G. S. and C. Issawi, *Middle East Perspectives: The Next Twenty Years*, Princeton, Darwin.

World Bank, 1993, *Developing the Occupied Territories: An Investment in Peace*, Report No. 11958, 6 vols, Washington, DC, The World Bank.

Yahya, Adil, 1990, 'The Role of the Refugee Camps', in Jamal R. Nassar and Roger Heacock (eds), 1990a, pp. 91–106.

Yuval-Davis, Nira, 1997, *Gender and Nation*, London, Sage.

Zubaida, Sami, 1988, 'Islam, Cultural Nationalism and the Left', *Review of Middle East Studies*,
    No. 4, pp. 1–32.
—— , 1989, *Islam, the People and the State*, London, Routledge.
Zureik, E. T., 1979, *The Palestinians in Israel: A Study in Internal Colonialism*, London, Routledge
    and Kegan Paul.

INDEX

189

190